Chequered Lives

Iola Mathews OAM (née Hack) is the great-great granddaughter of John Barton Hack. She has a degree in history from Melbourne University and was a journalist with the *Age* newspaper for many years and the author of *How to Use the Media in Australia* (Penguin, 1991). She later worked at the Australian Council for Trade Unions as an industrial officer and advocate. More recently she wrote a memoir, *My Mother, My Writing and Me* (Michelle Anderson Publishing, 2009) and established writers' studios in the National Trust property Glenfern in East St Kilda. She lives in Melbourne with her husband Dr Race Mathews.

Dr Chris Durrant is an astrophysicist with a keen interest in the history of South Australia. He was born in England and worked at Cambridge University and in Freiberg, Germany, before coming to Australia in 1983. He is a former head of

Chequered Lives

John Barton Hack and Stephen Hack
and the early days of South Australia

Iola Hack Mathews
with Chris Durrant

Wakefield
Press

Wakefield Press
1 The Parade West
Kent Town
South Australia 5067
www.wakefieldpress.com.au

First published 2013
Reprinted 2014 (twice)

Copyright © Iola Hack Mathews, 2013

All rights reserved. This book is copyright. Apart from any fair dealing for the
purposes of private study, research, criticism or review, as permitted under
the Copyright Act, no part may be reproduced without written permission.
Enquiries should be addressed to the publisher.

Cover image: John Barton Hack's farm, 'Echunga Springs', Echunga, South Australia,
by Governor George Gawler, June 1841
Edited by Penelope Curtin
Designed and typeset by Clinton Ellicott, Wakefield Press
Printed in Australia by Griffin Digital, Adelaide

National Library of Australia Cataloguing-in-Publication entry

Author:	Mathews, Iola, author.
Title:	Chequered lives: John Barton Hack and Stephen Hack and the early days of South Australia / Iola Hack Mathews with Chris Durrant.
ISBN:	978 1 74305 258 7 (paperback).
Notes:	Includes index.
Subjects:	Hack, John Barton, 1805–1884.
	Hack, Stephen.
	Pioneers – South Australia.
	South Australia – Biography.
	South Australia – History.
	South Australia – Discovery and exploration.
Other Authors/Contributors:	Durrant, Chris, author.
Dewey Number:	994.23

Contents

	Sponsors and acknowledgements	vii
	Introduction	1
Chapter 1	The Hacks and the Bartons	8
Chapter 2	Barton Hack marries	21
Chapter 3	Preparations for migration	29
Chapter 4	On board the *Isabella*	40
Chapter 5	Launceston	51
Chapter 6	Arrival in South Australia	58
Chapter 7	Leading citizens	69
Chapter 8	Letters from England	82
Chapter 9	Stephen's trip overland	90
Chapter 10	Hindley Street	98
Chapter 11	Governor Hindmarsh recalled	109
Chapter 12	Landed gentry	117
Chapter 13	The estate at Mount Barker	124
Chapter 14	Hack, Watson & Co.	134
Chapter 15	Barton moves to Echunga	143

Chapter 16	A cloud settles on the colony	152
Chapter 17	Crisis in the colony	159
Chapter 18	The crisis continues	168
Chapter 19	Ruin	179
Chapter 20	Desperation	193
Chapter 21	Burra, Kapunda and gold	202
Chapter 22	Stephen the explorer	213
Chapter 23	The Coorong	219
Chapter 24	Coonalpyn	229
Chapter 25	Final years	237
Appendix	Barton and Stephen's children	255
	Notes	266
	Index	284

Sponsors and acknowledgements

Sponsors
In 2013 we received a grant for $2000 from the South Australian History Fund towards publication, and we thank History SA and the South Australian Government for this.

We also thank Griffith Hack (Patents, Trade Marks and Intellectual Property) for its sponsorship, in particular Tony Ward, Principal, and Steve Parker, CEO. The link with John Barton Hack is via his grandson Clement Hack (1877–1930, my grandfather), who became a patent attorney in Adelaide after studying metallurgy. In 1904 at age of twenty-seven he moved to Melbourne and set up the firm of Clement Hack & Co in Collins Street, next door to the newly created federal patent office. In 1912 he moved into 360 Collins Street, the headquarters of the big mining companies (the Collins House Group) and most of them subsequently became his clients. Clem Hack's son John Barton Hack (1911–1996) was also a partner in the family firm throughout his life. In 1988 the firm merged with Griffith Hassel & Frazer in Sydney to become Griffith Hack, and now has offices in Melbourne, Sydney, Brisbane and Perth.

Acknowledgements
Very few families have the good fortune to possess nearly 500 original letters, ledgers and documents relating to their ancestors, going back nearly 200 years. We owe an immense debt of gratitude to John Barton Hack's brother-in-law Thomas Gates Darton (1810–1887), who kept the documents relating to the family's early years in South Australia, and to his descendants who preserved them. We are particularly grateful to his great-grandson Edward Lawrence Darton (1914–2008), who presented most of these documents to the State Library of South Australia (SLSA).

The journal that Barton Hack kept of the voyage to Australia and the first few months of the colony was handed down to Clement Hack, who had it typed around 1916 and presented to the SLSA along with the handwritten diary. In 1949 my father, John Barton Hack, completed a family tree, and in the 1980s he and Lawrence Darton transcribed the letters, annotated them and placed them in the SLSA. They also placed copies of the diary and letters in the state libraries of Victoria and New South Wales, as well as the National Library of Australia in Canberra and the West Sussex Records Office in England.

We also thank descendants of the Barton Hack's uncle, John Barton, for providing us with material, in particular Malcolm Barton and Dr David Barton. In the Darton family we thank Dr Nicholas Darton and Caroline Darton. In Chichester we have been assisted by Michael Woolley and Anne Stillwell Griffiths. We thank Julia Hedley in Perth for information on the family of Stephen Hack and June Scott in Adelaide for information on the family of Henry Watson.

When Chris Durrant began the task of researching and writing about John Barton Hack (see Introduction) he undertook the mammoth task of transcribing the diary and letters onto his computer in chronological order, and then added material from the diaries of other settlers and further historical research; he also added footnotes. He then commenced writing a narrative based on this material.

This was an invaluable start for the writing of this current book, which has involved further research, as can be seen from the lengthy list of endnotes. Chris Durrant, being a highly trained scientist, does not trust secondary sources, and when we first met, he was quick to point out that Manning Clark, in his famous *History of Australia*, wrote one paragraph about John Barton Hack, and it is full of errors. Chris and I both value accuracy and sometimes spent weeks tracking down a primary source to work out some confusing point in the letters or memoirs. We have relied heavily on the 'advanced search' tool on Trove, the National Library's digitised newspaper files, which are like gold for historical researchers, compared with the old days when you had to study dusty old newspapers or the dreaded microfiche.

SPONSORS AND ACKNOWLEDGEMENTS

We are grateful to the many institutions that have provided assistance, especially the State Library of South Australia, the State Records Office of South Australia and the Old Titles section of the General Registry Office in South Australia. In England Chris was given assistance by the West Sussex Records Office in Chichester and the Society of Friends in London.

There are many people and organisations that have helped in our research, and we apologise for not being able to name them all individually. We have tried to acknowledge most of them in the relevant endnotes. Chris Durrant has provided the maps and disgrams in this book as well as many of the photographs.

We thank the team at Wakefield Press, especially its director Michael Bollen who is very knowledgeable about South Australian history and has published widely on the subject, and Penelope Curtin for her thorough and thoughtful editing.

On a personal note, I wish to thank Di Buckley, writer, editor and friend, who in a very short time helped to reduce a bulky 140,000 word manuscript to a more manageable 90,000 words. Also the National Trust of Australia (Victoria) for allowing me to be a writer-in-residence at Glenfern in East St Kilda from 2003, and helped me to establish a writers' centre there in 2006 in conjunction with Writers Victoria. I thank all the writers who have spent time at Glenfern over the years for their support and friendship, especially Fiona Wood.

Chris and I also thank our partners Kerry Durrant and Race Mathews for their support and forbearance, especially for putting up with long interstate telephone conversations about obscure points of South Australian history.

Iola Mathews
Melbourne, 2013

Being now 79 years old, I have only to wait for my final retirement from the scenes of a very chequered life, in which I trust I have made very few enemies and many friends

– John Barton Hack, 1884

The Hack and Barton Family Trees

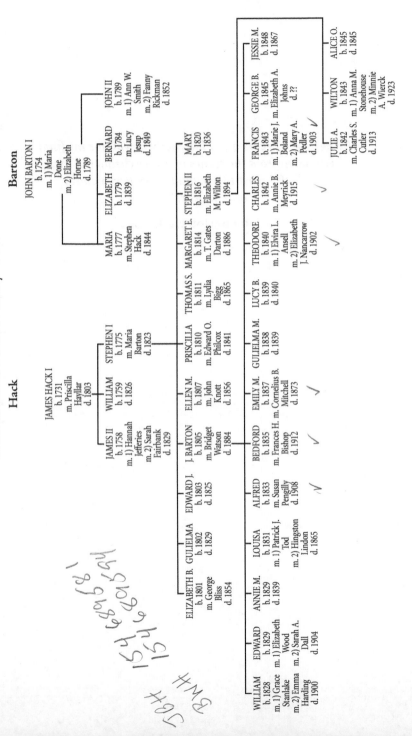

Introduction

A few years ago, I was in Adelaide for Writers' Week. We sat in the huge marquees down by the River Torrens, listening to speakers from all over the world. It was early March and stiflingly hot. When someone whispered that it was 37°, I decided to find somewhere cooler. Then I remembered, just up the road was the State Library, and somewhere inside was the diary of John Barton Hack, my ancestor and an important early pioneer in South Australia. I was curious to see it.

North Terrace is Adelaide's cultural boulevard, lined with elegant nineteenth-century buildings such as Government House, State Parliament, the museum, the art gallery and the library. To see the diary in the archive collection was not a simple exercise. I was directed to a private reading room and told I could take notes with a pencil but not a pen. I sat at an oak table and a librarian brought me some boxes.

I took out the diary carefully. It was old and worn, bound in soft leather. On one side was a metal clasp, which had once held it closed but was now broken. I opened the diary and saw writing on every page. The ink was faded, but still clear. I felt excited as I realised this was a direct link between J.B. Hack and me, over several generations. He'd held this book and written in it about 170 years earlier. I could imagine him seated at a desk in his dark coat, with pen and ink, writing in this neat hand.

I turned to the first page, '6 mo 20, first day' (Sunday 20 June 1836)[1]:

> Set off at 5 o'clock this morning for Portsmouth. Went on board the *Emerald Isle*, steam packet, which was detained till 1 o'clock in the afternoon alongside the *Buffalo* – she had brought upwards of 20 tons of goods belonging to South Australian emigrants from London. Soon after passing the Needles the swell became rather

annoying to us and the wind rose and became rather cold. Dinner at four o'clock. Soon after, Bbe and I became very sick . . .

I stopped reading and remembered that his wife was Bridget, known as 'Bbe' (pronounced Beeby).[2] I read on and soon realised they were not on the boat to Australia, but on their way to Liverpool, and I wondered why, when they were thinking of a warmer climate because of his health. Several pages on, it started to make more sense:

> [Gloucester, 24 July 1836] Went to see Mamma . . . We had much talk with her respecting our Australian projects, and as we feel decided as to our going there at any rate next year, she wished us to consider whether a move there at once would not be better than going to Madeira now – we feel quite inclined to do so, if we can see our way clear . . .
>
> [25 July 1836] I could not sleep last night – but do not feel much amiss this morning. Find it so difficult to bear any excitement . . .

I smiled as I read this. He sounded just like my father, whose name was also John Barton Hack. Dad was a worrier, and too much excitement or too many problems gave him insomnia and an upset stomach. He was proud of being named after his great-grandfather. Both were known as Barton, not John.

I put down the diary and opened another box. Inside was a folder with letters from Australia after they had arrived in 1837.[3] A note at the front said the letters were typed and donated by my father in the 1980s. The footnotes were by him and Lawrence Darton of Ludlow, Shropshire, England. I knew these letters existed, but had never read them.

I turned to the first one, from Barton Hack to his mother Maria Hack in Gloucester (Maria was pronounced like 'friar'):

> [Holdfast Bay, South Australia, 19 Feb 1837] Dear Mother, Thou wilt I am sure be pleased to hear we have arrived in safety in our adopted country, which we did on the 11th Instant after a tolerably favourable passage from Launceston, where we had laid in a stock of what we thought necessary to start with.

I noted the 'thee' and 'thou' sprinkled through the letter, because they were Quakers, as were quite a few of the early settlers. I looked at my father's footnotes and saw that the family left England on 3 September 1836 on the *Isabella*, and the journey took five-and-a-half months. Barton and Bbe were accompanied by their six small children and Barton's younger brother Stephen.

I suddenly felt close to my father, and sad that he was no longer alive to discuss all this. I felt guilty that I had not shown more interest in his work on the family history or his correspondence with Lawrence Darton, a distant relative. But that was in the 1980s when Dad was retired and had leisure, while I was flat out working and raising a family. How ironic, I thought, that we only become interested in these things when our parents are no longer around to answer our questions.

I turned back to the letter from South Australia and discovered that the weather was also very hot in February 1837. Barton wrote: 'The first few days after landing the wind was from over the land and the heat was excessive – 100° in the shade – this only lasted for about 4 days and now a breeze from the south makes it rather cool than otherwise'.

The next letter was two months later, dated 22 April, and written to his mother. He had been up in Adelaide and put up his two portable houses. Dad's footnote explained that these prefabricated wooden houses were erected in North Terrace, on the site of the present central railway station. I read this with amazement. Talk about prime real estate! But of course it wasn't then; the town was not even laid out. Barton was just squatting, like everyone else at the time, and he had a cow tied up by the river.

I was curious to see the view from where his house had been, so after reading for a while I left the library and walked down North Terrace to the railway station, with its imposing stone facade. I soon realised that the Adelaide Festival Centre stands between the railway station and the river, so I crossed to the Festival Centre and climbed some steps, and from there I could see the river.

It was greeny brown in colour, sparkling in the hot sun. On each side were wide lawns fringed with trees – willows, palms and eucalypts – and the river itself was dotted with swans and small paddle boats. I tried to imagine the scene in 1837, when Barton walked down this slope to milk his cow. According to his letters, it was native bush, with wattles and gum trees.

I didn't have time to visit the library again, but when I returned to Melbourne I opened the large metal trunk which had belonged to my father. Inside I found a series of large ring folders, neatly labelled. They contained a typed copy of Barton Hack's diary, copies of the letters I'd seen in the State Library of South Australia and other reference material. There were also maps, photographs and old books.

Near the top was the best find of all, a pale blue manila folder containing some original documents. The first was a large piece of parchment folded neatly into a square. The date was 1 April 1827. It was a 'Deed of Copartnership', between Mr John Barton Hack, Currier and Leather-Seller of Chichester, and Mr Thomas Smith, Currier and Leather-Seller of Bermondsey. (A currier, I later discovered, prepared and dyed leather, before it was cut and sold to shoemakers and saddlers.) The writing on the outside was faded, but inside, the ink was as fresh as if it had just been written, and there was a red wax seal next to each signature. It spelt out the arrangements for a partnership in the family business in Chichester.

Next I picked up a handwritten letter. It was yellow with age, but the ink was still clear. The heading said, 'Atlantic Ocean, Off Martin Vas, 29 October 1836'. It was from Barton's younger brother Stephen, written to his mother on the voyage out to Australia. The outside was stamped Gloucester July 13, 1837. I did a quick count on my fingers – it had been written in October and arrived in England in July – nine months later! I thought of his poor mother, waiting all that time for news. The letter must have strained her eyes, because it was 'crossed' – written first one way, then turned sideways and written the other way, across the lines, to save paper.

As I sifted through the trunk, I felt deep gratitude to my father and all those distant relatives who had kept these papers safe for nearly 200 years. I wondered if my generation would leave anything that would last so long. Few write letters, and most communicate by emails, text, phone or 'social media'. Our forebears wrote on paper made from rags – much more durable than the paper we use now, made from wood pulp.[4] The ink also lasted longer.

I picked up one of the photographs of Barton Hack in the trunk. Take away the beard and there was a resemblance to my father. They had the same straight brown hair, the same serious look and set of the mouth. I found a photo of Bbe Hack in later life, and one of Stephen Hack in middle age. Photography was not invented until the middle of the nineteenth century, so there were no photos of them when young; only a painting of Stephen aged about twenty.

In the trunk I found an entry on John Barton Hack in the *Australian Dictionary of Biography* (ADB), and an obituary written in 1884. In the early days of South Australia he was one of the most prominent citizens. He had a merchant business in Adelaide, established a market garden in North Adelaide and built a store and house in Hindley Street. He was chairman or committee member of almost all the new institutions. He was a partner in a whaling station at Encounter Bay, and took a 4000-acre survey at Echunga Springs in the Adelaide Hills, where he made his home, travelling on unmade roads to Adelaide twice a week to attend to business.

He planted the colony's first vines and made the first wine. His farm was a showpiece, with crops, dairies and 1000 cattle, but by 1843 he had lost everything, following the economic depression in South Australia of 1841–1842. His later ventures were various: he carted ore from the Burra copper mine to Port Adelaide, went to the Victorian goldfields, tried dairy-farming on the Coorong, returned to Adelaide and worked as an accountant, and became controller of railway accounts until his death at the age of seventy-nine.

The entry in the ADB says:

> Hack was too soft-hearted to be a successful pioneer; he paid high wages, gave generous credits and neglected to cover himself. Although he became a Wesleyan Methodist he was a Quaker by upbringing; he befriended Aboriginals and ex-convicts, advocated

temperance, presided over the Mechanics' Institute and gave land in Pennington Terrace for a Friends' meeting house.[5]

In retirement, John Barton Hack wrote an autobiographical sketch, which was published in the *South Australian Register* in April 1884 and in an expanded version in July–August 1884. 'Being now 79 years old', he wrote, 'I have only to wait for my final retirement from the scenes of a very chequered life, in which I trust I have made very few enemies and many friends'. He died shortly afterwards.

Further down in the trunk I found maps and a report of Stephen Hack's exploration into the remote north-west of South Australia, which looked intriguing, but I had no time to read it. I closed the trunk and made a vow that later on, I would write this story. Six months later, I received an email unexpectedly from my father's old firm, Griffith Hack, (Patents, Trade Marks and Intellectual Property Law). They forwarded an email from a man named Chris Durrant in Sydney, who wanted to get in touch with descendants of John Barton Hack. He said he was working on a history of the Hacks in South Australia.

I phoned Chris Durrant and discovered that he was not a relative, but a retired academic with an interest in South Australian history. He had written about his wife Kerry's ancestors, the Hursts, who had come to South Australia in 1852, and settled in Paracombe in the Adelaide Hills. 'I kept finding references to John Barton Hack', Chris said, 'because he took out the special survey for the area. I've been researching his story ever since'.

Chris said his narrative already ran into thousands of words, but he had no plans to publish it commercially. He only wanted to place it on a website for anyone to see. He said I was welcome to use any of it, and in exchange I invited him to Melbourne to see what was in my father's trunk and to meet other Hack relatives.

We were on a joint quest to find out more. What was life like for those pioneers? What sort of family did Barton and Stephen grow up in, and what was the particular cocktail of genes and environment that formed their adventurous spirits?

I also wanted to find out about the women in the family, including Barton's mother Maria, whose portrait had sat in my study for decades. She was a successful author at a time when it was rare for a woman to have her own career. Then there was Barton's wife Bridget, who supported her husband through his many ventures while giving birth to fourteen children, four of whom died in infancy.

And so began a happy collaboration: Chris writing a lengthy and more scholarly 'source book' about the family, while I was writing something shorter and more suitable for a general audience. The story, we agreed, started with the origins of the family in the south of England, and why they decided to set out for the yet-to-be established settlement of South Australia.

Style Note

When quoting from original documents, we have retained the measurements used then, for example, temperatures in Fahrenheit and distances in miles, as well as the currency (pounds, shillings and pence).

We have however dispensed with the Quaker practice of naming days and months (first day for Sunday, first month for January etc.) and adopted contemporary practice.

Chapter 1
The Hacks and the Bartons

John Barton Hack's ancestors can be traced back to the middle of the seventeenth century in England and the origins of Quakerism. Later they moved to Chichester, and it was there that Barton and his brother Stephen grew up. The Hack family was prosperous and connected to business and banking. On their mother's side, the Barton family was involved in business, literature and social reform, including the abolition of slavery, the founding of the University of London, and the promotion of the settlement of South Australia.

The Hack family origins
Nick Vine Hall, the Australian genealogist, said that after sex, the number one area of research on the internet was genealogy, 'and oddly the two are sort of related'.[6]

The internet has made tracing a family tree much easier, through websites like ancestry.com. Earlier on, it was harder. As a small child, I remember my father sitting night after night at the dining room table, working on the family tree, which his father started in the 1920s. They traced the Hack family back to the seventeenth century in England. The name Hack is said to be Scandinavian or North German, and one source says it was brought to England in the tenth and eleventh centuries by the Vikings.[7]

Tracing the family back to the seventeenth century was fairly easy, because from that time on the Hacks were Quakers, and the Quakers were good at keeping records. Until the nineteenth century, records in Britain were kept mainly by parish churches. The Quakers, being outside the established churches, kept their own centralised records. In 1836 the British Government took over the registration of births, deaths and marriages, but the Quakers kept copies of their records and made them available to researchers.[8]

The family tree starts with William Hack of Froyle, a village five miles from Alton in Hampshire, south-west of London. We don't know when he joined the Society of Friends, but in 1684 he married another Quaker, Mary Terry, in the Friends Meeting House in Alton. This meeting house is one of the oldest in England and is still in use today.

William and Mary had fifteen children and their second child, William (let's call him William Hack II), was a patten maker. Pattens were a bit like clogs and were worn by women over their flimsy shoes to raise their shoes and skirts above the dirt and mud. Later on, pattens were made of metal and clinked when worn indoors – a bit like tying each shoe onto a tin can. They were used until the late nineteenth century, when they were replaced by rubber galoshes (over-shoes).

From then on the Hacks were upwardly mobile. William II moved to Alton, a bigger town nearby. His son (William III) was also a patten-maker and moved to Basingstoke, a market town not far from Alton. In 1751 William III's son James Hack moved to the cathedral town of Chichester in Sussex, on the south coast. James was a patten-maker but also became a merchant and leather-cutter. His youngest son, Stephen Hack, was the father of John Barton Hack.

Quakerism

Quakerism arose out of the religious and political upheaval in England in the middle of the seventeenth century. The bloody civil war that culminated in the execution of King Charles I in 1649 was followed by a brief 'republic', until 1660 under the Puritan leader Oliver Cromwell. During this time, a number of small religious groups (Dissenters) broke away from the Church of England. One of these was the Religious Society of Friends, founded by George Fox around 1650.

Fox set out to create a purer form of Christianity. He believed that everyone should try to encounter God directly, without priests, churches or sacraments. Fox was imprisoned for blasphemy, and said later 'the judge called us Quakers, because I bade them tremble at the word of the Lord'.[9]

Quakerism thrived among people who felt ignored or

rejected by the church, state and powerful landowners. Quakers were committed to a belief in the sacredness of human life and the worth of all people, irrespective of gender or colour. Women were particularly attracted to the cause because it gave them a freedom of expression and activity denied them elsewhere. Quakers met in simple meeting rooms and had no clergy or rituals. When they assembled for 'meeting for worship', they sat in silence (nowadays for an hour). Any person present, male or female, could speak or perhaps read a religious passage. This was known as ministry.

Quakers did not use the common names of the days of the week and the months of the year, objecting to their heathen origin. Instead they named the days and months numerically, with Sunday being 'first day', and January being 'first month'. They believed in equality and 'refused to bow, to remove their hats to superiors, to acknowledge titles, and they spoke to their betters with the common, plain "thee" and "thou." '[10] Simplicity was paramount, in dress, homes and worship.

Quakerism infuriated the religious and political establishment of the time, with Quakers imprisoned and beaten in Britain, Ireland and the British colonies. In America, some were banished or hanged. The Quaker, William Penn, founded the Commonwealth of Pennsylvania as a safe place for them to live and practise their faith. Quakers adopted the principle of non-violence, including refusing to fight in wars.

The movement grew steadily, and when Fox died in 1691 he left 50,000 followers, with headquarters in London and meeting houses across the country. In 1689 the persecution eased with the *Toleration Act* under King William III. However, Quakers were still excluded from some aspects of everyday life and were banned from standing for parliament until 1833. Having been banned from Oxford and Cambridge universities and the old grammar schools, they established their own schools and trained their young people through apprenticeships.

In the early days, Quakers had been objects of suspicion, and were therefore extremely careful to be honest in business and to pay taxes and customs. They were frugal, industrious and proud of their sound financial housekeeping. The discipline of the

Society of Friends ensured they abided by strict codes, and those who fell by the wayside, married out or became bankrupt were excluded. As James Walvin wrote in *The Quakers: Money and Morals*, 'Their produce was sound, their prices fair, their services honest, their word good and their agreements honourable'.[11]

All this led to the rise of Quaker prosperity, and they exercised an influence out of all proportion to their numbers. They were later to dominate key eighteenth- and nineteenth-century industries. Businesses which have Quaker origins include Barclays, Lloyds, Price Waterhouse, Clark's Shoes, Huntley and Palmer, Cadbury, Fry's and Rowntree.

Quakers also emphasised the importance of human rights and social action. Having been persecuted in the seventeenth century they empathised with the less fortunate or the oppressed and they became leaders in movements to abolish slavery and to reform prisons. By the twentieth century they were famous for pacifism and for helping refugees. Today there are about half a million Quakers worldwide, with membership in Australia numbering about 1000, as well as a further 1000 who worship with the Quakers but have not applied for membership.[12]

Such was the religious and cultural context in which John Barton Hack (known as Barton) and his younger brother Stephen were raised and which helped to mould their personalities.

Stephen Hack (senior)

Stephen Hack, their father, was born in 1775 and by the time he was nineteen was in partnership with his two older brothers, James and William, as merchants in the corn trade. Stephen and his brothers prospered, with James Hack founding, in 1809, the Chichester Bank[13] in partnership with his brother William and two others, each supplying £2500 in capital. This was a successful venture for the next eighty years and was absorbed by Barclays Bank in 1891.

At the age of twenty-four, Stephen Hack married Mary Barton, known as Maria. Aged twenty-two, she came from a respected Quaker family in Tottenham, near London. The wedding, on 7 February 1800, was held in the Friends Meeting House in Tottenham. One of those present was Priscilla Wakefield, the grandmother of Edward Gibbon Wakefield, the man who would later devise the scheme for the settlement of South Australia.

Stephen brought his new bride back to live in Chichester, the centre of which, then and now, is the old walled Roman city, dissected like a hot cross bun by North, South, West and East streets. Chichester today, with a population of about 25,000,[14] is a cultural centre and is known for its Festival Theatre, two art galleries and an annual arts and music festival. Not far from the city are the Fishbourne Roman Palace and the Goodwood Estate, home of the Duke of Richmond, on 12,000 acres, with its own racecourse.

When Stephen and Maria married in 1800, Chichester was a busy and prosperous market town whose local industries included the tanning of leather, brewing and wool stapling.[15] Stephen proved to be an astute businessman. As well as being a merchant, he also took over the family leather business.

Eleven months after the wedding, Stephen and Maria had their first child. They were to have, in total, ten children over a period of nineteen years, most of them fewer than two years apart. Not all these children lived to adulthood: four died before the age of thirty. In that era any illness could be fatal. Medicine was still primitive, antibiotics were unknown, and diseases like cholera and typhus swept through the community at regular intervals. The first child, born in 1801, was named Elizabeth, after Maria's sister, and the second, born in 1802, was Gulielma, a name favoured by Quakers since it was that of the first wife of William Penn.

In March 1803 Stephen leased premises for his family home and a currier workshop in Little London, a narrow street in the old walled town, the lease including two three-storey buildings and surrounding gardens, stables and outbuildings. These two buildings are still there today. Number 29 was the former currier business and in 1962 became the Chichester and District Museum.[16] Number 30 was the Hack family home and is still a private residence. A plaque on number 30 states that 'The Quaker Pioneer John Hack, a founder of Adelaide Australia, lived here 1805–27'.

Stephen Hack senior and his brothers played a major role in

Quaker affairs. They attended the weekly meetings for worship with their families and the monthly business meetings, also participating in the quarterly regional meetings as well as the yearly meetings in London. As a result, they established a network of contacts with Quakers across the country, which were strengthened by business dealings and marriage.

In 1803 Maria gave birth to their third child, Edward Janson, and two years later their fourth child on 2 July 1805. This was John Barton Hack, who would later migrate to South Australia and who was probably named after his uncle John Barton, Maria's brother. Other children followed at regular intervals: Ellen Maria, Priscilla, Thomas Sandon and Margaret. Stephen, her ninth child, was born on 14 January 1816, when Maria was thirty-eight. Maria's last child, Mary, was born in 1820.

The Barton family

While Stephen Hack senior came from a family of business people, Maria came from a family in which business and intellectual and literary pursuits were combined. Her influence on her children was profound, even after they came to Australia.

Maria Hack's father was John Barton, a linen manufacturer who had grown up in Carlisle, near the Scottish border. In 1775 he married Mary Done (known as Maria) who was a Quaker and, although John was not a Quaker, he became one after marriage. A portrait of John Barton when he was aged about twenty shows him surrounded by books and music, indicating his love of learning. He had shown a talent for mathematics while at school, precociously producing a work on geometry and measurement at the age of seventeen.

John's wife Maria died at the age of thirty-one from tuberculosis, a common disease of the time. One of her children, only sixteen months old, was buried two weeks later. John Barton was now a widower with three children: Maria aged seven, Elizabeth four, and Bernard only two months. The family had earlier moved to London and Maria's married sister, Martha Bewley, stayed in the house to care for the children.

A few years later, John Barton became very active in the campaign against the slave trade. Quakers were prominent in this movement, but were still barred from standing for parliament. However, they worked closely with others like the MP for Yorkshire, William Wilberforce, and Thomas Clarkson, the leading abolitionist. John Barton was a founding member of the national committee of the Society for the Abolition of the Slave Trade, established in 1787. Nine of the twelve members of the committee, which also included Clarkson and Wilberforce, were Quakers. Their efforts ultimately led to the passing of the *Abolition of the Slave Trade Act* in 1807.[17] This meant the end of the British trans-Atlantic slave trade, although not the end of slave ownership, with slavery itself not banned in the British Empire until the *Slavery Abolition Act* of 1833.

John Barton married again, to a Quaker named Elizabeth Horne, whose father was a prosperous coal merchant in London, with a business on Bankside (where the Globe Theatre now stands) and a country retreat in Tottenham. But two years after the marriage, John Barton died of a fever at the age of thirty-four. Elizabeth was now a widow and expecting a child. She called her son John, after his father.

Elizabeth took a small house near her parents' country villa in Tottenham. Here she brought up the four children so 'wisely and happily', wrote Bernard Barton later, 'that I knew not but his second wife was my own mother, till I learned it years later at a boarding school'.

The love of literature and writing was to come to the fore in the next generation of Bartons. Maria Hack (née Barton) would become a well-known author of educational books;[18] her brother Bernard Barton a much-published poet, and John Barton would publish several papers on economics and a book on botany. He would carry on the work of his father in efforts to end the slave trade and be a founder of part of the University of London. He mixed with the leading economists of the day and supported the proposal for a colony in South Australia.[19] He would also play an important role in the upbringing of his nephews Barton and Stephen Hack before they migrated.

Maria Hack and the children's education

Stephen and Maria Hack were the only members of the family in Chichester with small children. Stephen's nephew James Hack and his wife Rhoda had none and Stephen's niece Elizabeth Hack remained single, but these three diligently reported on family matters to their sister Priscilla Tuke and her husband in York. Their letters provide invaluable glimpses into the lives of Stephen and Maria Hack and their growing family.

The household in Little London was crowded, with two busy parents, numerous children and two or three servants. Maria Hack was an intelligent, strong-minded woman, of firm religious principles and a deep interest in education. As a girl, she had found her first pupil in her infant brother Bernard, six years her junior. He said later in life that she was 'a sort of oracle to me'.[20]

The two older boys, Edward and Barton, were sent to boarding school, while the daughters and younger sons were taught at home by one of Stephen's nieces, with occasional supervision by Maria.

It was perhaps with the education of her own children in mind that Maria wrote her first book at the age of thirty-five. It was called *First Lessons in English Grammar*, and was published in 1812 by the London publishers, Darton, Harvey & Darton. Although they were Quakers, their books were intended for a wider audience. In an era when many children were taught at home, before compulsory education, there was a steady need for educational books. For the next three decades until her death, Maria was to write more than twenty books, some of which are listed in her entry in the *Dictionary of National Biography*.[21] Maria's daughter Elizabeth illustrated a number of them. After the death of her husband, Maria Hack continued to write books for children. Her books were reprinted in several editions and some continued to be published long after her death, with a number recently republished.[22] Her books were praised highly by the *Journal of Education*.

The *Oxford Encyclopedia of Children's Literature* describes Maria Hack as a British educational writer and says:

Maria Barton Hack published her first book *First Lessons in English Grammar*, in 1812. She became one of Quaker publisher William Darton's most important authors. Hack's pedagogical strategy, characteristic of her era, was to incorporate facts with fiction, using a frame story, as in *Winter Evenings* (1818), where a mother tells travellers' tales to spark her children's interest in geography. Hack's history books, such as *Grecian Stories* (1819), brought out moral lessons reflected in the lives of the great. Her most famous work *Harry Beaufoy; or the Pupil of Nature* (1821), attempted to inspire awareness of God through a fictional boy's observations of the natural world. Harry's parents point out the workings of a beehive, hoping he will deduce the presence of God from its perfect form and functionality. Hack's later works, like *Familiar Illustrations of the Principal Evidences and Design of Christianity* (1824), became more theological, as she moved away from Quakerism.[23]

Maria's brothers also had literary leanings. Her brother Bernard Barton published numerous books of poetry, but is remembered more for his association with other literary figures such as Charles Lamb and Edward FitzGerald, who translated the *Rubaiyat of Omar Khayyam*.

Maria corresponded regularly with Bernard on literary, religious and family matters. She also corresponded with her brother John, who was writing on economic issues. He and Maria were members of an elite debating society in Chichester, which met once a month in each other's homes.[24]

Stephen and Maria Hack's household was unusual, in that both partners pursued careers of their own in an era when women did not have paid work unless through financial desperation. But, like women today, Maria struggled to fit her work around the needs of her large family. She described this vividly in February 1821:

> I do believe if I had lived alone, or could have commanded leisure, I should have cultivated acquaintance with the Muses – but the continual interruptions of children are the most unpoetic thing in life – Pray lend me a pencil – Pray fit my work – Mamma I have cut my finger – May Hannah go & buy some seed for my bird – Oh my bantam cock is grown so handsome, only just look at him for

a minute! Then there is Eliz [abeth] – sketching a frontispiece & wants it to be criticized & commended, & dear industrious Guli [elma] making frocks for her sisters and desiring me to cut out more . . .

The 'fictional' mother in *Grecian Stories* sounds a lot like Maria, and through the book we can glimpse something of the Hack family's domestic life. The mother, who is loving and a good teacher, sits in the parlour sewing or in the summer house with the children, while they read to her and discuss what they read. That the household was a happy one is confirmed by Maria's niece Lucy, whose favourite visiting place was the home of her aunt Maria.[25]

Barton went to boarding school from the age of about eight until he was sixteen. The school was run by Josiah Forster, a kind-hearted Quaker, and was first located at Southgate in Middlesex, and later at Tottenham. After leaving school Barton Hack went to Liverpool to learn a trade, since Quakers were still banned from Oxford and Cambridge and were therefore 'apprenticed' with Friends. John Marsh, a friend of the Hacks, recorded in his diary that Barton worked in a counting house in the Exchange Building, where the cotton brokers had offices. This presumably was where Barton gained his knowledge of business and accounting.

When John Marsh visited Barton in Liverpool in 1823, Barton showed him the sights, also accompanying him to a concert. Marsh noted that they were both great readers and 'we easily fell into each other's habit of reading at breakfast, after dinner & in the evening.'[26]

Liverpool had grown enormously as a result of the slave trade. Despite the last slave ship leaving Liverpool in 1807, the trade in goods continued, especially in cotton. Among the wealthy merchant families was the Quaker Nicholas Waterhouse, whose children, along with their cousin Henry Watson, had been tutored by Maria's brother Bernard Barton. So when Barton arrived in Liverpool, he would have become acquainted with the Waterhouse and Watson families. Henry's sister Bridget would become Barton's wife four years later.

Stephen Hack's death

While Maria was turning out a book almost every year, Stephen Hack was concentrating on business, with his currier workshop and a separate merchant business in Little London. These were undoubtedly successful, since in 1816 he paid nearly £10,000 for Kingsham estate, a 134-acre farm located just south of Chichester. He had been unwell and the purchase was prompted by the hope that he would spend less time in the office and more time in the open air.

In 1821 Stephen became ill again, dying on 9 February 1823, shortly before his forty-eighth birthday. He was interred at the Quaker burial ground in Chichester. Maria's sister, Elizabeth Barton, reported that over 100 people followed the corpse the short distance from the house, with the funeral attended by relatives and friends from London as well as three clergymen. Stephen must have gained respect beyond Quaker circles.

Maria Hack was now a widow at the age of forty-five, with ten surviving children. The oldest, Elizabeth, was twenty-one and the youngest, Mary, only two. Barton, seventeen, was called back from Liverpool.

Stephen's will was generous in providing for his wife and children, but later caused complications. It was lengthy, giving specific directions about the currier business, and also involved large sums of money, most of which would not go to the children until after their mother's death. This expectation of future wealth would lead two of them – Barton and Stephen – to make unwise decisions after they had migrated to Australia.

In Stephen's will four executors were appointed: his brothers James and William, his brother-in-law John Barton, and his friend Halsey Janson. He appointed three guardians for his children until they reached the age of twenty-one; John Barton, Halsey Janson and Maria. The executors were directed to sell everything except the currier business and invest the proceeds in securities and funds. The currier business at Little London was to be preserved for one or more of the sons to continue to operate. In addition, Maria could, if she wished, lend any of the sons in the business up to £6000 from the estate, at five per cent interest.

Maria was allowed to remain in the house at Little London.

She was to be paid £1000 a year for the maintenance of herself and the children, until the sons in the currier business turned twenty-one, after which she would have an annual allowance of £600. Each child on reaching the age of twenty-one, or being married, would receive £1000 from the estate, but the entirety of the estate was not to be divided until after Maria's death.

Only two of Stephen's sons were old enough to go into the currier business. They were Edward, twenty, and Barton, seventeen, and it was Edward who was chosen to take over the business. Edward took on a heavy responsibility, but was well regarded in the family for his stability and good disposition.

The first of Maria's children to marry was her daughter Elizabeth, aged twenty-two. Four months after her father's death she married the Reverend George Bliss, a man nearly twenty years older. He was the vicar at the parish church of St Mary at Funtington, a village near Chichester. Elizabeth had to resign from the Society of Friends, but remained close to her family.

Uncle John Barton

Maria's brother John Barton played a significant role in the family as one of the executors of Stephen's estate and as a guardian of the children. His influence was to continue even after his nephews left for Australia.

As a young man, John Barton had moved to Chichester shortly after Maria's marriage to work with Stephen Hack in the merchant business. His later writings reveal a great breadth and depth of scholarship and a capacity for original thought. Like his father, he had a natural aptitude for mathematics.

He had little interest in Quaker worship and later rejected it, but throughout his life he was involved in a variety of philanthropic activities, including a school in Chichester for poor children and the establishment of the Chichester Savings Bank to help those who were too poor to deposit in a normal bank (different from the Chichester bank set up by Stephen Hack's brothers).

In 1811, at the age of twenty-two, John Barton married another Quaker, Ann Woodrouffe Smith. After marrying Ann, John Barton withdrew from the merchant business to concentrate on his interest in political economy (economics). He met leading economists and published a series of pamphlets on poverty and the plight of the labouring classes. His work influenced David Ricardo and was praised by Karl Marx.[27]

Ann Barton died of consumption in 1822. John became despondent, but continued his studies and philanthropic work. In 1823 he took up the cause his father had embraced, the abolition of slavery, and was the secretary of the Chichester anti-slavery committee.

He also became involved in activities in London, including the establishment of the London Mechanics Institute to provide education for the working man. John Barton was elected a member of the governing committee of the institute, and his name was included on the foundation stone in the entrance hall of the institute, which later became Birkbeck College, part of the University of London.

John Barton was now mixing with men of high intellectual standing, and it was from their ranks that the idea of colonisation as a means of addressing overpopulation and poverty originated, a view he supported. These ideas informed the development of the Wakefield scheme for the settlement of South Australia.

In 1825 John Barton left his home in Chichester and moved to a farmhouse at Stoughton, a village near Chichester. He stayed in contact with Maria Hack and the children, he and Halsey Janson taking on major responsibility for the family concerns. They were certainly prevailed upon when a crisis again overtook the family in 1825.

Chapter 2
Barton Hack marries

At the age of twenty, Barton took over the family leather business, and two years later married Bridget Watson of Liverpool. They started to raise a family, but in 1830, at the age of twenty-five, Barton developed tuberculosis. He moved to the countryside, but after further attacks he had to consider moving to a warmer climate. This was about the time the idea of a colony in South Australia was beginning to gain support.

Barton Hack goes into the family business
In October 1825 the Hack family in Chichester was hit by serious illness. Barton and Edward contracted typhus, a highly infectious disease. Typhus spread through the family, proving fatal to the twenty-one-year-old Edward. This was a great loss, as Edward was much loved and had done well in managing the family leather business. By April 1826 the family was out of further danger, but typhus had affected five of the children.

After Edward's death, Uncle John Barton took on the oversight of the currier business, and the family decided that Barton, as the next son in line, should go into the business. Uncle John wrote in his journal that it would 'still be necessary for me to attend frequently, even when Barton is well enough to perform the office, as he is yet under age, and unacquainted with the leather trade, as well as very inexperienced'.

Barton turned twenty-one in the middle of the following year, inheriting £1000 from his father's estate and almost the same amount from his uncle William Hack. He promptly invested this £2000 in the currier business. The family had concerns about Barton's ability to run the business, however, and were relieved when a currier by the name of Thomas Smith proposed a partnership. Smith, aged twenty-eight and a Quaker with a leather business in Bermondsey, could now provide the experience that

Barton lacked. Smith moved to Chichester, becoming mayor of the city nearly forty years later.

The 'Deed of Copartnership' between Barton Hack and Thomas Smith was signed the following year, on 1 April 1827. It dictated how the business of Hack and Smith was to be conducted, a key clause being the reference to repayment of any money lent to the business by either partner. There is no evidence that Thomas Smith brought any capital to the business, but Barton had invested £2000 and it seems that Maria also lent the business £6000 from her husband's estate, as allowed in her husband's will. Both amounts of money became an issue as soon as Barton left for Australia.

With Barton now settled in the family business, Maria had very few children at home. Margaret, Thomas, and Stephen were at Quaker boarding schools. Ellen, nineteen and Priscilla, sixteen, were staying with their sister Elizabeth and her husband, the Reverend George Bliss. Elizabeth was no longer a Quaker, and Ellen had begun to attend St John's Anglican chapel in Chichester, as well as Quaker meetings.

Barton Hack marries

Barton Hack settled into the currier business with Thomas Smith, and the following year returned to Liverpool to marry Bridget Watson, another Quaker. Her father, William Watson, had a medical degree and was a chemist and druggist with premises at 5 Scotland Place in Liverpool.

The wedding took place on 9 July 1827 in the Friends Meeting House at Hardshaw West in St Helens, a town near Liverpool. This meeting house was first used in 1679 and is still used today.[28]

Barton was twenty-two and Bridget was soon to be twenty-one. Quaker weddings were a simple affair and the only members of the Hack family who attended were Barton's uncle James Hack and his daughter Elizabeth, travelling from Yorkshire. James described the wedding in a letter on 16 September, saying that Bridget was a lovely young woman and would be a comfort to Barton.

The marriage certificate, in beautifully written copperplate, is still in existence. It states that the ceremony was conducted before the monthly meeting of Friends. Those present signed the certificate as witnesses and included James Hack and his daughter Elizabeth, James's old friend Isaac Hadwen of Liverpool, who had been an anti-slavery campaigner, and his son Isaac, a leather trader. In addition to Bridget's parents William and Martha Watson and her brother Henry Watson, also present were Bridget's relatives, well-to-do merchant families in Liverpool.

After the wedding, Barton and Bridget (Bbe) travelled to Chichester to their new home – Maria's house – next door to the currier business. Maria, now fifty, moved with her remaining children to a house in Lavant, a village just outside Chichester. Nine months after Barton and Bbe were married they had their first child, William, on 24 April 1828.

Not long after Barton and Bbe had settled into the house in Little London, Bbe's brother, Henry Watson moved to Chichester. Bbe's two sisters had died young, and she was close to Henry. Like his father, he set himself up as a chemist and druggist, opening premises in South Street, Chichester, in 1828. He developed a warm relationship with Barton and Bbe and would later join them in South Australia.

Family history has it that after he moved to Chichester in 1827, Henry Watson became engaged to Barton's sister Gulielma.[29] But Gulielma was seriously ill with consumption, and died on 24 April 1829. She was only twenty-six, and the third of Maria's children to die young. Gulielma's death was a blow to the family, and Maria Hack sought spiritual assistance from her brother Bernard Barton. She was still a Quaker, but her daughters Ellen and Priscilla had joined the Church of England, as had her brother John Barton.

In July 1828 John Barton married for the second time; he was thirty-nine and Fanny Rickman just twenty-one. She had been a Quaker but had resigned in order to marry in an Anglican church. Around 1834 they moved to a 300-acre estate near Chichester and would eventually have nine children.

In the early 1830s, Maria Hack moved from Lavant back to Chichester and took a house in St John's Street. Her brothers-in-law were now all dead, and only two trustees of the family estate remained: John Barton and Halsey Janson.

Most of Maria's children were living with her, or nearby. Elizabeth was still at Funtington, Barton was in Little London, Thomas was working in the office of Chichester's leading architect, Margaret was at boarding school and Ellen, Priscilla, Stephen and Mary were at home.

Stephen Hack junior

Barton Hack's younger brother Stephen was a favourite with his mother, who often called him 'Steenie'. As a young boy he went to Quaker schools, but did not remain a Quaker. From quite a young age it was clear that he was not cut out for a strict Quaker life, but instead longed for adventure.

Many years later, when he was over fifty, Stephen described his religious upbringing in a bitter tract called 'Silent Worship and its Results'.

> I was taken to meeting when quite a little chap and was told that I must 'sit still and be a good boy'. I believe that I really did try to do this and that I succeeded for perhaps five minutes. Then I fidgeted, played with my handkerchief, had 'creeps' up my back, fell asleep and tumbled off the form I was seated on. I was picked up, shaken, and when I got home I was talked to and punished 'for not being good at Meeting' ... at last I was fairly broken in and did sit still and quiet ... How did I manage to be so good? I was a very imaginative dreamy kind of child and I had given free play to my fancy and I soon found the long, dreary, silent Meetings at Chichester had become almost pleasant ... when the Fairyland epoch was gone by, Robinson Crusoe did just as well ... Then came Walter Scott and Fenimore Cooper ...

Stephen heard the Bible read constantly and the Friends' teachings on it. 'I found the whole subject to be so full of contradictions that I threw it all on one side and troubled myself no more about it.'

Stephen may have given up Quakerism, but he had a good sense of morality. When he was about twelve he attended a Quaker boarding school at Rochester, run by Richard Weston, who was disowned by the Quakers in March 1829 for 'conduct towards his pupils of a grossly indecent & immoral character' and the school was closed.[30] Stephen wrote later, 'it was a complete den of impurity' and 'had the old scoundrel been brought to justice as he ought to have been, "hard labour" would have been his portion'.

Stephen transferred to Fishponds, a Quaker school near Bristol, but returned home at fourteen, with Maria writing in desperation to her brother Bernard:

> Stephen is a boy of considerable talent and yet behind most boys of his age . . . I think the reason of this is a propensity to reverie for which he has been remarkable from a little child . . . He is honourable, affectionate and ingenuous but shy, and has very little notion of obeying unless he sees the command to be fit and just . . . Very few boys of his age give less trouble or do less mischief or have fewer *positive* faults except his reverie and sauntering. He will stand by the half hour with his hands in his pockets watching birds or insects in the garden – yet at short intervals he will apply with great energy . . . I fear he is not the kind of lad to get on in business . . . he has considerable mental power, if one could only hit on the right way of calling it forth . . .

Maria's worry was understandable, and she was not to know then that this love of the outdoors and 'great energy' would find their focus later on in South Australia. Meanwhile, Stephen stayed at home and the following year Maria wrote about her quandary to Gates Darton, the son of her publisher in London. The Hack and Darton families were close friends and confidants. Samuel Darton and his wife Ann had six children, the eldest being the twenty-three-year-old Thomas Gates Darton, known as Gates.

The Dartons, who lived above the publishing business at 55 Gracechurch Street in London, invited Stephen to stay with them to learn something of the publishing business. Soon afterwards, Maria wrote to Bernard that Stephen was employed in 'collecting' (money due), which took him out among the booksellers and was a job he liked very much. He was never cut out for an office job and throughout his life preferred to be out and about, adventuring.

In November 1831 Maria's daughter Ellen married John Knott, a young surgeon in Chichester. Ellen was no longer a Quaker and nor was he, so they were married in the Anglican Church. They too, would later go to South Australia.

Graylingwell House

By 1830 Barton Hack's tuberculosis had progressed to a serious state, prompting him to move to the countryside. In 1831 he rented Graylingwell House, just north of Chichester. A large house set in twelve acres, with a garden, orchard and enclosed farmyard, it was part of a larger farm belonging to the Dean and Chapter of Chichester Cathedral. Graylingwell Farmhouse still stands – it is part of a new housing estate – and is somewhat derelict, but heritage-protected.[31]

Despite the move, Barton's health remained a worry. At twenty-six, he was now the father of four children, William, born in 1828, twins Edward and Annie, born on 11 October 1829 and Louisa, born on 9 June 1831. Barton and Bbe were conscientious parents and by the time William was four years old they were teaching him to read. In September 1832, Barton wrote to Gates Darton thanking him for a book to help them,[32] and a 'dissected map' (jigsaw puzzle) for little William.

Gates Darton was now very much part of the family circle. Stephen was living with the Darton family and Maria corresponded regularly and confidentially to Gates from this time. From about 1831 on, a relationship began to develop between the twenty-one-year-old Gates Darton and Maria's seventeen-year-old-daughter Margaret, but since Margaret's health was poor, Maria counselled Gates to postpone any proposal of marriage. Margaret suffered from epilepsy and consumption. Margaret did recover, however, and she and Gates were married on 13 March 1834, in Brighton, two weeks before Margaret's twentieth birthday. A portrait of Margaret perhaps dates from the wedding, whereas the only portrait believed to be of Gates, is in older age.

Shortly before the marriage, Barton Hack wrote a frank letter of advice to Gates in London:

I had and have for some time past been much in hopes that you would have looked towards a small house in an airy part of the outskirts of Town such as Peckham – as I should have more hopes of Margaret enjoying a good state of health in such a situation than near your house of business – and I have another reason founded on my own experience – which I scarcely know whether thou wilt see in the same way as I do, and that is, when a young woman is brought into quite a new place and entirely thrown on her husband's relations for *daily* society as must be the case *at first* of living very near, there must be a very great similarity of tastes and pursuits and feelings – to prevent the two parties from very soon wishing that a greater distance separated them . . .

The letter suggests that Barton's move to the country was not just for health reasons, but also for Bbe's feelings. Both Maria Hack and Bbe Hack were strong women with minds of their own, and perhaps they clashed. At any rate, Gates Darton followed Barton's advice and after the wedding took a house in London at 10 South Place, Finsbury.

Bbe's brother, Henry Watson, had built a substantial house at 11 South Street opposite his shop. Of a more contemplative disposition and less a man of action than his brother-in-law, Barton,[33] Henry was a leading light in the Chichester Literary and Philosophical Society, with its library and museum. It was founded in 1831 with John Barton as a trustee and located in Henry's house. It later amalgamated with the Chichester Mechanics Institute.

Henry and Bbe's parents, William and Martha Watson, moved down from Liverpool to Chichester to be near their children. In 1836 Henry married Charlotte Float, who was not a Quaker, and Henry left the Society of Friends.

After Margaret married Gates and moved to London, her brother Thomas moved to Gloucester where he became an ironmonger. Maria Hack then moved to Gloucester and set up house with Thomas and Mary while Priscilla stayed in Chichester with her sister Ellen and her husband John Knott.

Barton Hack's family at Graylingwell Farm was growing, with Bbe giving birth to their fifth child Alfred on 25 October 1833.

Around this time Barton experienced another bout of tuberculosis, which prompted their consideration of a move to a warmer climate.

It was at this time that the colonisation plans for South Australia were gaining momentum.

Chapter 3
Preparations for migration

By the 1830s, Britain was suffering from overpopulation and widespread poverty, and migration was seen as the answer. A new scheme was proposed by Edward Gibbon Wakefield – the settlement of South Australia as a place of free settlers, with religious freedom. The Hack family became very interested in the scheme and in 1835 they purchased land orders in the new colony. By mid-1836 the fleets of the South Australian Company and the government surveyors were on their way. Barton Hack had planned to move to Madeira for his health, but decided on South Australia instead. His younger brother Stephen was asked to go with him.

Why people were leaving Britain
From about 1800 to the 1830s poverty was widespread in Britain. The population had doubled over the previous century, which meant that more food was required, but the enclosures had reduced the amount of land available to small holders. Textile factories had grown up in the towns, creating new jobs, but wages were low.

The price of corn, including wheat, had risen sharply. The importation of cheap foreign corn might have brought some relief, but the Corn Laws of 1815 onwards effectively prohibited the importation of foreign corn, which had a huge impact on the poorer classes. Bread made with wheat had become the staple diet, and meat was rare. The Corn Laws were violently opposed by working people, with riots in some parts of the country. By the 1830s Britain was marked by unemployment, destitution and over-population.

Barton Hack's uncle John Barton wrote several papers about the plight of the agricultural labourer and the Corn Laws, in 1830 publishing a pamphlet in which he called for migration to the colonies. The following year he was invited to address a House of

Lords Committee on the Poor Laws. 'Nothing can save us from famine or civil war', he said, 'but an equalisation between the amount of our population and the means of our subsistence . . . I am therefore compelled to conclude that emigration is our only resource . . .'[34] He was not alone in this view, with several people searching for a new approach to colonisation.

Wakefield

In 1829 a pamphlet appeared, *Sketch of a proposal for colonising Australasia*, edited by Robert Gouger, a young idealist and a Dissenter – that is, not a member of the Church of England. His interest in colonisation stemmed from a desire to help the working classes. The real author, however, was Edward Gibbon Wakefield, aged thirty-three. His name was not on the pamphlet because at the time he was in Newgate Prison.

Wakefield was at this stage notorious. At the age of twenty he had eloped with a sixteen-year-old heiress, married her and had two children. She died and at the age of thirty he abducted a fifteen-year-old schoolgirl and tricked her into marrying him. At his trial, which caused a public sensation, he was sentenced to three years in prison. There he read widely, developing his theory of colonisation. Gouger visited him and then tirelessly promoted the idea of systematic colonisation.

Shortly after the publication of Wakefield's pamphlet, a series of articles appeared in London's *Morning Chronicle* with the title 'A Letter from Sydney', with these later published in a book with Gouger as editor. Once again, the author was Wakefield. He was to become an influential figure in the early colonisation of South Australia and subsequently New Zealand and Canada.[35]

Wakefield came from a talented and well-known Quaker family and had been exposed to Quaker thought and philanthropy, although he was not himself a member. The Wakefield family knew the Hacks and the Bartons. His grandmother Priscilla Wakefield was a popular writer for children, as well as the inventor of the idea of savings banks. Her books (and Maria Hack's) were to be found in most Quaker schoolrooms of the day. Edward's cousin Elizabeth Fry, the Quaker prison reformer, was also a friend of the Hacks and the Bartons.

Wakefield's ideas on colonisation spread, and he and his supporters began to seriously consider South Australia as a suitable place for applying the scheme. At this time Australia was a penal colony, with the main convict settlements at Sydney Cove and in Van Diemen's Land (later called Tasmania).

Wakefield and Gouger realised that the release of land in a new colony was meaningless without a proper plan and the provision of labour and capital. They proposed a colony of free settlers – without convicts – with all the land in the new colony sold initially in England. The proceeds would pay for free passage for labourers and tradesmen. The emigrants would be carefully selected and preference given to young married couples. This would do away with the need for convict labour. The surveying and allocation of land would take place after the emigrants' arrival in the colony. Wakefield also suggested that the new colony should be largely self-governing. The Wakefield 'Principle' became widely discussed.

At the end of 1830, news reached England of the momentous discoveries of Captain Charles Sturt in the southern part of Australia. He traced the course of the River Murray from New South Wales to its mouth near Encounter Bay. Soon afterwards, his friend Captain Barker explored the east coast of the Gulf St Vincent, climbed Mount Lofty and crossed the Fleurieu Peninsula to the mouth of the Murray, discovering rich unclaimed land and the Port Adelaide inlet.

Wakefield, Gouger and their supporters, encouraged by the report of Sturt's exploration, proposed a new colony in South Australia based on their theories. Their proposal gained the support of several influential young political economists, including John Stuart Mill. Barton Hack would have heard about the scheme from his uncle John, who was one of the supporters.

In 1831 Wakefield and his supporters formed the South Australian Land Company to enable investors to buy land in the new colony. This attracted support from wealthy merchants, bankers and members of parliament, the most enthusiastic supporter being George Fife Angas, a merchant and devout nonconformist. Although the Land Company did not proceed, the promoters of the new colony pressed on.

After much lobbying by Wakefield's supporters, in 1834 an Act of Parliament was eventually passed for the creation of South Australia as a crown colony with a governor. The British Government established the South Australian Commission in May the following year. With the responsibility for selling £35,000 worth of land, which would then fund migration, the commission was also obliged to deposit £20,000 in the British Treasury as a guarantee fund. This gave the Colonial Office total control, without any financial liability. The colony was to be self-financing, a requirement which would later bring the infant colony to its knees.

The chairman of the new South Australian Commission was Colonel Robert Torrens, one of whose first official tasks was the appointment of Robert Gouger as the Colonial Secretary in South Australia. Amongst the promoters were many Dissenters who wanted civil and religious freedom for the new colony. Nonconformists like Gouger and George Fife Angas were restricted by their religious beliefs, and like the Quakers, were not permitted to attend either Oxford or Cambridge universities. The promoters extracted an undertaking that there would be no government interference in religious matters, other than the appointment of a colonial chaplain.

In 1838 Angas assisted a group of German Lutherans who had been similarly persecuted, to emigrate to the Colony of South Australia. The colony thus attracted Dissenters from Britain and religious refugees from Germany – and, also significantly, had no convicts. As the historian Douglas Pike showed in his book, *Paradise of Dissent: South Australia 1829–1857*, South Australia was settled by men and women whose professed ideals were civil liberty, social opportunity and equality for all religions.[36]

The Hack family's interest in South Australia

The first mention of Barton Hack's interest in South Australia is the entry which Robert Gouger made in his journal of 29 May 1835:

> Two gentlemen called today at the office, having rather important errands. Mr Barton Hack, a Quaker, called to say he has some

friends, persons of capital, desirous to emigrate. The other is a Captain Hindmarsh, a post-captain in the Navy, who wishes to be appointed Governor.

Barton Hack was not at this stage thinking of migrating to South Australia; he was more interested in its commercial potential. He would have appealed to Gouger as a non-conformist like himself, and a person with money to invest.

Captain John Hindmarsh had had a lengthy naval career and had fought at Trafalgar and the Nile, where he lost the sight in one eye. His references were impressive and Gouger referred him to the Colonial Office and the Board of Commissioners, after which Hindmarsh was confirmed as governor. He appointed George Stevenson as his private secretary, which paved the way for problems in the new colony. Stevenson set out to influence the policies of Governor Hindmarsh, and while Hindmarsh was said to be 'not remarkably clever'[37] Stevenson was too clever by half.

In June 1835 the Commissioners issued regulations for the sale of land in South Australia at £1 per acre, and set out to raise the £35,000 required. The preliminary land orders went on sale in July at £81 for 81 acres, with each order comprised of one acre of land in the town and eighty acres outside the town. The capital of the colony, later to be called Adelaide, was not yet named or its location fixed.

Soon after the land went on sale, Gates Darton bought three of the land orders as a family investment. He advanced the money for the three sections, effectively lending Barton £162 for two of the shares, and Barton agreed to pay him five per cent interest on the loan. Barton had no money of his own, with all his capital tied up in the family business. After ten years in the currier business he had saved nothing; his earnings had been consumed by his growing family, a large house, servants and carriage. Later on, Stephen Hack was allocated one of Barton's shares. They were now the owners of land on the other side of the world.

The sale of land orders slowed after the first flurry of excitement, and the Commissioners were far short of the £35,000 they needed. George Fife Angas saw a golden opportunity and offered to buy the remaining land at the discounted price of twelve shillings an acre. The other Commissioners agreed reluctantly, with Angas and two partners snapping up the remaining land.

The inequity between the two land prices was overcome by increasing the country section of the earlier purchasers to 134 acres. Thus the Hack-Darton purchase increased to three in the town and 402 in the country. Barton Hack wrote to Gates: '134 acres instead of 80 seems like 54 gained, which does not make the spec[ulation] appear worse'. They appointed John Morphett as their agent, and he would select their land as soon as the first surveys were made.

Barton's brother Stephen was nineteen and restless. He had left Darton's publishing business and was employed by a Quaker family on a farm near Horsham. Although not staying there long, he did get some farming experience, which would later prove invaluable in South Australia.

Barton's family was growing; on 10 August 1835 Bbe gave birth to their sixth child, Bedford. Two months later, Barton was again very ill with tuberculosis, having frequent attacks. His doctor advised him to spend the following winter in Madeira and in the interim to take a sea trip round the British Isles.

'Dr Forbes's plan is indeed a formidable one!' wrote Maria Hack to Gates Darton in June 1836: 'But I do not like *half*-measures ... I cannot help suspecting these summer trips are advised merely as a *palliative* and that the Doctor has but little hope of poor Barton living to put the Madeira plan in execution'.

1836 – ships leave for South Australia

Now that Barton and Gates were owners of land in South Australia, they would have kept abreast of the three entities involved with the new colony: the South Australian Commission, the South Australian Company and the British Government.

The South Australian Company was established in October 1835 by George Fife Angas, to buy property for lease or sale and to establish a bank. He appointed a number of company officials to go to South Australia, including Samuel Stephens as the local manager and his brother Edward Stephens to establish the bank. Angas purchased three ships for the company and chartered another. The first of these, the *John Pirie*, set off in February 1836, ahead of the Governor and the official party. It was followed by the *Lady Mary Pelham*, the *Duke of York* and the *Emma*.

The Commissioners set about appointing officials for the new colony, including James Hurtle Fisher as the Resident Commissioner, who was given considerable powers, setting him on a collision course with Governor Hindmarsh. Pascoe St Leger Grenfell, an industrialist, donated a town acre as the site for a church in Adelaide, and the Reverend Charles Beaumont Howard, a Church of England minister, was appointed colonial chaplain.

In February 1836 Colonel Light was appointed surveyor-general, with the responsibility for choosing the site of the town of Adelaide and surveying the whole of the province. Light was not a surveyor, but as a military man he was suited to be in charge of the surveying team. George Kingston, the deputy surveyor-general, had earlier presented a plan for the town, based on a grid of streets surrounding four squares, with the whole surrounded by parklands.

In March 1836 the first survey team left London in the *Cygnet*. It also carried forty-nine labourers and two paying passengers. Colonel Light was not well enough to leave and sailed in May on board the *Rapid*, while Governor Hindmarsh did not leave England until 3 August in HMS *Buffalo* with the government officials.

Another last minute consideration was the treatment of the Aborigines. Around this time, the Aboriginal population of South Australia was well over 10,000,[38] but the South Australian legislation was based on the erroneous assumption that the country 'consists of waste and unoccupied lands'. Lord Glenelg, the Colonial Secretary, now decided that the treatment of the native population should be an official responsibility. Their cause was championed by John Brown, the Emigration Agent, who ensured that provision was made for a Protector of Aborigines.

Liverpool and Gloucester

In mid-1836 Barton Hack was about to take a trip to Liverpool to visit relatives, following which he planned to spend a year in the warmer climate of Madeira and, then perhaps, visit Australia.

He started a journal to record their new life. The first entry was for 18 June 1836, in which he wrote that he was arranging to sublet Graylingwell House for five years. He and Bbe then went to Portsmouth and boarded the *Emerald Isle*, a large paddle steamer, which, coincidentally, was lying alongside the *Buffalo*. The *Buffalo* was being fitted out for Governor Hindmarsh and loading baggage for emigrants to South Australia.

In Liverpool they visited relatives of Bridget's and did some sightseeing. They then travelled to Gloucester to visit Thomas and his new wife Lydia, going on to 4 Brunswick Square, where Maria Hack was living with sixteen-year-old Mary, who was very ill with consumption. Here they had the momentous discussion which caused them to change their plans. In the light of Mary's life-threatening illness, Maria suggested they go straight to South Australia rather than Madeira, and they agreed. Four days later they left for Chichester. In his pocket Barton carried £100, a gift from his mother towards the expenses of their outfit for Australia. Although he was unaware of it at the time, he would never see his mother or sister again.

The moment they left, Maria Hack wrote to Gates. Her first thought was for books for Barton's children and she asked Gates to send her a book on physical and mental education. Then she turned to the fears she could not voice to Barton:

> It has been and is an overwhelming decision to us all ... We all dread the effect of discussion and difficulties on poor Barton's feverish habit ... Our surgeon is fully persuaded from his appearance that there is yet no organic disease, and thinks after six years in a warm climate he will probably be a strong man.

It seems to have been Barton's nature to make major decisions impetuously and hastily and then throw himself into frenetic activity. His greatest problem now was what to do about the family currier business in which he was in partnership with Thomas Smith. He discussed the matter with Smith and they agreed on a stocktake and a final balance sheet. A visit from Dr Forbes, the family doctor and friend, followed. He gave his approval for migration, but on one condition, that Barton's younger brother Stephen accompanied them.

Writing to his mother two months later en route to Australia, Stephen made it clear that he was only going because of concern for his brother and family:

> In a short time now I shall have the cares of the world on me with a vengeance. Did thee know that I am named as guardian and executor in Barton's will so that if anything should happen I should be sole and acting guardian for eighteen months at least . . .

Stephen had been considering going to the United States, but an obstacle had arisen in the form of a romantic attachment to Julia Woods, the eighteen-year-old daughter of a family who had a farm near Chichester. Farewelling the Woods had made him 'perfectly miserable' and he now hoped that he would be allowed to correspond with Julia. He was concerned about her health, however, for she had the beginnings of consumption. So the change of plans was at great personal cost to Stephen, although there was the exciting prospect of adventure and of making money in the new colony.

Barton now had to face Uncle John and discuss the family business. John Barton was kind to his nephew, but as an executor of the family estate, he was concerned about 'the £6000 bond being paid off in six years by Thomas Smith', which belonged to the estate.

John Barton lectured his two nephews on potential problems in the new colony. He warned of the dangers of drought and hostile natives; he said the colony would attract a swarm of rogues and swindlers and he prophesied that it would be bankrupt within a year or so of its foundation. He admitted that he could not prevent Barton from going to his ruin, but he was not convinced of the need for Stephen to accompany him. Having registered his protest however, Uncle John acquiesced.[39]

Preparations, 1836

Preparations now began in earnest. Barton ordered items of saddlery and Margaret helped Bbe with making clothes and linen. Making clothes for the family for such a long time ahead, with everything done by hand, even the men's suits, was a mammoth task. Gates arrived to discuss their plans and returned to London with Barton and Stephen on 8 August. Gates's account book, carefully preserved down the years, provides a record of their pre-trip purchases.

The most expensive items were two portable 'Manning' cottages at £210, other items including tarpaulins, ropes, linens, a stove, a dinner service, clothes, sheep nets and mattresses. The list totalled £387, a great deal more than the £100 Maria had given Barton for his outfit. Maria began to be apprehensive and wrote to Gates, asking, 'how could it be that he [Barton] ordered so many things without considering *how* they were to be paid for?'

The next pressing matter was shipping. Barton went to the South Australian Commissioners, who recommended the *Isabella*, captained by John Hart. Hart was only twenty-seven, but had extensive experience sailing in southern Australia. He was later to become Premier of South Australia on three occasions.

The *Isabella* was sailing to Van Diemen's Land, but that suited the Hacks, as they needed to buy stock and materials there. They signed up with Captain Hart, beginning a close association that would last for many years. The fares for the three adults, six children and their freight totalled £400.

After visiting the docks to meet Captain Hart and arranging the berths for the family, Barton and Stephen went to the offices of the South Australia Commission, where they 'had a long conversation with E.G. Wakefield'. It is frustrating not to know more about the meeting with Wakefield, since he was known to have a fascinating personality,[40] and the Hacks must have been intrigued, even if somewhat shocked, by his colourful background.

To the concern of his mother Barton continued to buy ever more goods. Years later, in his memoir, he wrote 'I fear our outfit was much more elaborate than was necessary'. In addition to items he would need for his family and farming operations, he purchased goods he hoped to sell on arrival, most of which were obtained on credit.

Back in Chichester, Barton met with Uncle John, who announced that he wanted to keep Barton's capital in the currier business until the £6000 bond had been repaid. This was a huge blow to Barton, who had expected to recoup his investment in the business.

Barton's thoughts now turned to Stephen, who would soon turn twenty-one and also inherit £2000, which Barton assumed could be used in their Australian venture. Barton borrowed £300 from each of his two brothers-in-law, Gates Darton and Henry Watson, on which he would pay interest. He also raised some money by sub-letting Graylingwell House and selling his furniture.

John Barton insisted that Barton's partnership could not be dissolved until Smith could find another partner to pay off the £6000. Barton and Smith signed a dissolution of the partnership, but one which would not come into operation for over two years to give Smith time to find another partner. Smith agreed to pay Barton £200 per annum until then, at which occasion Barton would be paid out his capital.

Barton and Bbe attended their last meeting of the Society of Friends in Chichester and farewelled friends. Barton was hopeful for the future: he was going to Australia for his health, but also in anticipation of becoming a successful businessman and landowner, like his father and uncles before him.

His mother was not so calm. She was concerned about his impetuousness and over-spending. As she wrote to Gates on 14 August, 'Only let him [Barton] be careful to guard against sanguine anticipations & rash confidence in strangers – Keep all things snug – *on a small scale*, and feel their way gradually – I believe this will be the path of peace & safety . . .'

Maria's fears were well founded. At that time neither she nor Gates were aware of the extent of Barton's outlays, or that so many purchases had been made on credit. Gates Darton, the linchpin of the family, would be left to sort it out. The hurried arrangements for departure meant that when Barton left England his complex finances were largely unresolved, a situation that would have grave consequences later on, in terms of his finances in Australia and his relationship with his extended family.

Chapter 4
On board the *Isabella*

The voyage from England to Sydney was 13,000 miles and not much less to Launceston. The Hacks left on the Isabella *at the beginning of September1836, arriving in Van Diemen's Land on 4 January 1837. On the first leg of the voyage they travelled down the coast of Africa to the Cape Verde Islands, where they went on shore for the only time on the voyage. They crossed the Equator on 17 October 1836, and rounded the Cape of Good Hope about a month later. From there they had a direct run to Launceston.*

Boarding the *Isabella*

On 31 August 1836, a warm summer's day in Chichester,[41] the Hacks finally set out for their long voyage. Their decision to migrate to South Australia had been made on 24 July and they had arranged everything in just five weeks. Bbe was exhausted from the packing, but anxious to get away. Two wagons arrived at Graylingwell House at nine in the morning to load the luggage for Portsmouth.

At noon, two horse-drawn carriages with drivers arrived to transport the large party – Barton, Bridget, their six young children and Stephen – to Portsmouth. They were accompanied by Gates Darton, Henry Watson and Bridget's father William Watson, who were coming to the port to see them off.

Having purchased land orders for South Australia for £243, the family was entitled to up to twelve free passages to the colony for servants or labourers. They had engaged a couple as servants, Michael and Mina Pfender, who were accompanied by their eight-year-old-daughter Dorothea.

Quaker portraits of the time give us a good indication of how the Hack family would have looked as they set out. The men wore dark suits and waistcoats over a white shirt, with a dark cravat tied in a soft bow. The women wore dark-coloured dresses with long sleeves and a full skirt. Bridget's hair would have been twisted into a bun at the back and covered by a bonnet tied under the chin. To keep warm she would have wrapped a large shawl around her shoulders or worn a cape. Barton may already have had the beard seen in later photographs, but the portrait of Stephen as a young man shows him almost clean-shaven and wearing glasses. The children would have been dressed in simple cotton or linen clothes; the boys in jackets and trousers and the girls in dresses.

The Hacks arrived at Portsmouth in the afternoon and went on board that night. The *Isabella* was anchored at Spithead, the sheltered harbour between Portsmouth and the Isle of Wight. A wooden three-masted barque of 226 tons, the *Isabella* was eighty-nine feet long and twenty-three feet wide. Cabins on board a sailing ship like the *Isabella* were small and cramped; they were usually about six by eight feet. Barton, Bbe and their six children were squashed into two of these, which also housed their mattresses, a writing desk and numerous trunks and equipment. They had a portable crib for the baby, which still exists today.[42] Cabin passengers could bring their own furniture and construct shelves and attach hooks to the walls for their belongings, but the furniture had to be nailed down or lashed to the side of the cabin to prevent its moving.

The *Isabella* was laden with cargo, with even a marble chimney-piece being transported to the other side of the world.[43] Because Captain Hart had not reserved sufficient space for the Hacks' large amount of cargo, most of it had to be put into storage in London and later sent on to South Australia. All they could take on board the *Isabella* were their two Manning portable cottages, their cabin luggage and a few other essentials, including their dogs.

Once on board they met the other passengers. There was a Miss Esther Dixon, returning to Launceston to join her brother James, and Miss Caroline Carter who was on her way to Launceston to be married. She was acquainted with some friends of the Hacks and was to become a good companion and helper for Bbe. There was a Mr Henry Jones, who was planning to be a merchant in Launceston, but later settled in South Australia.

A last minute passenger was Sir John Jeffcott, the judge appointed to the new colony. What they did not know was that he was boarding the *Isabella* at the last minute to avoid creditors. He had been Chief Justice in Sierra Leone, but on his return to England had killed an adversary in a duel and was also deeply in debt. Jeffcott was 'in urgent need of temporary absence from England'.[44]

The next day Captain Hart purchased a small sailing boat for £10 for Barton, which was stored on deck. Barton thought it would be useful because he assumed the settlement would be located on the sea. In this he turned out to be mistaken.

Into the Channel

The *Isabella* moved out into the English Channel and, according to Barton's journal, they immediately hit stormy weather.

> [4 September, 1836] We were very sick as soon as we moved in the morning. A fresh wind which is contrary and a heavy sea makes the vessel roll very much. Captain Hart told me this morning that it was always his practice to read prayers on first day [Sunday] mornings. We mean to attend and to sit quietly. We are quite unable today to do anything beyond what the children positively require.

The next few days were no better and they were all seasick. The cabins would have been oppressive and smelling dreadfully, with no fresh air, as the cabin windows could not be opened in rough weather. To make things worse, the weather turned cold and there was no heating. Fires were too dangerous on board a wooden ship, although they were lit in the big iron stoves in the galley.

> [5 September 1836] Had a most stormy night. Our cot swung so much against the lockers at our head and the bulkheads at our feet, that we could get no rest whatever and poor Bbe was thrown out. I called up [for] Stephen, and after unhooking the cot we laid it on the packages and boxes underneath but when the ship tacked we slid with such a shock to the lee side that I was obliged to lash it to the side of the cabin and hold on as well as we could.

A sailing ship is entirely dependent on the wind, and at this point the *Isabella* was being driven back up the channel to Alderney, off the coast of France, in completely the opposite direction.

Moving south

Two days later they were in calmer waters, off the coast of France. They were over their seasickness and all managed to go to the saloon for dinner for the first time.

Captain Hart was taking the standard route to Australia, laid down by the Admiralty.[45] The journey was 13,000 nautical miles to Sydney, slightly less to Launceston, and relied on favourable winds. Once a ship was out of the English Channel it headed down the coast of Spain and Africa until it crossed the Equator, where it hit the doldrums or calms. Further south it met the south-east trade winds, but they blew it in the wrong direction, towards the coast of South America.

The ship would stop only once to replenish food and water, at the Cape Verde Islands or Cape Town. Once it rounded the Cape, it was blown by westerlies and could sail east across the Indian Ocean until it reached Australia. It would be another thirty-three years before the Suez Canal was opened, in 1869, and then a steamship could make the journey in five weeks. But in 1836 the long, sixteen-week voyage was dominated by the wind and weather. The longitude, latitude, temperature and distances covered were noted regularly by Barton in his journal.

Life on board now had a routine, based on mealtimes. Breakfast for the adult passengers was at eight, and at one o'clock there was a light lunch. Dinner was at three or four in the afternoon, and tea at seven or eight at night. The children had their meals before the adults. The food on board was fairly limited, with only rare appearance of fresh meat. Canned or salt meat and sometimes canned beans or fish were the regular fare. Fresh bread was also rare but there was plenty of 'ship's biscuit'. Boiled rice was a staple, as was pea soup made from dried peas. Oats were used for porridge, and suet for puddings made with flour, raisins, sugar or treacle. Lime juice was used to combat scurvy. There was tea, coffee, wine or beer and preserved milk.

In bad weather it was too dangerous to go on deck, which

made life very difficult for the Hacks. They were cooped up with six small children, and everybody was seasick. Leaving the dark, cramped and smelly cabins to go up on deck must have been a relief, but even there movement was severely restricted by the masts, booms, spars, sails, ropes, cargo, fittings and hatches, as well as the sailors and other passengers. The *Isabella* also carried livestock on deck.

By 19 September they were off the Straits of Gibraltar and sailing well and, on the following day:

> [20 September 1836] We remained on deck rather later last night, and enjoyed the beautiful moonlight. The moon appears in these latitudes to hang like a lamp in the sky, as if we could imagine the sky to fall back an immense distance beyond it – which is seldom the case in England . . .

The boat was now off the coast of Africa. Captain Hart decided to call in at St Jago, the main island in the Cape Verde group to obtain fresh food and water and to leave letters. The temperature was getting warmer, with a pleasant breeze, and the sea water they had in the morning to wash with was quite warm. On 24 September they crossed the Tropic of Cancer and made a very good 160 miles in the day. A canvas awning was rigged up on deck for shade.

The Cape Verde Islands

By 28 September they had been at sea four weeks and had arrived at the Cape Verde Islands, where some of the passengers were able to leave the ship for the first time. The island of St Jago was inhabited mostly by Negro slaves, brought there by the Portuguese. The Hacks and other passengers went on shore and walked into the town. Barton found Port Praya a 'miserable place' with dilapidated buildings. They called on the American Consul, William G. Merrill, who also acted on behalf of Great Britain.

> [28 September, 1836] We ordered dinner at the hostel opposite the Consul's house and at four sat down to a most plentiful dinner, but spoiled in the cooking, a turkey, roast pig, several fowls etc,

> lemons, oranges, and bananas in plenty, the latter fruit we begin to like very much . . . Took a walk afterwards in the valley below the town, through some gardens . . . planted with Date trees, plantains, Bananas, Cocoa nut trees, Indian corn etc, and had a truly tropical appearance . . . Thermometer 86°, a very close night.

They left St Jago, but some of the sailors had purchased some rum and the next night they were intoxicated.

> One of the men was very insolent to the Captain, who dragged him to the quarter deck and had him hand-cuffed. The other men appeared inclined to take part with the one in confinement, but they seemed quite overawed by the Captain's firmness . . . Last night Mr. Lewis was tipsy for the third or fourth time since we sailed and the Captain was very angry about it.

This is the first reference in Barton's diary to Captain Hart showing anger. On a sailing ship the captain had absolute control and had to be obeyed by the crew without question.[46] This was essential to keep order, but Captain Hart was a fair man and well respected by his men. The Hacks chose wisely when they decided to sail with him; in the sixteen-week voyage there were no floggings, nobody died and they were not shipwrecked. Other voyagers at the time were not so fortunate.

The *Isabella* had now completed a third of its journey and was moving towards the Equator. Soon they would be in the Southern Hemisphere.

Into the tropics

After the Cape Verde Islands, the *Isabella* sailed into the doldrums, where the weather was oppressive. It was too hot to wear a coat and Barton wished he'd brought some lightweight jackets so his shirts could be kept clean. They were in trouble with the children's clothes too, as the little girls had dirtied all their frocks and had only pinafores to wear. Keeping clothes clean was a major issue on board ship, as there was no water for washing clothes except for salt water. Each week Barton rolled up their dirty clothes and washing in bundles and stored them in the bottom of his sailing boat, turned upside down on the deck.

[3 October, 1836] I have begun to bathe on deck before six in the morning now, by having a few buckets of water poured over my head, and then have up the six kits [children] one after another, and do the same for them; it seems to do us so much good . . .

A few days later squalls of wind hit the ship and rain came through the cabin window. However, it was welcome, as it meant clean water. Drinking water on board ship was stored in barrels and after a while became foul-tasting. Whenever it rained, the passengers rushed out to collect fresh water in whatever jugs, pots or containers they could find.[47]

The South Atlantic

On 17 October they crossed the Equator. Barton was pleased that Captain Hart had refused a celebration, because this normally meant drunk and disorderly behaviour from the crew. The ship was heading almost due south with a fine breeze, and the temperature had dropped to a pleasant 76°. They were travelling parallel to the coast of South America. The weather was 'delightful; we can just bear the sheet over us at night'.

Barton now felt in strong health. Bbe, however, was feverish and not feeling well. What Barton may not have known (or was too discreet to record) was that Bbe must have become pregnant about this time, as her next child was born nine months later, in July 1837. Women at the time tended to breastfeed a baby for the first year, partly as a method of contraception, and as Bedford was now fourteen months, he would have been weaned.

Barton's brother Stephen was busy on board chatting to people who had been to Australia and could offer advice. He wrote to his mother and asked Gates to send a book on shooting, several volumes of the *Sportsman* and some books on agriculture. He also asked for drawing paper and a drawing board.

By the first of November they had been at sea two months and were halfway through the journey. The evenings were now cold and damp, and Barton and Stephen had acquired pea jackets (short woollen coats) and rough blue trousers from the captain to keep warm on deck.

On 7 November there was another incident with the crew. A sailor named James was too attentive to Miss Dixon's servant, a young woman named Jane Lively. Miss Dixon complained to the Captain, who summoned the sailor and lectured him.

> All the passengers were highly diverted ... I would advise any of my friends who come after us to take great care not to bring any young unmarried servants with them, as they would be causes of dispute continually, from one cause or another. The gentlemen passengers are so idle and in want of excitement that they would give her no peace, and at any rate let any servant if possible sleep in her mistress's cabin. The man [Bob, a sailor] ... wrote a poem on the above occasion and sent it for the amusement of the passengers. I hear the Captain sent a bottle of rum forward [i.e. to the crew] to make all straight. E.D. [Miss Dixon] is sadly annoyed, and will scarcely speak to the Captain having heard him laughing with the others.

Stephen had a notebook into which he had copied his favourite poems, mainly Byron, Scott and Burns. Now he entered the poem by Bob the sailor, titled 'An account of Jane Lively of Yorkshire & James of Portsmouth'. Stephen was showing an ability to get on with people of all ranks, a skill which would serve him well in the new colony.

Barton and the male cabin passengers passed the time practising their shooting, but because of the ship's motion they mostly missed the target. His backgammon board was very popular and seldom out of use among the passengers. It was now too cold to be on deck and they stayed in the cabin, where Bbe was busy sewing and Barton copied his journal for Gates and Margaret.

Rounding the Cape of Good Hope

On 18 November they were near the Cape of Good Hope. The weather was much colder, and showery, but they were making faster progress.

> [19 November, 1836] I had to put in our dead light [shutters] in a hurry this morning as the sea rose very rapidly, and the ship was lying over so much. We could scarcely manage dressing – and we hear much of casualties among crockery, etc., in consequence ... We are all again in good spirits, though it is not pleasant to be so tumbled about.

As they neared land, they saw many albatrosses and the sailors caught two terns. Several roosted on the yard arms and made a pleasant twittering. They rounded the Cape and sailed east, with no land between them and Australia for thousands of miles. To the south was Antarctica and the seas had become rougher. By the first of December they had been three months at sea and were making good progress, although everything on board was damp and wet and everybody was cross.

The weather was now so cold they could not keep warm. Barton was copying Bbe's journal to send home to the family in Chichester, as she was too busy to do it. Sadly, this journal has not survived.

In Australian waters

On Christmas Eve they were in Australian waters, heading for Launceston on the north coast of Van Diemen's Land. The Hacks toasted the birthday of Tom (Barton and Stephen's brother) back in England.

Everyone was now busy writing letters to send home. Stephen continued his letter to his mother, and added some advice regarding the voyage out. He advised passengers to measure their cabin before embarkation and plan accordingly. All vessels for drinking or washing should be made of pewter, he wrote, because it was unbreakable, and he recommended a large tin can with a spout for collecting rain water.

The most important advice of all, he said, was to get a written agreement with the captain, as to the exact quantity of food to be provided, especially for children. Specify that the children were to have a fresh dinner every day and an allowance of preserved milk. When on board, he said, be friendly with all the passengers. As for clothing, he warned that after passing the Cape, 'you want more clothes than in winter in England'. The children had suffered badly from broken chilblains and ought to have had worsted (thick woollen) stockings, good calf shoes and Gloucester (cloth) boots. Bring your own shoe-blacking and brushes, he wrote: 'shoes will not wear well on board ship without blacking at least once a week'. For hot weather he advised anything cool, in a colour that would not show the dirt.

These handy hints were posted home when they reached Launceston. Stephen's letter arrived in England months later, and ended up being published. His brother-in-law Henry Watson reproduced the advice in 1838 in a lecture on South Australia,[48] and the following year it was reprinted in part by John Stephens in his book *Land of Promise*.[49]

Meanwhile Barton was keeping up his journal, even on Christmas Day. Quakers did not celebrate religious festivals like Christmas or Easter, but the children had a nice present, as their sheepdog Rose gave birth to some fine puppies.

In Bass Strait

New Year's Day was fine and warm as they approached King Island in Bass Strait, between Van Diemen's Land and the mainland of Australia.

> [2 January, 1837] We were awoke [sic] from a sound sleep by the Captain coming down the companion crying 'Land. Land. Turn Out', and all but one or two were soon on deck. We found ourselves about seven miles from King Island . . . The morning is very delightful. Thermometer 65° and at length realizes our ideas of Australian climates.

On 3 January the pilot came on board and they passed close under the lighthouse at Low Head, at the entrance to the River Tamar.

> [3 Jan] The views all the way down the river were delightful, and it was very pleasing to see the different stages of improvement which were visible in the settlers' dwellings, as we sailed on . . . The reaches in the river too were very beautiful, as most of them assumed the appearance of lakes surrounded by hills wooded to the water's edge. We were so much favoured by the wind that we were able to sail down the river until within six miles of Launceston when we grounded.

Their excitement can be imagined as they waited to set foot on land. Captain Hart had arranged to take the *Isabella* to South Australia at the end of the month and they decided to accompany him. It suited them well, as it gave them time to purchase stock, and saved the expense of unloading their goods and looking for another vessel.

Stephen finished off his long letter and gave it to Barton to add a quick postscript. Barton explained that he had copied his diary of the voyage and was sending it to Gates and Margaret for all the family to read. He then went on to assure his mother that all was well:

> As the most important thing relating to our success and happiness is my health, I may assure thee I never felt more fit for exertion or was stouter in appearance than I am at present. And all my weakly symptoms have disappeared – this climate of Van Dieman's [sic] Land is a most delightful one in Summer to our feelings, except that the mornings and evenings are generally cool enough for a good wood fire – but the dryness of the air is such that the feeling continually reminds us of a very warm day in a port in England . . .

Barton signed off with love from Bridget and himself, and then Stephen dashed off a few extra lines.

> Just to say that we are safely landed, and all in good case and spirits. Everything is turning out well and it seems a complete impossibility to miss succeeding in this part of the world.

Stephen addressed the letter to his mother in Gloucester. But on this summer day in Launceston, they were not thinking of England. They had been at sea four long months and had travelled halfway around the world.

Chapter 5

Launceston

When the Hack brothers arrived in Launceston, their aim was to purchase stock and goods. This was on Captain Hart's advice, but it would involve a further capital outlay. The brothers examined their finances and decided they could go ahead. They spent up on a grand scale, buying 400 sheep, some bullocks and supplies, totalling about £1600. Back in England, their brother-in-law Gates Darton was struggling to pay off the debts they had left behind.

Finances

While on board the *Isabella*, Barton and Stephen spent several days working on their accounts. We can imagine them hunched over their journals, trying not to spill the bottle of ink. Barton noted in his journal that it was hard to check all the bills when they didn't know what Gates had paid for after they had left England. As far as they could estimate, their joint assets, as well as Barton's personal property, added up to £1590. On the debit side, Barton was rather vague, noting that before leaving he'd paid some bills, but the £250 for the passage was on borrowed capital. Their outlay totalled £1840, roughly equivalent to $202,400 today.[50]

Underpinning these calculations was Barton's expectation of the money he would receive later. He expected to recoup his capital in the currier business, but that was not due for two years. Barton also anticipated a large inheritance from his father's estate when his mother died. But Maria was only fifty-nine and in good health, so that was unlikely in the near future, although some interim divisions from the estate were probable. Barton hoped to make money in the new colony, and he was also relying on the fact that Stephen would soon inherit £2000, which could be added to their assets.

Back in England, Gates Darton was doing his own calculations. He estimated that Barton and Stephen's outfit, expenses and gold sovereigns totalled about £1800 – a similar estimate to the £1840 Barton reached when poring over his accounts on the *Isabella*. Gates was a methodical person, proposing that the partnership of the firm of 'J.B. and S. Hack' should commence from the date of their departure on 1 September 1836. He began a ledger for this business and another ledger for each of their personal finances.[51] In the front was recorded his advice to the brothers – that they should keep clear accounts. Over the next few years Gates sent regular copies and summaries of this ledger to Barton and Stephen.

Gates's ledger shows that he calculated the Hack brothers' assets and the debts, but he came to a very different conclusion about their debts. He estimated that Barton and Stephen had left behind debts of £700, on top of the £600 Barton had borrowed from his brothers-in-law. In addition, Barton and Stephen were paying interest on the money lent by Gates for the land orders, and Barton was paying interest of £15 per quarter on a loan of £600 from his father-in-law, William Watson.

Soon after the *Isabella* departed, Gates had to find £556 for Henry Watson to pay bills for Barton and Stephen in Chichester. In desperation, Gates borrowed this from Robert Harvey, his father's partner. Then another £200 in outstanding bills arrived. He wrote to Maria Hack, who was shocked. 'How can it be that he ordered so many things without considering <u>how</u> they were to be paid for?', she wrote, referring to 'poor dear Barton's fearful example of rashness . . .'

Maria realised that someone had to pay, and asked Halsey Janson, her cousin and trustee of the family estate, to transfer the money to Gates. 'Keep a guard about expenses and do not execute any fresh orders that are not *absolutely* necessary', she wrote to Gates on 9 September, 'better wait and see how they get on'.

In the middle of September things improved greatly, however, with the entry of Thomas Smith's brother Nathan into the currier business, bringing in extra capital. Smith proposed that the partnership with Barton Hack be dissolved at the end of the month, paying £1800. Some of the family were concerned, because no mention was made of the £6000 the family estate had invested initially in the business. However, the parties met and agreed to Smith paying the £1800 in three instalments and dissolving the partnership.

What happened to the £6000 is not known, since there is no further mention of it in family letters. The premises in Little London remained in the hands of the executors for two more years until the Smith brothers paid the final £1400 and the lease was transferred to them.

Over the next few months, Gates was able to use Barton's money to pay off most of the debts. But Gates was only able to pay himself a small part of the £300 he had separately lent Barton, the reason being that the remainder of Barton's capital was required to pay new bills which had come in to the tune of £540. These were mostly for the heavy goods that had not been taken on board the *Isabella*, but which had gone into storage in London, waiting for a suitable vessel bound for South Australia. This was the *Schah*, which left on 8 January.

Some of these goods were not for personal use, but for sale in Australia, possibly in Sydney. They included a case of books from Darton and Harvey worth £108. Barton was now almost solvent, but he still owed over £200 to Gates. When Barton and Stephen first set foot on Australian soil at Launceston in January 1837, they knew nothing of all this. They knew they owed a considerable amount of money, but were buoyed by the fact that Stephen was about to inherit £2000 on turning twenty-one. Barton saw this as further capital for their new venture.

Stephen, however, had other ideas. He had told his mother before he departed that when he inherited the £2000 he wanted only half of it sent to Australia, with the balance invested in England. He said he was planning to return home at the end of two years. Back in Gloucester, Maria Hack explained this in a letter to Gates in January 1837, about the time that Stephen arrived in Launceston. She added that Stephen had told her, 'If Barton risks more, I will not'.

Stephen was ten years younger than Barton and let his older brother take the lead in their new partnership. Stephen wrote to his mother while on board the *Isabella* that when Barton recouped his capital from Thomas Smith they would 'do swimmingly'. On the other hand, Barton was looking to Stephen's inheritance to fund the next stage of their venture.

Launceston

Launceston is situated at the junction of three rivers: the Tamar, the South Esk and the North Esk. On 4 January 1837, the *Isabella* caught the tide up the Tamar and anchored half a mile below the town. At last the Hacks were able to go ashore. Barton, Stephen and Bbe and the two boys set out with Captain Hart. How exciting it must have been to walk freely after the months on board ship.

Captain Hart introduced the Hacks to Lewis Gilles, a local merchant and banker whose older brother Osmond had just arrived in South Australia to become Treasurer. Gilles then helped the Hacks find lodgings for the few weeks they would be in Launceston. Accommodation was scarce and they had to take five rooms above an unfinished shop.

They were anxious to hear news of South Australia, and soon heard that the *Buffalo* had arrived in the Gulf St Vincent with Governor Hindmarsh and officials and, a week later, that a good river had been found on the east side of the Gulf (the Port River), providing the long-sought sheltered harbour. Colonel Light, the Surveyor-General, had chosen the site for a town (later called Adelaide) on the plains beside another river (later called the River Torrens). The town was not yet surveyed, but many of the settlers had moved from Kangaroo Island to Holdfast Bay and were camped on the beach there (later to be called Glenelg).

On Saturday 7 January the Hacks were busy transferring packages and heavy boxes from the ship and settling into their rooms. Bbe was now three months pregnant, and had to organise four months of dirty washing. She was helped by her friend Caroline Carter and by Mina Pfender.

Caroline Carter had come to Van Diemen's Land to marry her fiancé, a Mr Weedon, but was having second thoughts. He'd failed to meet her when she came on shore, so she'd visited his lodgings with her loyal shipboard friends Bbe and Esther Dixon. They subsequently learned that he was keeping an actress with whom he had a child, so when he visited Caroline at the Hacks' lodgings a few days later, she broke off her engagement. She decided instead to go to South Australia, and Barton wrote happily in his journal, 'she will remain with us as one of the family, which will be an inexpressible comfort to my wife'.

Esther Dixon had come out to join her brother Captain James Dixon, who now helped the Hacks look for stock. Stephen, who had worked for a short time on a farm in England, was in charge of this task, and Dixon took him to the Curraghmore estate, six miles south-east of Launceston. It had a reputation for fine sheep and wool and Stephen was so impressed by the stock that he took Barton back a few days later.

In Launceston the brothers ran into some old friends from Sussex, the Hentys. When Barton went to the Australasian Bank to deposit his gold sovereigns, he was received by Charles Henty, the manager of the bank. The Hentys came from a village near Chichester and were early pioneers in southern Australia. In 1829 three of the sons had emigrated to the Swan River settlement in Western Australia, but quickly became disillusioned and moved to Launceston. They were joined there by their father Thomas Henty and his wife Frances, a daughter and three more sons. In 1834 one of the brothers, Edward Henty, occupied land at Portland Bay on the other side of Bass Strait. The following year a settlement began at the distant site of Melbourne at the head of Port Phillip Bay.

The Hacks returned to the Curraghmore estate, where they purchased 370 Merino ewes, thirty wethers and six heifers, also acquiring bullocks, a dray and cart, and a colonial plough. Because they could carry heavy loads over long distances on rough tracks, bullocks were essential at the time,

The final bill for these purchases was £750. This far exceeded their cash in hand, so Barton had to pay by means of a bill of exchange, drawn on Gates Darton in England. Barton must have made other purchases in Launceston, because a further £800 was run up on a second bill of exchange drawn on Gates. Six months later when the bills arrived in England, poor Gates had to find £1600 for them, which he paid in several drafts, recording them faithfully in his ledger.

Stephen turned twenty-one on the fourteenth of January and could now inherit. He signed a document giving his power of attorney to Gates Darton, or in the event of Gates's death, to Thomas Hack. This document authorised Gates to handle all his financial affairs in England, and after some formalities with the notary it was sent off to England. This power of attorney has been preserved down the years and is still in excellent condition.

Towards the end of the month they started repacking their goods for the *Isabella*, and there were last-minute purchases of more stock. Barton later recalled that, along with the packages they had brought out in the ship, they put on board the 400 sheep, six heifers, a Devon bull, ten working bullocks, two mares, a Timor pony, goats, pigs, poultry, dray, wagon, seed wheat, and provisions for twelve months.

Towards the end of their stay in Launceston, Michael Pfender asked for an increase in pay and Barton declined. The Pfenders then decided not to accompany the Hacks to South Australia, with Barton later describing the couple as 'very useless'. Barton needed people who were experienced in the local conditions and engaged three bush hands who were 'ticket of leave' men; ex-convicts, or convicts who had permission to work. One of these was Joseph Hill, a bush carpenter and sawyer, whose wife Bella was taken on as a washerwoman. Later in life Barton wrote that Bella 'turned out to be a confirmed drunkard, and was for years known in the colony as Scotch Bella (who had more interviews with the resident magistrate in her time than any other man or woman)'.

Barton engaged a fourth bush hand named Tom Davis who was not a convict but a native of Sydney.

On 28 January the family once again boarded the *Isabella* and settled into their old cabins. Also on board were Caroline Carter, Henry Jones, who was taking sheep for sale in South Australia, and Lewis Gilles, who was visiting his brother. Sir John Jeffcott remained in Van Diemen's Land, where he had met a young relative who later became his fiancée. The *Isabella* moved out of the River Tamar into Bass Strait on 3 February.

Bass Strait is notoriously stormy, and the next day the *Isabella* laboured against a westerly gale which blew them off course.

Some of the animals broke loose and the Hacks lost a bullock and twenty-nine sheep. When the weather turned calmer, everyone's spirits lifted. They passed Cape Otway but kept their distance as it was notorious for shipwrecks. On 10 February Captain Hart sighted Kangaroo Island, but the seas were too heavy to go further that night. The Hacks must have been disappointed at having to retire to their cabins when they were so close to their new home, but it was to be their last night before setting foot on shore. Their South Australian adventure was about to begin.

Chapter 6
Arrival in South Australia

The Hack family arrived at Holdfast Bay at the beginning of 1837, six weeks after the proclamation of the colony. Most people were camped on the beach at Glenelg, waiting for the survey of the town to be completed. The Hacks erected one of their Manning cottages by the lagoons, and soon afterwards Barton erected the second cottage in Adelaide in a clump of wattles that would later be the site of the Adelaide Railway Station on North Terrace. They made friends with some of the settlers, including John Morphett, Robert Gouger and James Hurtle Fisher, and got to know the local Aboriginal people.

Holdfast Bay

On Saturday 11 February 1837, the *Isabella* sailed through Backstairs Passage between Kangaroo Island and the mainland and entered the Gulf St Vincent. At Rapid Bay Captain Hart took Barton and some others on shore, but where the settlement had been was now deserted. The few people who had lived there had moved to Holdfast Bay, thirty miles further on. The *Isabella* continued up the eastern shore of the Gulf, which Barton considered resembled the craggy cliffs of North Wales.

It was midsummer and very hot, quite the opposite of a February day in England. The *Isabella* reached the southern part of Holdfast Bay about midnight and dropped anchor. It was dark, so they fired a signal gun and then had the pleasure of seeing lights hoisted on five vessels, about a mile ahead.

When the master of one of the vessels came on board they learned that the other ships were the *Buffalo*, which had brought Governor Hindmarsh on 24 December, the two survey vessels, the *Rapid* and the *Cygnet*, and the two emigrant vessels, the *John Renwick* and the *Coromandel*. They were facing Glenelg, where the settlers were camped. The *Tam O'Shanter* was in the Port

River fifteen miles further north, along with the *Africaine* and the *William Hutt*. The Hacks were too excited to sleep that night, and at daybreak came on deck to look at their new home. 'The country is extremely beautiful', Barton wrote in his journal, 'a plain of great extent, bounded by wooded hills'.

The next day the *Isabella* was still a mile or two south of Glenelg, a hot north wind preventing it from moving. The sheep were in a sickly state, so Captain Hart decided to offload them at the spot where the present-day suburb of Brighton is situated. Some of them were dying, and his employer, the ship-owner John Griffiths, was only paid if the animals were delivered safely. Hart began to offload the sheep in the morning and Barton and Stephen went onshore to receive them. It was 104° in the shade.

As the sheep swam ashore, the Hacks waited for Hart to deliver their sheep netting so they could make a yard, but it did not arrive. Worse still, there was no time to drive the weakened animals to the lagoons a mile or so inland to water them. After rounding up the sheep, the Hacks stationed their four hired hands to watch them. But during the night the sheep, maddened by thirst, scattered and headed for the lagoons and most were lost. The Hacks had landed about 340 sheep, but lost over 200. The sheep belonging to Henry Jones suffered the same fate.

The next day Stephen went with their land agent John Morphett to the lagoons, located where the Sturt River flooded, before it ran into the Patawalonga Inlet. Today the Sturt River at this location is a concrete canal in the suburb of North Glenelg, close to Morphettville, which is named after the same man, later Sir John Morphett. Stephen and his men then transferred the remaining sheep there.

Glenelg

The *Isabella* moved up to Glenelg and anchored close to the other ships. We know exactly what Glenelg was like at the time, from a painting by J.M. Skipper called *Holdfast Bay, SA, 1837*. Above the beach was a large sand dune with a flagstaff flying the Red Ensign, to indicate to newly arrived ships that this was the temporary settlement.[52] Behind the flagpole were a number of large storage huts guarded by marines, and the mouth of the

Patawalonga Creek. In the distance, about half a mile inland, were the tents of the government officials and settlers, who had set up temporary residence.

Barton went on shore in the blazing heat and headed off to see Morphett. As he approached the settlers' camp he would have seen the large tent and hut belonging to Robert Gouger, the Colonial Secretary. It was here, under a large gum tree, that the new province had been proclaimed on 28 December by Governor Hindmarsh.

Chatting to Morphett, Barton would have learned that the capital was being surveyed and had been named 'Adelaide', after the German-born wife of King William IV. But its location was a matter of dispute between the new Governor, John Hindmarsh, and the Surveyor-General, Colonel Light. Light had chosen a site on the fertile plains five miles inland, on the as yet unnamed River Torrens. Hindmarsh, being a naval man, wanted the town to be on the sea, and preferred Port Lincoln, at the entrance to Spencer Gulf. Only the day before the Hacks arrived, a public meeting of landholders had approved the site selected by Light.

The European population of the colony at this time totalled only about 700 people,[53] which included government officials, members of the surveying parties, free settlers and employees of the South Australian Company. The government officials had erected some temporary huts in Adelaide, but most people had no way of getting their goods any further than the beach.

The *John Renwick* had arrived two days before the *Isabella* and it carried letters from home. They learned of the death of Barton's sixteen-year-old sister Mary just after they had left Portsmouth. 'How truly grieved we were to hear of the removal of our dear Mary', Barton wrote to his mother. This was the fourth sibling of Barton's to die, and he must have been hoping that with his emigration to a warmer climate he would be spared.

The next task was to offload their goods from the *Isabella*. Sailors transported the goods to the shore in boats and dumped them in the shallows, from where they had to be hauled onto the sand. The family slept on board the *Isabella* until their portable houses could be erected. Barton later recalled:

> A heifer calved a day or two after, and I had the pleasure of milking the first cow in the colony. The settlers . . . were busy rolling their goods over the sand hummocks. My men at once yoked a team of eight bullocks, and [with it] brought our goods from the ship's longboat to the camp we formed near a lagoon. It created quite a sensation in the encampment, as most of the people had not seen a colonial team before.[54]

When the Hacks arrived there were a few bullocks in the settlement, but nobody had a full team or a dray, so theirs was now invaluable, and Barton was quick to take advantage of the opportunity offered. They carted their own goods to the lagoons, after which they began to carry loads for other people for a fee of 10s. A few weeks later they took their first load to Adelaide, charging £3. Their bullock team must be the one seen in Skipper's painting of Holdfast Bay.[55]

Barton wrote to his mother and Gates to report progress, and added:

> Stephen is a most zealous assistant . . . I have reasons to be very thankful that it was arranged for him to come with me, for I could not myself have gone through the difficulties of landing in a wild desert country without his assistance . . . [he] seems very happy and takes to bush life capitally. Damper, tea and pork are the order of the day, varied by an occasional kangaroo, duck, emu or parrot.

Barton and Stephen were 'gentlemen' but they had some practical skills. Barton had some carpentry skills and Stephen had some farming experience, but they also relied on their experienced employees.

Despite a temperature of 105° in the shade, they erected one of the Manning cottages by the lagoons, close to their cattle and the remaining sheep. Barton covered the rafters with a tarpaulin and the family and their bedding were brought there in a bullock cart. They slept there that night, somehow fitting in three adults and six children. The Hacks' little two-room cottage was relative luxury, being the only wooden house at Glenelg – all the other immigrants were in tents or rush huts.[56]

The family must have been very excited as they got down from the bullock cart and surveyed their new home by the gum trees and lagoons. Bbe, with the help of Caroline Carter and Bella, their servant, would have cooked a meal outdoors. A gardener from near Chichester, William Suter, had arrived just before the Hacks with his wife Emma and their small daughter, on a free passage as part of Barton's entitlement. Barton took them on at £55 a year and board. The Hacks now had seven employees to support.

It was soon clear to Barton that the colonists were extremely short of livestock and provisions, and these could be sold at a good profit. It would be some time before any country land would be surveyed and available for grazing, so once more he seized the opportunity. He decided in the short-term to be a merchant like his father and uncles, and 'do something in the storekeeping line'.

He discussed the idea with Captain Hart, who wanted to take the *Isabella* to Tasmania and bring back stores and stock. They quickly reached an agreement. Hart and Jones would purchase goods that were needed in the colony and Barton would pay for them plus ten per cent commission. Barton also agreed to pay for any stock landed in good condition, at specified prices. With this agreement, Hart set off for Launceston. The two men had become friends on the long voyage out and trusted each other. There was just one problem however. The agreement was not written down, which would cause Barton an immense problem later on.

Before Captain Hart left with Jones, Barton purchased goods from the store that had accompanied them on the *Isabella* and offered them for sale. On 5 March they made their first sales, with some porter, a type of dark beer like stout. A few weeks later Barton noted: 'I sold a lot of butter ex *Isabella* by which we clear £25, which is pretty well for a beginning'. Barton sold groceries and drapery to a Mrs Chittleborough, who had moved up to Adelaide. Her son, James Chittleborough recalled later in life:

> My mother kept a store – the first in South Australia – her drapery and other goods being brought by Mr. Barton Hack from Tasmania or NSW. Well, we were completely burnt out, and had not a single thing to our back ... I should like to put it on record that Barton

Hack said to my mother, 'Never mind, old dame, I will give you more goods to start again'. And he did.⁵⁷

Barton was helping settlers out of kindness, but also for self-interest. From the moment he arrived, he saw that he could make money in the colony. With his bullock team and supply of goods, he was becoming indispensable to the settlers. It was an exciting beginning for the two brothers.

Adelaide

At the beginning of March, Barton travelled to Adelaide with Joseph Hill to begin construction of the second Manning cottage on a spot overlooking the river. The land was not yet allocated, and they were 'squatting' in a clump of wattles on a site which would later become the Adelaide Railway Station on North Terrace. The Hacks' wooden house was one of the first in Adelaide, as the town was then mainly a collection of tents with some temporary huts near the river. A sketch by Colonel Light shows the scene on the south bank of the Torrens around this time.

The Hacks continued to charge £3 a load for their bullock wagon and it was in constant demand, transporting goods up the maze of tracks which led from Holdfast Bay to Adelaide. Back at Glenelg, Bbe was busy looking after the family in the two-room cottage, with the help of Caroline Carter. Bbe was nearly five months pregnant and with six young children underfoot she was proving to be as resilient onshore as she had been on board the *Isabella*. She was clearly a strong and capable woman, and in the letters home she was always cheerful.

Despite the cramped conditions by the lagoons, the Hacks had their first guests on Sunday 12 March when John Morphett and Samuel Stephens came to dine. Stephens was manager of the South Australian Company and Barton thought him something of a schemer. About the dinner he noted, 'We had for dinner some fine fish, preserved meat pie and a rice pudding, which I account sumptuous fare for a young colony'. The children were thriving on the milk from their goats and the heifer, and daily rice puddings.

At Adelaide, Barton and Joseph Hill soon had the Manning

cottage erected, with Barton installing shelves and assembling the iron bedsteads brought from England. His next task was to build a separate kitchen and two rooms for their employees. The weather was still hot, and Barton found a dip in the Torrens at the end of the day very refreshing.

On 15 March a meeting of landholders was held to decide upon the method of selecting their town lots. Barton was too busy to attend, but Morphett was there as his agent. The meeting was dramatic, as Barton recorded in his journal the following day:

> I was glad I was not there . . . as the Governor and Mr Stephens came to high words, and the former very unwisely threatened to take Mr Stephens into custody. It is a misfortune that Sir John Hindmarsh is not a different character. He seems well intentioned . . . but he is firm and determined to an excess . . . [he] seems quite led by his Private Secretary, Mr George Stevenson, who has taken on himself, I hope temporarily, several important offices.

George Stevenson's unpopularity soon came to a head. Three weeks later Barton noted: 'I am glad to hear that Stevenson has been in a manner indicted . . . He has been obliged to resign all his appointments but his original one – that of Private Secretary to the Governor'. However, Stevenson still wielded a great deal of power, becoming the editor of the only newspaper in the colony, the *South Australian Gazette and Colonial Register*, and used his position to vigorously defend the Governor and attack any opponents.

On 17 March lots were drawn to determine the order in which preliminary land holders could choose their town acres. The three lots were in the name of Gates Darton, although the partners regarded themselves as possessing one each. They made their selections, acquiring their three town acres, numbers 21, 345 and 702, and they allocated number 345 to Gates. When the streets were named later on, these acres were in North Terrace, Wakefield Street and Pennington Terrace.

On 27 and 28 March the remaining town acres were auctioned and Barton purchased another sixty-one acres, located over north and south Adelaide. The total cost was £360, averaging about £5 17s per acre. Of these, he allocated fifteen to Henry Watson for £100 and thirteen to Gates for £78 as investments on their behalf.

While Barton was travelling to Adelaide each day to work on the house, Stephen was busy at Glenelg looking after the livestock and the bullock team, assisted by the hired hands. He often rode out into the country with his dogs and a new friend, Charles Stuart, who was stock manager for the South Australian Company. The company had nearly 900 sheep and had established a station at the foot of the hills.

Stephen brought home kangaroos and emus for meat and Bbe wrote to her brother, Henry Watson:

> We continue to like our adopted country exceedingly ... we have scarcely made a meal on salt meat ... [Barton] has kept us well supplied with parrots, which are most excellent cooked any way; but the best meat I ever tasted is kangaroo ... the harbour here abounds with the finest fish in the world ... called snappers – then there are wild ducks, quails and pigeons in abundance, so no fear of our starving.

As soon as the town acres had been allocated, people began to cut down trees on their land, building temporary houses and digging wells. The Reverend Howard put up a six-room Manning cottage opposite the Hacks, on the acre set aside for Trinity Church. The road up from the bay crossed the river, with a small ferry, operated by a rope fastened to a tree on either side of the river, transporting people and goods from one side of the river to the other. This was near 'Buffalo Row' (temporary reed huts built by some of those who came out on the *Buffalo*) west of current-day Morphett Street, where the weir is now situated. Barton forded the river just below his house, with his horses and bullocks.

On Monday 3 April the whole family, accompanied by Caroline Carter, moved to Adelaide into the little cottage overlooking the river, and Barton noted 'we like the change much'. A week later, Barton brought up the other cottage from Glenelg, erecting it beside the other; they had a house with four rooms and a passage between the two houses covered by a tarpaulin. At the end of the house was a separate kitchen with a stove brought from England, and the two rooms for their household help. There was no bathroom, and all their water was carried up from the river.

On 14 April the Hacks dined in the parlour for the first time. We can imagine them looking out through the trees and catching a glimpse of the river below. Compared with most of the settlers at the time this was a life of luxury. The river was as not as wide and river-like as it is now. In the early days it consisted of large pools of very deep water connected by small streams, and the Hacks had to be careful not to let the children too near.

Barton asked William Suter to fence in and prepare a piece of land for a vegetable garden, where he planted seeds brought from England. The heifer and the four goats were brought from the lagoons and milked for the children. 'The said cow is now tethered down by the river among the reeds and grass opposite our windows', Barton wrote. 'She is dismally afraid of the natives, and I was witness to quite a scene when a party of them crossed the river near her while my man was milking her.'

The Hacks were very happy in their new home. They wrote to Henry Watson: 'the country and climate are superior to anything we had anticipated ... it seems the very country for children to thrive in; ours are in robust health, and look so stout and rosy, very unlike the delicate children they were in England'.

The Hacks were starting to make new friends amongst the settlers, in particular the doctor Thomas Cotter and his wife Jane; the chaplain Charles Howard and his wife Grace; and a young lawyer named Henry Jickling, who would later instruct the older children. 'Indeed we could not have found better society in any country-town in England', Bbe wrote enthusiastically. Over the next few months Barton dined with Sir John Jeffcott at the house of Robert Gouger, several ladies called on Bbe and Caroline, and Caroline went to a grand party at the Governor's residence.

On another evening Barton dined with a large party at the home of James Hurtle Fisher, the Resident Commissioner. There he picked up strong criticisms of Governor Hindmarsh, who was in frequent conflict with Fisher. The power-sharing arrangement between them was not working, and the two strong personalities clashed ferociously. People at the dinner commented that

Hindmarsh's appointment was 'a most random one'. This may have been a reference to the fact that he had been given the job mainly because of his high-level contacts, including Admiral Sir Pulteney Malcolm.

The Aboriginal inhabitants

At the beginning of 1837, the Aboriginal population of South Australia was between 10,000 and 14,000 across the province.[58] At this early stage, relations were friendly and the Indigenous people helped the white settlers in many ways.

While Barton worked on the house in Adelaide, he got to know some of the local Aboriginal people, members of the Kaurna nation. They wandered around the settlement in a friendly fashion, and when they wanted bread he set them to work cutting wood. Barton's attitude to the Indigenous people was sympathetic and he was in contact with Quakers in London who were concerned about Aboriginal rights. The most prominent of these was Dr Thomas Hodgkin, who became the first secretary of the Aborigines' Protection Society in Britain.[59]

On 15 April Barton and Bbe wrote home commenting that they had no fear of the Aborigines:

> Parties of them frequently come down to the house: they are very quiet and peaceable, never stealing ... Our children are a great amusement to them, particularly the youngest [Bedford, 18 months] – they pat his cheek and laugh, and he seems as much pleased with them ... They seem very fond of their own children, and often bring them to be named ... One called Jack has just passed with his children; he is a fine specimen of the natives, and very intelligent ... The noise they make in their corroborees in the evenings is tremendous ...

Stephen Hack was also making friends with the Aboriginal people and wrote: 'One of the black fellows, named Jack, persuaded me to name his two daughters, five or six years old; I named then Jenny and Polly'. Stephen was starting to learn their language and made a list of the Aboriginal names for the places near the settlement. Later on, his knowledge of the local language proved to be valuable when exploring or searching for lost cattle, as he was able to befriend Aborigines and learn about local conditions.

At this stage, however, the Hacks were probably unaware of the extent to which the settlers were overturning the way of life that the Aboriginal people had preserved for thousands of years. The local inhabitants were acquiring a taste for European food, while the Europeans were rapidly killing their supply of birds, kangaroos and emus. This was to cause an increasing problem as the colony expanded.

Chapter 7
Leading citizens

The Hack brothers decided to become merchants, importing goods from Sydney and Launceston. They soon became leading citizens in the small community and Barton was on the committee to name the streets of Adelaide, including what became Barton Terrace. They were the first public contractors to the government, and established a stockyard, dairy and market garden in North Adelaide and imported the first vines into the mainland of the colony. Stephen Hack became an expert bushman and explorer, and went on expeditions to Encounter Bay and to the head of Gulf St Vincent.

Barton the businessman

While Barton and Stephen waited for the country acres to be surveyed, they continued their carrying and merchant businesses. In April Barton received news that Captain Hart had left Launceston in the *Isabella*, carrying a large consignment for the Hacks. But as the weeks went by Barton became concerned, as there was no sign of the *Isabella*.

On 4 May the *Schah* finally arrived, with all the goods the Hacks had left behind in London and some letters from home. Barton and Bbe read the letters eagerly and then wrote to Henry Watson, 'while you are fancying us suffering all manner of distresses ... here we are enjoying the comfort and freshness and independence of a new colony'.

On 12 May Barton rode to Glenelg and was astonished to find Captain Hart walking with Stephen near the tents, and still more so to hear that he had lost the *Isabella* with the whole of her cargo. Hart explained that the vessel had been wrecked on Cape Nelson, a steep headland near Portland Bay.[60] The passengers and crew were rescued, but not the cargo, and it was uninsured. Hart said he had lost everything and his friends had turned their backs on him. Barton wrote, 'We are very sorry for the Captain. He will be our guest while he stays'.

Barton assumed he was not liable for the cargo, becoming shocked when Captain Hart handed over a letter from Henry Jones. It was a series of bills totalling £1377 for the lost cargo, including the ten per cent commission. Jones claimed that he and Hart had merely been acting as Barton's agent when they purchased the goods.

Barton wrote back immediately dismissing the claims:

> I have never ... considered that we were in any way liable to loss in case of shipwreck ... The cargo of this vessel was not to be considered mine until delivered to me ... we do positively decline to consider ourselves liable to loss in consequence of your omitting to ensure the cargo.

Henry Jones rejected this view, and the dispute dragged on throughout the year. Jones had included Hart in the claim, but Barton continued to be friendly with Captain Hart and even gave him a present of two town acres, in Rundle Street.

The loss of the *Isabella*'s cargo was a blow, but it was not in Barton's nature to brood on problems. He simply got on with other activities, always in a spirit of optimism. Besides, he was extremely busy. On 13 May the first Grand Jury in the colony was called, under Judge Jeffcott, and both Barton and Stephen were on it, with Colonel Light as foreman.

Barton was very busy selling the goods brought out on the *Schah* and from other ships. On 6 May the *Regia* arrived with goods needed by the settlers and Barton purchased some of these. Stephen wrote home: 'I am now in excellent spirits about our prospects, for we have a good income ... There have been several cargoes imported, of which we have purchased very largely ... they will average about £50 ... clear profit'.

A few days later Barton purchased goods worth £289 from the *William* for resale, mainly timber, sugar and potatoes. These were purchased with a bill on Gates Darton. Barton had long discussions with Captain Hart about the merchant business and decided that he and Stephen would become part-owners of a schooner, which Hart would captain, to trade between Adelaide and Sydney. 'We have therefore drawn on Gates for £1500', Barton wrote blithely in his journal.

Barton had most fortunately learned one lesson from the loss of the *Isabella*: the next agreement with Hart had to be in writing, and he organised Charles Mann, the Attorney General, to draw it up. On 20 May Captain Hart left for Launceston en route to Sydney on the *William*.

Barton's connections, energy and apparent wealth ensured that he was recognised as a leading citizen in the small community. The Hacks' Quaker beliefs were not a problem, because of the colony's commitment to religious tolerance. The emigrants brought with them the class divisions from the old country, and the Hacks were part of the small group of 'gentlemen', separate from the tradesmen and labourers.

On 23 May Barton had the privilege of attending a meeting to name the streets, squares and terraces of Adelaide, as well as the river. The group consisted of the Governor and the leading officials of the government and the South Australian Company, as well as three settlers: Barton Hack, John Morphett and Thomas Strangways.[61]

There is no record of why Barton was chosen for this role, but at this stage he was probably the most prominent settler in the colony, after Morphett. Barton had his bullock team, he sold goods to the settlers and had experienced labour. He was very active, had an eye for opportunity and was regarded as a rich and influential man.

Barton had met Gouger and Morphett back in England and had made Morphett his land agent. Morphett had great influence in the early days because he represented so many investors from England. Strangways was probably nominated by Hindmarsh.

The town was laid out by Light on a grid pattern with Adelaide and North Adelaide separated by the river. It was an excellent design, with parks all around and the town ringed by hills. The meeting named the streets on the edge of the town, North Terrace, South Terrace, East and West Terrace. Patriotic names were also selected – Victoria Square and King William Street – and a number of streets recognised the early colonial officials such as Light, Hindmarsh and Gilles. The river was named the Torrens.

Barton Terrace in North Adelaide was presumably named by Barton, although there are no minutes of the meeting to confirm this. Some historians have assumed it was named after Barton himself, but this is unlikely, as Quakers did not promote themselves in this way. It is more likely that he chose the name to honour his mother's family or, more specifically, his uncle John Barton.

Now that the *Schah* had arrived, they were able to unload their belongings from London. Barton and Bbe wrote to Henry Watson:

> Our little parlour is the pride of the colony, it looks so neat and cheerful, now that the pictures are up, and the ornaments on the chimney-piece ... We had to-day a white table-cloth for the first time, and the luxury of silver spoons is great indeed; it is delightful to have tea-cups and glass tumblers to drink out of once more ... everything looks green and fresh; the children are constantly bringing home handfuls of the most beautiful flowers ... growing, to their surprise, wild in the bush.

Barton's health was no longer a problem. 'I have forgotten all about the pain in my chest', he wrote. 'I work hard, and am always in the open air ... assure our friends that we have found things better than we had even hoped for, and that it would be a real hardship to *think* of returning'.

The garden next to their cottage was flourishing and they expected to have vegetables in a few weeks. William Suter wrote home to his family in England: 'I am as happy as a king ... I get 70s per month and my board, and a comfortable place to live in, and a quart of port'.[62]

Stephen the bushman

Stephen Hack was mainly responsible for the bullock team, carting goods from Glenelg or the Port River to Adelaide. By 1 May Stephen wrote that the bullocks had cleared £300 already. The Hacks were doing well; they were also engaged to supply the *Buffalo* with twenty tons of water from the Torrens, and this later earned them £100.[63]

Stephen was in his element, living the frontier life he had read about in 'wild west' novels. He was proud to be the hunter of the family, bringing home fresh meat, mainly kangaroos. He was also at 'deadly war' with the wild dogs (dingoes) which had taken two of his sheep. He wrote to Henry Watson: 'When I was in England I thought there would be something very sublime in going over country which no white man had ever trod before, but now that I have done so half-a-score times it does not seem worth a thought'.

Despite frequent journeys into the bush to look for the sheep they had lost on arrival, Stephen could not locate them, and nor could Henry Jones, who had only about sixty left. These he sold to Barton and Stephen, which meant they now had 176 Merino ewes.

On his travels, Stephen found some fine country among the hills about ten miles south of Adelaide, and took Barton to see it. Barton was delighted, writing that 'the valleys are very beautiful; with rich black soil at the bottom ... natural springs of water in all directions'. This was the Upper Sturt River, near modern-day Eden Hills and Blackwood. The Hacks decided to squat in this valley, which had grass 'up to the horses' middles', until the country acres were allocated, and they moved their sheep there.

Stephen's skill as a bushman was beginning to be recognised, and in the middle of June 1837 he was invited to join Colonel Light, James Hurtle Fisher and John Morphett on a trip to Encounter Bay. This bay, near the mouth of the River Murray, was the location of two rival whaling stations: one established by Captain Blenkinsop from Sydney at Hind Cove, and the South Australian Company's operation at nearby Rosetta Cove. Samuel Stephens, the manager of the South Australian Company, wanted Blenkinsop evicted, and Fisher had been asked to investigate.

On 14 June, Light and his group left Adelaide. On their arrival at Encounter Bay, Captain Blenkinsop convinced them that he had as much right to be there as the South Australian Company, and lodged a complaint about Samuel Stephens. Fisher, Light and Morphett then left for Adelaide, with Stephen and the bullock driver and cart returning at a more leisurely pace. Stephen wrote to his mother that he was away a fortnight, and on the way back, he ran into a party of Aboriginal people:

They were young and old, nearly twenty of them, wild savage looking fellows. I know enough of the language to be able to chatter with them a little and we travelled on in very good humour to the Onkeperinga [sic] river which I found so much swelled that I was obliged to make the natives carry everything over on their heads.

The following month Barton and Stephen were contracted to search for the government's bullocks; about sixty had been lost. The Hacks were to be paid £2 a day, plus 10 shillings for each bullock they found. To everyone's surprise Stephen returned in two days with thirty-five of them. Barton wrote proudly to Henry Watson that Stephen's success was 'quite the wonder of the colony'. Stephen also aroused interest by finding beautiful plains and running streams in every direction. He wrote eloquently about his trip:

> I have been on horseback with no-one but our head bullock driver [Tom Davis] to the head of St Vincent's Gulf, hunting up some wild fat cattle belonging to the Government. I believe no one but myself has yet seen so far. I had a tent made of a pair of blankets hung over a stick, under which we slept, and carried in the fashion of a horse cloth under the saddle. We carried our bread in knapsacks and took a brace of kangaroo dogs to keep us in meat. A tin pint pot to boil tea in was all my cooking tackle, as the best way to cook a kangaroo in the bush is sticking steaks on sharp sticks in the ground before the fire. I have frequently rolled myself in my blankets and slept all night without waking when the ground was squashy under my feet, and had not a pain or an ache in the morning . . .

This was possibly the best time of his life:

> I don't know anything that makes one so light-hearted and happy as to be mounted on a good powerful horse in a new interesting and beautiful country, with just sufficient danger from the natives to produce excitement without fear. All you want is a blanket strapped behind the saddle, a tin pot, flint and steel, punk [dry fungus to start a fire] and tinder, a little bread in a knapsack, a large knife and tomahawk, a brace of good kangaroo dogs and a pair of pistols.

To his mother, Stephen confided his private thoughts and hopes: 'It is now nearly a year since I left England and such a year. I have lived more in it than in my whole life . . . Half my term of transportation is now over. I shall soon see you again. I have not yet heard from the Woods, but I hope to by the first ship this season'. This was the family of Julia Woods, whom he hoped to marry. He did not know that Julia had died in May, of consumption. It would be a long time before he received this sad news.

The Hacks had about five town acres in Pennington Terrace across the river, beside the present location of St Peter's Anglican Cathedral. By winter they had completed large stockyards on this site and moved their cattle from Glenelg. They now had two teams of bullocks earning £4 to £5 a day. Stephen was in charge, but the Hacks also engaged a stockkeeper. They built a cottage for their shepherd made of timber and stone, plastered inside and out, 'the first anyone has built for their labourers', and a row of three timber cottages at Pennington Terrace. Barton rented these out at three shillings a week to his men which, 'keeps them attached to my service'.

The Hacks' businesses expand

On 22 July Bbe gave birth to a baby girl, Emily Margaret. This was their seventh child and the first born in Australia. Stephen reported to his mother, 'Bbe is very weak and poorly since her confinement, but the child is quite well'. He said they were fortunate in having such a good medical man, their friend Thomas Cotter. Bbe's friend Caroline Carter was still with them and Barton purchased four town acres on her behalf.

The cattle were now at Pennington Terrace and the Hacks established a dairy in their sitting room on North Terrace. It is hard to see how they all fitted in the house, but perhaps they freed up the storeroom at the end of the house for family use. Selling milk, skim milk and butter, the dairy brought in £6 to £7 a week clear profit; they sent away for a cheese press.

Barton became the first public works contractor in the colony, hiring men to dig a canal seven feet deep at the harbour. The port in those early days was located further up the Port River, at modern-day West Lakes. The river was full of mangroves and this was the only point at which dry land could be reached and, even here, the ships could become grounded on a mudflat in the middle of the river. Barton realised that if a small canal could be cut, the ships could be tied up closer to the warehouses. He prepared an address on the problem to Fisher, attaching nineteen signatures, including his, Stephen's and John Morphett's. Not long afterwards, the Hack brothers were given a contract to dig the canal.

The contract was for £400 and they expected to make a profit of about £50. With a foreman and fifteen men, they were soon at work. However, the project was not without its problems, with an anonymous letter in the *Gazette and Register* on 29 July questioning why the contract had been allocated privately to Mr Hack instead of public tenders being called. Barton claimed later that nobody else could be found to take on the work.

If Barton felt aggrieved at this anonymous attack, he was not alone. The editor of the newspaper, George Stevenson, was a troublemaker. At the end of July, Fisher called a public meeting to answer a number of anonymous attacks on him made in the newspaper. Barton Hack was there and was pleased when the meeting cleared Fisher, criticised Stevenson, and unanimously called for the establishment of a new paper. The petition for a second newspaper was signed by twelve people, including Fisher, Light, Gouger and Hack.

The dispute between Fisher and Stevenson escalated, with the *Gazette and Register* publishing a further anonymous attack on Fisher, claiming that he had secretly sold cattle and pork belonging to the Commissioners, to himself, his sons and his friends, including Barton Hack. Fisher responded by calling a public meeting on 12 August, chaired by Colonel Light. Fisher said the livestock were not for the use of the Commissioners and their auction had been quite open. He said Barton Hack was the only person interested in purchasing the cows, and that Barton's dairy was an advantage to the colony. The meeting voted in support of Fisher.

While Governor Hindmarsh was unpopular, he was not the only one embroiled in disputes in the young colony. Robert Gouger, the Colonial Secretary, quarrelled violently with

Osmond Gilles, the Colonial Treasurer. Hindmarsh then suspended Gouger on 22 August and appointed Thomas Strangways as interim Colonial Secretary. Strangways had come out on the *Buffalo* with Hindmarsh.

Gouger's friends were shocked at the sacking. They held a public meeting, chaired by Colonel Light, and passed a resolution of confidence in Gouger. A petition for reinstatement addressed to the Commissioners in London was quickly drawn up. There were twenty-one signatures, with Barton's at the top, followed by John Morphett and Stephen Hack. Gouger made plans to return to England to put his case to the Commissioners.

September 1837 was the anniversary of the Hacks sailing from Portsmouth, and Barton wrote to Henry Watson that their situation was:

> above what our most sanguine hopes would have permitted us to expect . . . What a change there is in my health since I was so delicate in England . . . I work hard enough, but it is work that suits me. I scarcely sit down except on horseback from breakfast to tea-time.

Henry Watson was the Chichester agent for the South Australian Commissioners, and Barton wrote to him frequently urging him to encourage new settlers. He said there was grass for cattle in all directions and, 'Col Light computes that there are as many as 470,000 acres of good soil between Rapid Bay and the head of the Gulf, without any timber to impede cultivation and ready for the plough'.

The Hacks had a large block of thirteen acres in North Adelaide, converting this into a market garden. This block was between Stanley Street on the north, Melbourne Street on the south and Jerningham Street on the west. They called it Chichester Gardens, and later named the internal streets, Sussex Street, West Pallant and East Pallant after their home in England.

Here they planted 130 apple trees imported from Launceston, along with cabbages, cherries, melons and pomegranates. Barton received a 'very good parcel of vines, bananas, oranges, lemons, peaches etc.' from Sydney and planted them. These vines were the first on the mainland of the colony. The *Register* a few years later reported that vines were 'first introduced into South Australia by

Mr J.B. Hack in 1837 . . . Mr Stevenson, of North Adelaide, procured a few rooted plants in 1838 from Messrs Henty in Portland Bay'.[64] Several years later, when the vines produced grapes, Barton became the first person to produce wine in the colony.

Chichester Gardens today is a charming residential area with many old cottages that have been tastefully renovated. In 1837 it was, according to Barton, 'the centre of a pretty little plain of about 100 acres'. The garden was enclosed and maize was planted in every available space, as it was valuable for the horses. Barton also grew some wheat that first season and a sample sent to the Corn Exchange in London as a specimen of what the colony could produce.

By the time the canal had been completed, Barton's finances were severely stretched. With Barton now charging boats to use the canal, the Governor sent Lipson, the Harbour Master, to investigate. Lipson reported that there were three ships in the harbour, the *Siren*, *Gem* and *Abeona*, the first two carrying cargo for Hack. 'These two landed the whole of their cargo in the canal, while the *Abeona* was obliged to land hers at the mangroves, except such part as they chose to pay for landing in the canal, which I understand to be at the rate of 5s per boat load'.[65] There is no further correspondence on this subject and presumably Barton was forced to stop charging.

Another project for Barton was a bridge over the River Torrens. That winter saw very heavy rains – the river rose eight feet in one storm and the ferry was washed away. In those days the Torrens in winter turned into a raging flood, sweeping away the banks and gouging out new channels. (The river was not tamed until later, when, in 1881, the weir and the Torrens Lake were constructed.) As Barton recalled in his memoirs, 'I was obliged to put up a rough bridge over the worst place in the crossing opposite my stockyard'. The bridge was below his house and his stockyard was on Pennington Terrace, with a cattle run roughly where the Adelaide Oval now stands.

Barton and the Fisher brothers (sons of James Hurtle Fisher) approached Gouger on 8 August 1837 asking for timber for a bridge that would 'enable carts to cross without difficulty'. Governor Hindmarsh said it should be put to tender, but when he was informed that the work was already in progress, he approved it, on 9 August. Barton employed a carpenter and three men, and on 26 September charged £8.18.9 for this work.

It was known as 'Hack's bridge' and Barton and another settler named William Ellis were the first people to cross it – with a loaded bullock team.[66] It must have washed away at some stage, because two years later another wooden bridge was built on the same site and completed in August 1839. The location of Barton's bridge and its 1839 replacement can be seen in the painting of North Terrace by E.A. Opie in 1841.

Now that people were settling in the town and squatting on country land, there was a shortage of good timber for fencing. Stephen's friend Charles Stuart rode into the Mount Lofty ranges south-east of Adelaide, and discovered a forest of stringybark trees (eucalypts), which were very suitable for fencing. Many flocked to the hills to take advantage of this new source of timber. Barton, not one to miss an opportunity, sent up a bullock wagon and started carting timber back to Adelaide for a fee.

Baby Emily was now two months old and Barton wrote that she was thriving and a 'pretty a little thing'. Bbe was running the dairy in their home in North Terrace. 'It does one good to see dear Bbe bustling about serving customers', he wrote, 'and scolding if the shelves, pans, churn, etc., are not kept quite clean'.

Willie, aged nine, had begun lessons in French and Italian from Henry Jickling, but Barton had other ideas for his sons:

> The boys are such admirers of cattle they take the herd out and fetch them in with as much ease as if they had been brought up to the great and useful profession of stockkeepers, and stockkeepers I expect they will have to be, for cattle and sheep are the only dependable riches in this country.

In October the Staker family, who were to work for the Hacks, arrived from Chichester: Frank, Harriet and their three-year-old son Francis. As Harriet wrote to her family:[67]

> [Mr Hack] Received us very kindly and was very glad to have us work for him. He gives Frank £4 a month and his rations, and a cottage with two rooms, and a piece of garden ground, rent free. We

live about half a mile from Mr Hack's home and I go every morning to char in the house, for which Mr Hack pays me ten shillings a week . . .

The cottage was one of those in Pennington Terrace. The arrival of Harriet Staker must have been a great relief, as they had dispensed with the services of the tipsy Bella Hill and the unreliable Emma Suter.

Barton's expedition to Mount Barker

From their time of arrival in the colony Stephen had been the explorer, but towards the end of 1837 Barton made a small discovery himself. At this stage most of South Australia was still unexplored by Europeans. The settlers knew the stringybark forest in the Mount Lofty ranges, but the country beyond was unknown. At the end of November Barton was the catalyst for an expedition further east and the first ascent of Mount Barker.

Two of Barton's horses had become lost and he and Tom Davis rode into the hills. Locating the horses' tracks, they followed these beyond Mount Lofty until it was quite dark, then abandoning their search and returning home. The following day Tom found the horses near a fine river with splendid feed. Since this seemed to present a worthwhile prospect, Barton assembled a party comprised of John Morphett, Charles Stuart and John Wade from Hobart Town, with Tom Davis as their guide, to explore further. Samuel Stephens, who had recently been suspended as manager of the South Australian Company, also accompanied them. As Barton wrote in his memoirs:

> On ascending a rise, a mile or two from the river, we came in sight of a very prominent hill some miles to the east. Mr. Morphett said it must be the Mount Barker hill described by Captain Sturt on his boat expedition down the [River] Murray. We at once decided on reaching it, and about 5 o'clock in the evening we were all on the summit; we were the first white men who had ascended the hill. We could trace the course of the Murray into the Lake Alexandrina, and had the Encounter Bay coastline full in view.

From the top of Mount Barker, these men had seen good land to the west over to the Mount Lofty Ranges and also to the southeast, towards Lake Alexandrina. Their reports of this rich soil and luxurious pasturage attracted much attention back in Adelaide. Barton began to dream that he and Stephen could take up land near Mount Barker themselves.

Chapter 8
Letters from England

The Hack brothers continued to prosper, but sent more bills back to Gates Darton, including £1500 to purchase a vessel in Sydney. Gates struggled to pay off these debts, which caused a serious rift in the family. Maria Hack was depressed by these events as well as by the death of her daughter Mary. She was also involved in a split in the Quaker movement, during which she resigned and joined the Church of England. Two prominent Quakers visited the Hacks in Adelaide and urged the settlers to do more for the Aboriginal people.

Letters from Gates Darton

By the end of September 1837 Barton was waiting anxiously for letters that would tell him that Stephen's power of attorney had arrived in England. He wrote to his mother:

> It is not ... the safest position in the world to have drawn on Stephen's and other property until we were quite sure that it was bona fide in Gates's hands – though there was a certainty that it ought to be – and that we should be missing great present advantages by not making use of it.

Barton and Stephen relied on Gates to handle all their financial and business matters in England. His father was Maria Hack's publisher and Gates had married her daughter Margaret in 1834. Maria relied heavily on Gates and wrote to him regularly. He was solid, reliable and cautious, while Barton and Stephen were the risk-takers in the family. From the moment they departed, they tested Gates's patience to the limit with bills of exchange, which he had to pay. In October 1837 Gates and Margaret moved to 10 Catherine's Court, Tower Hill, in London with their two small children Emily Jane and Edward Hack Darton.

Barton finally received letters from England and learned of

the sad news of the death of Julia Woods back in May, although Stephen was still unaware of this unhappy event, as he had gone to Sydney with Captain Hart. A letter from Gates informed Barton that Stephen's power of attorney had arrived safely. Gates also sent a copy of the ledger in which he detailed Barton and Stephen's assets and debts. Gates's original ledger, with meticulous accounts in copperplate writing, has been carefully preserved by his family.

Gates's ledger arrived on the *Hartley* on 20 October. It covered the period from when the Hacks left England to April 1837, the date the letter was written. Barton now learned of all the problems that Gates had been forced to deal with: the debts he had to pay and how he had been saved by Thomas Smith and his brother unexpectedly paying off Barton's share in the currier business. Barton was by that time solvent, except for £200 which he still owed Gates.

But since April, Barton had sent more bills. These included the bills from Launceston, the bill for sheep purchased from Henry Jones, the bill for goods on the *William* and £1500 for the purchase of a vessel. These four bills totalled nearly £3600.

Back in England, Gates waited anxiously for a distribution of the family trust. At the beginning of September 1837 when he had to pay almost £1800, he had received only £1034 from the executors and most of this was Stephen's inheritance. Gates was then forced to take out another loan from Robert Harvey to prevent default on Barton's bills. Soon afterwards Gates received another £1160 for Stephen's inheritance and was able to repay Robert Harvey. But in the same month Gates had to pay £134 for goods shipped to Australia and at the end of November another £86 for Barton's merchant business. Gates had now used up nearly all of Stephen's inheritance. Stephen may have wanted half his inheritance to be invested in England, but it was too late, it was needed to pay the bills run up by Barton and Stephen.

The final blow for Gates arrived on 5 December 1837 with the bills for the brothers' expenditure in May, totalling almost £1800. At the end of the year, Gates was faced with unfunded liabilities of almost £1600 as well as the debt of £200 to himself. He had to borrow from various sources and his situation was now desperate. As the most conservative Quaker in the family, the prospect of defaulting on these loans must have been horrifying to him. Not only would he lose credit in the business community, he would also attract severe censure from the Society of Friends.

Barton and Stephen's response

The bills which Barton sent to England far exceeded Stephen's legacy, so what were they thinking? They knew there was going to be a distribution from their father's estate in the near future, and miscalculated the amount due to them. They believed there would be plenty to cover all their borrowings, with about £1000 left over in England. In addition, they were optimistic that their ventures in Australia would be profitable. Barton took the lead in all business matters, and as Barton knew much more about finances, Stephen left most of this area to him. Stephen looked up to Barton and trusted in his judgement. It was a trust that would eventually turn out to be misplaced.

When Barton received the letter and ledger from Gates in October, he should have been mortified by the thought of all the debts he had left for his brother-in-law, and the extra bills sent to Gates since that time. A more cautious man would have apologised and reined in his spending, but Barton was not that man. His dream was that he and Stephen would become so successful that the rest of the family would join them and assist in the running of these South Australian ventures, especially Tom, Gates and Henry Watson. In the meantime Barton was reinvesting whatever money he made in the colony, instead of sending it back home.

Barton's letters to his mother and Henry Watson around this time were ebullient. He said there was nothing to worry about and all their investments were being transformed into profits. He said their land speculation was paying off: the sixty-one acres he had purchased in March for £360 were now worth £3000. He was very busy selling goods from Sydney and Launceston, some on commission. These were from the *Ann* and the *Gem* and he added, 'I think we shall clear about £300 by this'.

To his mother Barton confided:

My friends here laugh at my formerly expressed resolutions against being engaged in business ... but then I do this *con amore* and in Little London it was slavery, without hope of release – here I have the prospect in a short time of being able to subsist comfortably and respectably ... and that will give any one spirits to work.

The following month he wrote that a friend, Henry Dowling, was visiting Adelaide from Launceston and had £4000 worth of goods to sell and had appointed Barton as his agent. But his reports of the merchant business were overly optimistic. The Hacks were not the only people importing goods, and prices were dropping.

Hart had also chartered the brig *Siren* for Barton, but this turned out badly, as she lost more than half her cargo in two trips.[68] Since this went unmentioned by Barton in his diary or letters, perhaps the goods were insured. The Hacks also had the dispute with Henry Jones over the loss of the *Isabella* back in May hanging over them. The Hacks, Hart and Jones agreed to submit their dispute to arbitration by Fisher and Morphett.

Barton swaps the town acres

In December 1837 the land grants were issued for the town acres. Barton registered fourteen of these for Henry Watson and thirteen for Gates. He also allocated four to Caroline Carter. During the year Barton had sold some acres and purchased more, including acre number 74 in Hindley Street.

The fourteen acres for Henry Watson had cost Barton £100 and the thirteen acres for Gates about £78. Barton then did a curious thing: he wrote to Gates saying these town acres were a swap for Gates's 134 country acres, which were nominally worth £80. In this way Barton made a unilateral decision to take Gates's rural acres for himself and give Gates the town acres in exchange. As they were worth roughly the same, Barton thought it was fair. He still owed Gates about £200 of the loan Gates had given him, but as Barton was paying interest on the loan, and intended to pay back the principal one day, he did not take that into account.

Why did Barton make the swap? Presumably he and Stephen wanted to add Gates's rural acres to their own, making a consolidated rural estate of 402 acres. But what Barton did not know was that in London, Gates was selling off *all* the rural acres in order to pay off Barton and Stephen's debts, so in reality Barton had no country acres to swap. When Barton found this out several months later, it became another source of friction between the two.

Maria Hack leaves the Quakers

Apart from the letters from Gates, there were two from Maria Hack, written from Gloucester in April 1837. Maria, aged sixty, was feeling old, depressed and alone after the death of her youngest child Mary. Maria at this stage had received only one letter from Barton and Stephen, written on their voyage to Australia, and she longed to hear from them. She was thinking about Barton's children and anxious about their religious education. She begged him to teach them to look to the Bible as the rule of life, and not just the 'uncertain feeling of their own hearts'. This referred to a division in the Society of Friends, known as the 'Beaconite Controversy'. During the split, Maria resigned from the Society and joined the Church of England.

Barton assured his mother that he understood the importance of the Bible in educating his children. He and Bbe remained Quakers, but were to leave some years later and join the Methodists. When Stephen heard about his mother's resignation, he agreed with it. Stephen had never been an active Quaker and later became a nominal Anglican when he married in a Church of England ceremony.

Backhouse and Walker

While Maria was preoccupied with religious matters, Barton and Stephen were more concerned with getting ahead in a new country. It is noticeable that after they arrived in Australia they sometimes dropped the terms 'thee' and 'thou' in their letters, and started using the more common 'you'. But in December they welcomed two prominent members of the Society of Friends, James Backhouse and George Walker, who were making a tour of the Australian colonies. On 10 December Backhouse reported that 'Meetings for worship were held at J.B. Hack's at eleven and six o'clock. They were attended by his family and a few other persons'.

In an account written later, Backhouse said the Hacks had much more comfort in their wooden house, 'than most of the other settlers do, in their small and rude rush or sod huts'.[69] One day, he said, when it was very wet, 'about a score of the Aborigines took shelter under J.B. Hack's veranda . . . most of the women have children, of which they seem very fond . . . one of them noticed Bridget Hack kissing her little son, and exclaimed, "very good" with evident satisfaction'.

Backhouse and Walker had pursued two main concerns in their travels: temperance (the avoidance of alcohol) and the plight of the Aboriginal people. In Adelaide they held two large public meetings at which the state of the Indigenous people was discussed. The Protector of Aborigines, William Wyatt, and various other people spoke on the subject, including Barton Hack. A committee was then appointed to assist the Protector and Barton was a member. He noted in his diary, 'We are trying to obtain a habitation and regular meals for all who will come for them, in every district'. His concern for the rights of the Aborigines was linked to his Quaker upbringing, with its belief in the equality of all human beings, paralleling to some extent his uncle and grandfather's involvement in the anti-slavery campaigns.

The balance sheet for 1837

By the end of 1837, the first year of the colony, the Hacks were doing well and were confident that things would only get better. There were very few men of capital amongst the emigrants, and from the beginning the brothers had been quick to seize every opportunity. Their bullock teams were doing well and making a good profit in that first year. Another source of income was the merchant business, and they had secured government work, including the development of the canal. The dairy was a money-earner, they looked after other people's cattle as well as their own, and they sold fruit and vegetables from their market garden.

By the end of the first year then, we could estimate their income as being more than £1000. Against this was the cost of wages, stock and other outlays, but they were doing well.

The state of the colony

The small colony of South Australia was full of optimism by the end of 1837. Emigrants were flocking to it and by one estimate the population had reached around 3000.[70] 'It is really astonishing how this place increases in buildings', Barton wrote to Henry Watson, 'there are many good handsome houses of brick, stone and pisé [rammed earth]; gardens are fenced by split paling... We have had great arrivals of emigrants lately'. Barton asked Henry to send out governesses, who were urgently needed, as they were married off soon after they arrived, as were servant girls. Barton continued:

> As we sat down to dinner today, with a fine leg of mutton, and dried apricot pie on the table, Bbe exclaimed, 'oh, that our English friends could see the hardship we undergo, and such cherry-cheeked, healthy children as we have around us, we never had such in England. All the poor sickly-looking children improve directly in this fine climate'.

Henry Watson as the agent in Chichester for the South Australian Commissioners gave a lecture on South Australia on 17 November, based on the Hacks' jubilant early letters and reports from other emigrants. In a long and erudite introduction, Henry explained the current problems in the United Kingdom, why people wanted to emigrate, and the virtues of South Australia.

In early December the Hacks received news that Henry was thinking of coming to South Australia with his wife Charlotte, their baby daughter Charlotte Emily (Apetty) and his parents. They would not leave England for many months, but the news was exciting. Barton advised Henry, who was a pharmacist, on the goods to bring with him – drugs and medicines, especially for sheep and cattle, clothes for sale and British wine.

Barton went on to report the discovery of the entrance to the River Murray in Encounter Bay, but it was 'exposed to such tremendous rollers at its entrance that it will never be I fear of much use as a harbour'. This was a reference to Governor Hindmarsh's desire to move the capital to Encounter Bay. Barton was hostile to the idea and firmly on the side of Colonel Light and the original site. Hindmarsh soon had to drop the idea, however, after a tragic accident at the mouth of the Murray, in which Sir John Jeffcott and Captain Blenkinsop were drowned.

Barton did not elaborate on the politics of the colony, but if he had, he may not have painted such an optimistic picture, for in reality the colony was in disarray. The tensions between Hindmarsh and Fisher had paralysed decision-making, there was no money in the local treasury, and development had stagnated. Hindmarsh had dismissed Robert Gouger as Colonial Secretary and John Brown as Emigration Agent. In November Charles Mann resigned as Advocate-General and Gouger set off for England to argue the case against Hindmarsh.

Another problem was the delay in surveying the country sections. Colonel Light was held up by a lack of men and resources, and the settlers were locked up in Adelaide, living on their savings. Those who did well were those who provided the settlers with food and necessities, and this was the basis of the Hack brothers' success. Now they were to embark on a new venture. Stephen was in Sydney to buy cattle, and the two brothers were planning on becoming landowners and graziers once the rural acres had been surveyed.

Chapter 9
Stephen's trip overland

At the end of 1837 Stephen Hack went to Sydney with Captain Hart and Captain Devlin. They purchased a brig called the Lady Wellington *and about 1000 cattle for themselves. Stephen was the first person to set out to overland cattle from New South Wales to Adelaide, although not the first to arrive. He took about 500 cattle and followed Major Mitchell's route through Victoria, which had been established the year before. Stephen reached Portland Bay, where he stayed with the Henty family for six weeks. From there, the cattle were taken by ship in relays to Adelaide.*

Stephen sets out
In September 1837, Stephen Hack left Adelaide to set out on a major expedition. He was off to Sydney to buy cattle and would bring them back overland to South Australia, the first man to embark on such an expedition. At this stage, no overland route was known from New South Wales to Adelaide, so his plan was to take the cattle south-west across Australia Felix (later called Victoria) to Portland Bay, and then transport them by ship in relays to Adelaide.

Unknown to Stephen, two other young men, Joseph Hawdon and Charles Bonney, were also planning to take cattle overland for the first time from New South Wales to South Australia. Both journeys aroused great interest in the Australian colonies.

Stephen was commissioned to buy cattle in New South Wales for the South Australian Company and the Fisher brothers. In addition, he wanted cattle for himself and Barton, since there was huge demand for bullocks in Adelaide, mainly for fresh meat. Stephen worked out he could buy them in New South Wales for about £4 or £5, fatten them up in Adelaide and sell them to the butchers for £25 to £30 each. He set off with Captain

Arthur Devlin for Sydney, where they joined Captain Hart, who had earlier chartered the *Ann* and the *Gem* to transport goods for the Hacks.

Sydney

When the three men reached Sydney, their first task was to buy a vessel for carrying stock and goods between the colonies. Earlier in the year Barton had drawn a bill on Gates for £1500 for a vessel, and Captain Hart cashed this bill on arrival in Sydney. On 1 November they purchased the *Lady Wellington*, a schooner of 142 tons, for £1800. Captains Hart and Devlin had quarter shares. Hart also chartered a larger vessel, the barque *Hope*, to bring back the cattle they were about to purchase.

Stephen and Hart met the Dutton brothers in Sydney and arranged to buy their cattle. Frederick Dutton was a grazier with extensive property on the River Murray; his brother William lived in Sydney. Stephen purchased 850 cattle (yet to be selected) for a total of £7140. The Duttons threw in 150 yearlings free of charge, making 1000 cattle in all. Most of this was paid for with a loan Barton had arranged with the Bank of South Australia. In addition, two bills for £200 each were drawn on Gates. Barton claimed that these were the last bills they ever drew on Gates.[71]

Barton seemed enthusiastic about the cattle venture at the time, but Stephen may have purchased more cattle than had been agreed, because Barton later blamed Stephen for over-reaching himself in this venture.

Sydney to Mullengandra

At the end of November Stephen set out on horseback with Frederick Dutton, heading south-west to Dutton's property at Mullengandra on the Murray to select the cattle. A third man accompanied them, probably Samuel Mason, a young stockman who quickly became Stephen's companion. The distance from Sydney to Mullengandra was about 360 miles, and Stephen wrote to his mother that he accomplished it on one horse in thirteen days. On the second day they rode into a storm, which caused huge trees to fall across the road:

The storm grew, if possible, more violent, and it was getting dark, and 7 or 8 miles had yet to be travelled before we reached the inn at Myrtle Creek ... we struck our spurs in our horses' sides and, holding down our heads, started on a regular neck or nothing scamper over stony creeks and roads that we saw nothing of till it was too late to stop. By great good luck, we met with no accident and got safe to the inn, though nearly perished with cold.

They continued their journey through Berrima, Goulburn and Yass, then crossed the Murrumbidgee River, where Stephen 'took old Roger in half way up the saddle flaps'. They reached a cattle station, but ran into trouble when they found the huts they depended on for provisions were deserted:

> We had to ride 120 miles in six and thirty hours, with nothing in the world to eat but two spoonfuls of sugar among three of us. I don't think I could have stood it 5 miles farther, but when I did get alongside the beef again, I could not eat anything like what I expected ... It is rather a strange fact ... that when a man is in the course of starvation, the first night and next morning are the worst ... then you are fairly ravenous. Afterwards, you get weak and faint, but with little or no desire to eat ...

From Kyeamba they travelled along the Hume River (the Upper Murray) to Mullengandra, north-east of Albury, where they stayed on Frederick Dutton's property for three weeks. They selected the stock they wanted, and as they could not take the whole 1000, they chose the fittest, about half, for the long journey overland.

Overlanding the cattle

Stephen planned to take the cattle to Portland Bay, and most of the way he would follow the journey of Major Thomas Mitchell, who had explored a route from New South Wales to Portland Bay the year before.

At Mullengandra, Stephen met the manager, James Darlot, who was to take charge of the overland journey. In Darlot's reminiscences later in life, he said the cattle purchased by Stephen were to be 'delivered to Portland Bay within 40 days of leaving the Hume River, or pay demurrage [a penalty] of £16 per day to the barque *Hope*, which was to take them to Adelaide'.[72] Darlot had to have enough flour to take a large team of men to Portland Bay, so he set two men to work grinding the wheat, which took nearly a week to get ready.

In Darlot's journal of the trip, he said they had 565 head of cattle.[73] Stephen and Darlot's party of eleven men, together with horses and traps, bullocks and two drays, provisions, guns and a pack of dogs, left Mullengandra on 30 December 1837. Darlot and Stephen went ahead each night to look for water. The day's droving was over by 10 or 11 in the morning, before the main heat of the day, and the cattle, bullocks and horses 'all rather gained in condition'.

They crossed the Hume (Upper Murray) and travelled southwest, then crossed the Ovens River, and fell in with a party of Aborigines, who showed them where to dig for water.

On 6 January they met Joseph Hawdon, who was travelling north to Howlong on the Murray to collect cattle and meet up with a companion, Charles Bonney. Hawdon and Bonney were only twenty-five years old and embarking on a risky venture, the first attempt to overland cattle all the way to Adelaide, travelling through unknown country inhabited by potentially hostile natives. Hawdon recorded in his journal: 'In the afternoon we met with two travellers, Mr. Darlot and Mr. Hack, proceeding with stock, attended by a full complement of men, etc., to Portland Bay to the westward of Port Phillip'.[74]

Joseph Hawdon had overlanded the first cattle from Sydney to Port Phillip in 1836, and taken up land near Melbourne. Stephen and Darlot must have found their meeting with Hawdon fascinating, but he was going in the opposite direction and they soon had to part. All these young men were, in their way, on historic journeys. Hack and Darlot were the first men to set out to take cattle overland from New South Wales to South Australia, while Hawdon and Bonney were the first to take cattle all the way overland to Adelaide following the Murray.

After leaving Hawdon, Stephen and Darlot travelled west. On 14 January Stephen turned twenty-two and we can imagine them toasting his health in billy tea and damper. On 24 January they reached the southern part of the Grampians. Stephen wrote later that he had a narrow escape with the natives there, but gave no further details, other than, 'I still keep my favourite old horse that stood me in such good stead among the blacks at the Grampians'.

Portland Bay

On 3 February, five weeks after leaving Mullengandra, Stephen, Darlot and the large herd of cattle reached Portland on 3 February and camped near the bay. Stephen went ahead and met the Hentys. Stephen had met Thomas Henty and his wife in Launceston and they were now at Portland with their sons Stephen, Edward, Frances and John.

Stephen Hack wrote to his mother that the journey from Mullengandra to Portland Bay was over 450 miles and for the entire journey he had not taken off his clothes.

> On my arrival at the Bay I looked such a wild figure, not having been shaved for more than two months and my hair nearly long enough to tie under my chin; that Mr [John] Henty was very near shooting me for a bushranger. All my clothes were in complete rags; but the shooting concern was no joke. I was in point of fact at the wrong end of a double barrelled gun, with both barrels full cocked.

The incident left such a mark on Stephen that he described it in three different accounts to his mother over the next few months. In another letter he wrote:

> I assure thee it isn't pleasant to be at the wrong end of a double gun cocked and levelled at one's head. To say the truth, he was so flustered that I was thinking he would pull without knowing it . . . The scene of action was in Henty's back yard opposite the scullery door, which was the first I could find, as it was just 10 o'clock at night. In the foreground was the shoe boy, with his eyes open a preternatural width and his hair fairly on end. Next was John Henty, gun in hand as I have described, and, holding by his coat collar, one each side, were Mrs Stephen & Mrs John Henty, both scared out of their wits. An old woman was peeping thro[ugh] a half opened door and a girl was trying to hide under the dresser . . .

Stephen wrote that once he had explained who he was, the Hentys were very kind and he stayed with them for nearly six weeks:

> The Hentys are settled at Portland Bay and are doing a great stroke of business there. They have about 10,000 Ewes and 200 head of cattle. They have nearly 70 whalers employed and man six boats or eight . . . I cannot express sufficiently the kindness that Stephen Henty in particular has taken every opportunity of showing me. They could not have done more for me if I had been their brother.

A few days later Stephen returned to the camp and the cattle were moved to a creek near Portland Bay (later called Darlot Creek), where they were turned loose to recover condition after the long trek. Captain Hart and the *Hope* did not arrive for six weeks, but Darlot and his men were under contract to stay until the end of June.

Stephen Henty's wife Jane seems to have taken a motherly interest in Stephen Hack while he was with them. She gave him a haircut before he left, and said that 'a good wash and fresh suit of clothes made a different man of him'.[75] Stephen would have been in need of a kind word from a woman, because in Portland he got mail from Adelaide and learned about Julia Wood's death in England, almost a year before. He wrote to his mother that Julia's death was seldom out of his mind:

> It has had the effect of rendering me totally careless and indifferent to what I have been striving every nerve to bring about, that is my return to England with sufficient capital to warrant my marrying. I have <u>now</u> done this but what advantage is this to me? . . . I have long had the most distinct impression of poor Julia's death. Ours was but a short acquaintance, but it was one I shall not easily forget.

Stephen looked up to Barton and was obviously much attached to him, as he explained to his mother:

> The sight of Barton and his family doing well more than pays me for any reverses that have happened to myself. I cannot account for the extreme attachment there is between us, on my side at all events. We are very dissimilar in our tastes and pursuits, yet still everything that I am able to give up for him I would with the greatest willingness.

No consideration would have induced me to leave England when I did, except for it being necessary on Barton's account.

In June 1838 Darlot published an account of his overland trip with Stephen and it attracted much interest. The report was published first in the *Australian* in Sydney, and later in the *South Australian Record* in London.

Transporting the cattle

In January 1838 while Stephen was travelling overland to Portland Bay, Hart and Devlin were busy arranging the transport of goods, sheep for the South Australian Company and some cattle. These were loaded at Kissing Point on the Parramatta River, where Devlin had a property. He started out on 1 January on the *Lady Wellington* and arrived back in Adelaide with the loss of only two animals. Devlin made several voyages back and forth on the *Lady Wellington* and these trips were profitable for the Hacks and their co-owners.

Captain Hart left Sydney at the end of January on the *Hope* with bullocks for the Hacks and sheep for the South Australian Company. After arriving in Adelaide in February he turned his attention to collecting Stephen's cattle at Portland Bay. On the first trip he collected 120 cattle, mostly for the Hacks' dairy. In March, the remaining cattle at Mullengandra (about 300) arrived overland at Portland Bay. Stephen now had about 900 cattle at the Bay.

Hart arrived in Portland Bay on the *Hope* in April and took another load of cattle, and on this occasion Stephen and Darlot went with him. They ran into a storm and Hart was forced to land at Encounter Bay near the mouth of the Murray. They offloaded the cattle and, with no horses, had to walk the seventy miles to Adelaide. Hart and Darlot, who were anxious to return, went on ahead and made it in two days. Stephen followed with the cattle, arriving in early May 1838.

He had been away eight months, and wrote to his mother: 'Hard work, living and exposure have made me look much older than when I left England. I am now taken by most people to be considerably more than 30. If my old friend rheumatism keeps off, I can weather it out a year or two more and then I shall not live so much in the bush'.

Hawdon and Bonney

When Stephen arrived in Adelaide in early May 1838, he found the town buzzing with the news of Hawdon and Bonney's arrival a month earlier, after overlanding their cattle along the Murray and on to Adelaide. Hawdon and Bonney spoke enthusiastically about the land around Mount Barker, covered with the 'most luxuriant grass'. Barton had seen this earlier, having been part of the first ascent of Mount Barker. He and Stephen knew it was excellent grazing country and decided they would be among the first to take up land in that area.

Hawdon and Bonney had opened up a new route, and it became clear that this was preferable to taking stock by ship, as the cattle arrived in better condition and there were fewer losses. Later in the year, after several more trips to Portland Bay by ship, Captain Hart transported Stephen's remaining 500 cattle overland from Portland to Adelaide. He did this in November 1838 with nine stockmen and a friend, William Pullen. They travelled north until they reached the Murray and followed it to Adelaide, arriving in March the following year without the loss of a single beast.

In the meantime, Barton was expanding his activities in town.

Chapter 10
Hindley Street

The second year of the colony, 1838, was full of exciting new ventures for Barton Hack and his family. They built a two-storey stone house and warehouse in Hindley Street and went into a whaling business at Encounter Bay with Captains Hart and Devlin. The children continued to thrive, and in the middle of the year Bbe gave birth to their eighth child, a girl. Stephen continued to explore and Barton befriended a bushranger.

Family matters

At the beginning of 1838, Barton began to build on a block near their cottage on North Terrace. This was acre 74 in Hindley Street, located between Morphett and King William streets. He planned a limestone house two storeys high with a large storeroom underneath. Most of the houses being constructed in Adelaide were now made of limestone. It was easily accessible, lying two to three feet below the topsoil.

Bridget Hack was as active as ever, despite being pregnant again. She ran the dairy, which was bringing in about £16 a week, and was planning to expand it as soon as Stephen arrived with more cattle. 'The rankest salt butter is 2s 6d per lb here', she wrote in January, 'and my delicious butter is only 6d more'.

Willie, aged nine, and Edward, eight, were at the first school in the colony, a school for boys run by the Reverend Thomas Stow, a Congregational minister. It was in North Terrace, part of a larger building he used for church services.[76] Bbe wrote home that:

> Willie at his own request has begun Greek as well as Latin and keeps at the head of his class. Poor Teddy has no natural liking for books and forgets his lessons again in the walk to school, but is getting on nicely in Geography.

Bbe was helped by her friend Caroline Carter and their maid Harriet Staker, who was enjoying her new life in the colony. Harriet wrote to her mother: 'People can do a great deal better than at home, so I hope in about two years we shall have a little property of our own, which we should not get at home if we worked hard all our lives . . . Little Frank has grown very much and is a good boy. He plays with Mr Hack's children'.[77]

With Stephen away, Barton was flat out supervising all their various businesses and their large number of employees. He slaved from dawn to dusk and then sat down with his accounts until bedtime. He must have been amazed at their progress in just over a year – they had the carrying business, the dairy, the market garden in North Adelaide, the cattle speculation and the sale of goods on commission. He and Stephen were leading citizens, and Barton believed that in a year or two they would be comfortable financially.

The partnership between the Hack brothers and Captains Hart and Devlin was flourishing, and in April they embarked upon a new venture together, the purchase of a whaling station at Encounter Bay. This was at Hind Cove, previously managed by Captain Blenkinsop, who had been drowned along with Judge Jeffcott. Stephen and Barton had a two-fifth share in the fishery. Whaling was potentially a lucrative business, with a huge demand for whale oil in England for lamps and candle wax, while whalebone was used for women's corsets and hoops for their skirts.

The fisheries in Encounter Bay hunted the Southern Right Whale, which migrated along the coast from May to October. The whaling business was dirty, difficult and dangerous. Large numbers of men were needed, which meant considerable capital and running expenses. The whalers were rough men and David McLaren of the South Australian Company described them as uncouth 'off-scourings of the earth'.[78] Nevertheless, Barton and Hart had seen men make a great deal of money from whaling, especially the Hentys at Portland Bay, and they believed they could do the same.

In April the Hacks received letters and presents from home. Bbe wrote to Tom and Lydia about the children's delight at opening the 'box of treasures' from Gloucester:

> The books and desk and slates and toys were received with a zest of joy ... they have not had such a treat since leaving the old country. The ball was given up to little Bed [ford] who hugged it close all evening and even when I went to bed I found him asleep with it in his arms, and poor Teddy [Edward] when I read his kind Aunt's letter to him [Margaret Darton] ... fairly cried for joy. Mamma's [Maria's] present of books are highly valued and Willie's desk makes him quite a man – it is brought out every evening to write his Latin exercises upon.

Bbe thanked Maria Hack for her seeds which had been planted in the thirteen acres they called 'Chichester Gardens' in North Adelaide. They had prevailed upon Captain Devlin to buy orange, lime and lemon trees in Sydney, which would 'make our garden the most complete as well as profitable in the Colony'. She continued:

> Barton and I rode there the other afternoon and everything looks in a most promising condition. We have been abundantly supplied with melons this last season ... we have also vines, figs, bananas, pineapples and sweet potatoes and all English vegetables in perfection.

By the end of April the house in Hindley Street was proceeding, and Barton had erected stables on the site, which he let out. Considering that the store underneath the house was not large enough for their merchant business, he started construction of a separate store behind the house.

Committees

Barton continued to be involved in many of the key decisions in the colony. He was a public-spirited man who loved nothing more than to attend a meeting with his fellow colonists or to set up a committee if there was a problem to be solved. Perhaps he was following the example of his father and uncles, who had been involved in local issues in Chichester and sometimes national ones.

On 24 March 1838 he attended a meeting called by Fisher to discuss the financial state of the province. The meeting also included John Morphett, John Brown and Edward Stephens, the manager of the Bank of South Australia. The colony had been set up on the basis that it was largely self-financing through its land sales, but Fisher had very little money for the expenses of the settlement, explaining to the meeting that there were no funds left in the hands of the treasurer, Osmond Gilles. But certain payments had to be made immediately; the meeting agreed that the Bank of South Australia should advance £200, with a committee set up to advise Fisher on the best course of action.[79]

In April 1838 Barton submitted a bill for payment for the canal at the Old Port, which had been completed the year before. The initial contract between Barton and the Colonial Secretary Robert Gouger was for £400, but it allowed for extra payments. Barton submitted a bill for £800. The cost over-run was not surprising, considering his lack of experience in civil engineering works, and it was signed off by Colonel Light. But it provided ammunition for George Stevenson, the editor of the *Gazette and Register*, who used his paper to attack Fisher and his friends.

On 28 April the newspaper reported:

> The muddy ditch at the harbour, by some good-natured persons dignified by the name of *canal*, which was contracted to be dug by Messrs J.B. Hack & Co, for £400, *has cost exactly double that sum*, and £800 has actually been paid by Mr. Resident Commissioner.

The paper called for an inquiry and added 'the canal is all but unserviceable; and before it was known that Mr Gouger had given the contract *privately* to Messrs Hack, Mr. E. Stephens offered to complete the work, on the part of the South Australian Company, for £200!'

Barton did not reply to the allegations, but one thing was true, the canal and the wharf were inadequate for the growing needs of the province. The Old Port, which became known as Port Misery, was too shallow, meaning that vessels could only unload at high tide, and there was little room for boats to manoeuvre. The following year a new port was under discussion, although it did not open until late in 1840 and was located further down the Port River and had a road leading to it. Barton's canal was eventually filled in and no trace of it remains today.[80]

In May 1838 a school for boys and girls opened on North Terrace, not far from the Classical Academy conducted by the Reverend Stow attended by William and Edward Hack.[81] The new school, with Barton Hack on the committee, was established by the South Australian School Society. This society had been founded in London in 1836, and appointed a 'director of schools' named John Shepherdson, who had arrived in Adelaide in 1837.[82]

Barton was also involved in the establishment of the Literary and Scientific Association and Mechanics Institute. The decision to form the institute was taken at a public meeting in June, with the first general meeting held on 30 July, at which Fisher was elected president and Barton a vice-president. The Mechanics Institute would later become the South Australia Institute, which in turn led to the Public Library (now the State Library), the Art Gallery of South Australia and the South Australian Museum in Adelaide.

Aboriginal people

The local Indigenous people continued to be dispossessed of their land and food sources. In general, relations between them and the colonists were friendly, although clashes were becoming more common. The *Gazette and Register* reported that two white men had been murdered by Aborigines, one in September 1837 and one in March 1838.

After the second murder, the public demanded some action. Governor Hindmarsh established a twelve-member committee 'to recommend measures relative to the Aborigines' and to advise the Protector of Aborigines (Dr William Wyatt). Barton was one of those elected to the committee. The *South Australian* noted that the committee:

> seemed to recognize on the part of the Commissioners [in London] a moral, if not a legal right of the natives to the land we now occupy, for it seems certain that at different periods of the year the whole of the districts surveyed ... and allotted without any reserve to the Colonists, was occupied by the natives.[83]

In setting up the colony, the Commissioners in London had promised to set aside land, the rent from which would go to an ongoing fund for the Indigenous inhabitants. In May Dr Wyatt wrote to the Colonial Secretary on this subject, and later in the year the Acting Governor wrote to the British Government, but to no avail.[84]

Maria Hack back in England read about the two murders by Aborigines and wrote to her sons expressing concern for their welfare. Stephen wrote to reassure her that the natives were 'very quiet and orderly, in fact they are ... better behaved than the mass of the lower order of white people here'. He described attending a corroboree and added, 'I have seldom been in any danger from them, though I am more in the bush I believe than most in the colony'.

Stephen's return

In early May when Stephen Hack arrived back in Adelaide with his cattle, he was welcomed warmly by the family. He had been away eight months and can be imagined sitting by the fire in the house on North Terrace, telling the wide-eyed children about his adventures on the overland trek from New South Wales. He wrote to his mother that Caroline Carter was going to be married to Dr John Woodforde, a young surgeon who had arrived in 1836 on the *Rapid* and who had opened a practice in Adelaide. The Hacks were happy for them, and Stephen described Dr Woodforde as 'a very amiable, clever young man'.

Stephen said the carrying business with the bullock drays had cleared £500 to date, and they had made nearly as much with the dairy. He said Johnny (the family's pet name for Barton) 'is looking delightful, I never saw him better. I might see you in a year or two, as Barton, if he continues as well as he is now, might be left 12 months without danger'. Stephen had not forgotten that he was sent out to Australia to look after things should Barton's health fail.

Stephen's explorations

It was not long before Stephen was off exploring again. He and Tom Davis travelled beyond Mount Barker searching for an easier route to Encounter Bay, and again a few days later Stephen made a longer trip with his friend Charles Stuart. They rode north-east of Adelaide and explored the hills between the South Para and the little Para rivers. The trip took them as far north as modern-day Gawler. This was unexplored territory.

In July Stephen went off again to search for some of their cattle that had gone astray. This was a nine-day trip south of Adelaide and around the coast. He camped on the Onkaparinga River and then travelled to Aldinga and camped near Mount Terrible. From there he travelled on to Encounter Bay where he visited the Hacks' fishery and was 'made comfortable' by the manager, Captain William Wright. From Encounter Bay his travels took him north-west to Yankalilla, which he described as 'rich and beautiful' country. From there he crossed to Rapid Bay and Cape Jervis, which faces Kangaroo Island. He returned to Adelaide via Cowyrlanka (Second Valley).

Stephen described this trip in a letter to his mother and then digressed with a request for Gates to send him books. From the list we can learn a lot about this young man of twenty-two. He was a curious mixture – a bushman who loved hunting and could survive in harsh conditions, but at the same time a sensitive person who wore glasses and read poetry.

He asked for his favourite 'frontier' novels, including the latest volumes of Washington Irving's *A Tour on the Prairie*, James Hall's *Legends of the West*, and all of James Fenimore Cooper's books except *The Last of the Mohicans*, which he'd read. He added the novels of Sir Walter Scott and Wilson's *Tales of the Borders and of Scotland* to his list, also asking for several volumes of the *Naturalist's Library*, including those on mammals, birds and insects. He wanted poetry – Byron, Burns and Scott – and the latest volumes of the *New Sporting Magazine* and the *Annals of Sporting*.

Stephen urged his brother Tom to come to the colony, and his mother too. Sounding homesick, he added, 'Now my dear Mother, thee may have found me self willed, passionate, and perhaps worse, but I doubt if thee know the sincere affection which every time I write to thee, seems to increase in strength'.

Jack Foley

During Stephen's visit to Encounter Bay in July, he heard there were men camped nearby with a fine chestnut mare belonging to the Hacks. Stephen decided to search for them, setting out, guns loaded, with Tom Davis. The search yielded nothing: the thieves had bolted. The thieves were later discovered to be three runaways from Sydney named Jack Foley, Edward Stone and Henry Manley. Shortly after Stephen's visit the trio split up, with Stone and Manley going to Adelaide with two horses said to be stolen from the Hentys. Foley stayed in the bush near Encounter Bay, hunting kangaroos and selling the meat to the whalers. The officers at the fishery wanted to get rid of him, so they offered him a reward if he would deliver a packet to Edward Stephens, the manager of the Bank of South Australia in Adelaide. Then they tipped off the authorities.[85]

Foley turned up at the bank on North Terrace on the evening of 30 July. A meeting was taking place to consider the state of the local police force, with Barton Hack in the chair and Inspector Inman, the superintendant of police, present.[86] As Barton recalled later:

> Inman called me out, and said he thought my missing horse was in the yard. In this he proved to be mistaken; but while we were looking at the horse, the man who had ridden him came out, and some words passed between him and Inman. The man tried to force the horse out of his hold, and presented a pistol, which Inman caught hold of, and in the struggle the lock was wrenched off. The man was taken into custody, and he proved to be a convict from Sydney named Jack Foley, who had been camped for some time in the vicinity of Encounter Bay.[87]

The horse was not Barton's, so suspicion then fell on Stone and Manley. Foley offered to help track them down, and led a party made up of Inspector Inman, Sergeant Alford, three policemen and Stephen Hack. With Foley's help, they captured Stone near a creek at Encounter Bay. Manley was captured later in Adelaide, but he and Stone soon escaped again.

Foley was held in custody, but Barton had taken a liking to him. He wrote later, 'I saw the man Jack Foley in prison several times and thought there was not much harm in him, and as he was a good stockkeeper and bush hand, I applied for his release, no special charge having been preferred against him'.

Later that year, when Captain Hart set out to take cattle overland, Foley accompanied him from Portland Bay to Adelaide. Foley later worked for the Hacks on their cattle station at Mount Barker, and, when Stephen Hack paid a visit to England in 1840, he took Foley with him as his servant. Foley, whose real name was Lovett, was a Suffolk ploughman who had been transported for life in 1821 but had escaped in 1833.

John W. Bull in his book *Early Experiences of Life in South Australia* claimed that Foley was a gypsy, and had been transported to Sydney for horse stealing.[88] Bull said that when Foley returned to England with Stephen, he went to Chichester and exhibited himself in the horse market in the costume and character of an Australian stockman, to the astonishment of the Duke of Richmond and a large crowd. Later on Foley was rumoured to have got into a brawl and stabbed a man, for which he was sentenced to jail for life.

Hindley Street

Towards the middle of 1838 the Hack family moved into their new house in Hindley Street. Built of stone with a shingled roof, it was, according to Stephen, 'without comparison the best and most comfortable house in Adelaide'.

Barton described it to his mother:

> The walls are nearly two feet thick so I think it must be pretty cool. There is a large cellar and warehouse for stores. We shall have 6 bedrooms on the second floor and 3 attics, 2 sitting rooms on the ground and convert the wooden houses [the Manning cottages] into kitchens and dry stores ... it looks quite imposing from the other side of the river.

How the house and store looked at this time can be seen in the sketch *Hindley Street Adelaide 1838* by Frederick Nixon, one of Light's assistant surveyors. The half-acre on Hindley Street was turning into quite a compound, with stables for horses, a stockyard, a cow shed and an underground dairy for keeping the milk cool. Once they moved in, the Manning cottages in North Terrace were moved to Hindley Street. The structures remaining on North Terrace became a police station. By December the separate store was nearly finished. Barton wrote that it would be a noble building, 'of large stone and brick quoins [cornerstones]... 90 ft x 30 ft with large doors for the drays to draw through'.

On 7 August Bbe gave birth to a baby daughter, Gulielma Mary, named in memory of Barton's two sisters who had died in England.

By the end of 1838 the population of the colony was 6000, having increased by nearly 3000 during the year.[89] Emigrants were flocking to South Australia, lured by the free passages paid for by land sales. Buildings were going up all over Adelaide, but the streets were of dirt and became mud or dust, depending on the weather. Barton had chosen Hindley Street well, as it was rapidly becoming the chief centre of business in the young capital. The house stood at what is now 91 Hindley Street, the current home of the Adelaide Symphony Orchestra.

The family expands

During the year the Hacks were joined by some close relatives. In September George Deane, a cousin of Barton's, arrived from England with his wife Rachel and their children. Barton rode down to the harbour to meet them and put them up in one of his timber cottages in Pennington Terrace. He found work for Deane as an accountant and agent, arranged for him to look after the government accounts and do some work for the bank. Soon George had two clerks employed, as well as acting as a wine merchant.

The following month Barton's brother-in-law Dr John Knott arrived on the *Pestonjee Bomanjee*, travelling as the ship's medical officer and Barton accommodated him in another of the cottages in Pennington Terrace. Knott had come ahead of his wife Ellen and the children. Barton's future brother-in-law Edward Philcox had already arrived, and he and John Knott planned to become sheep farmers.

Discussing farming with the two of them, Barton saw the need for another committee, and on 6 November the South

Australian Bush Club was formed for 'gentlemen who may be desirous of embarking in pastoral or agricultural pursuits'.[90] Barton was the treasurer, John Knott one of the three trustees, and Stephen Hack, Edward Philcox and Stephen's friend Charles Stuart among the nine committee members.

In the meantime John Knott started work as a dealer in merchandise, although Barton wrote that he was 'quite out of his element'. In December Edward Philcox left Adelaide for England to marry Priscilla Hack and bring her back to South Australia. Bridget Hack's relatives were also on their way. Her brother Henry Watson, his wife Charlotte, their two small children and Henry's parents, had left England in October.

Chapter 11
Governor Hindmarsh recalled

In the early days of the colony, friction developed rapidly between Governor Hindmarsh and the Resident Commissioner, James Hurtle Fisher, and in 1838 Hindmarsh was recalled. His replacement was Governor George Gawler, who arrived in October that year. Barton Hack, as a friend of Fisher's, was caught up in this dispute, but later became a friend of Gawler's. Barton was now a prominent citizen, active in the public life of the colony. The Hack brothers' various businesses expanded, although they also experienced setbacks.

Hindmarsh recalled

At the beginning of 1838, the second year of the colony, Governor Hindmarsh was recalled. From the outset the system of dual responsibility had been a problem, with Hindmarsh appointed by the Colonial Secretary and Fisher by the Colonization Commissioners. Hindmarsh had never been accorded full authority like the governors of the other Australian colonies, and the dual system promoted conflict between him and Fisher. But Hindmarsh's quarterdeck manner did not help, with one historian describing him as 'a complete stranger to systematic colonization and civil liberty'.[91]

The authorities learned a lesson from this dispute, and when Colonel George Gawler was appointed as the next governor he was given dual powers of governor and resident commissioner. Gawler did not arrive in Adelaide until October 1838. Hindmarsh was told to wait for his successor, but he ignored this and departed in July. James Hurtle Fisher could no longer hold the position of resident commissioner, so he reluctantly surrendered his duties and embarked on a political career. In 1840 he became the first mayor of Adelaide and later a prominent member of the state parliament.

Barton Hack was caught up in these events. Before Hindmarsh left, the fight between his supporters and Fisher's reached a climax with the publication of the colony's second newspaper the *Southern Australian*. Barton, one of those who had signed a petition for a second newspaper and annoyed by the vitriol of the *Gazette and Register*, then became a member of the committee of proprietors who established the new paper. It appeared on 2 June, and before long the colony's leading citizens were attacking each other in the two rival newspapers.

Before leaving Adelaide, Hindmarsh dashed off angry letters to London, complaining about his enemies, including Fisher, Light and Morphett. In a long despatch to Lord Glenelg, Hindmarsh criticised 'a gentleman named Hack' and mentioned the payment of £800 for the canal, saying that the contract had been for half that sum. Hindmarsh said he did not authorise the payment for 'extras' but it had been authorised by Gouger and Light and paid by Fisher. Hindmarsh wrote:

> For the foregoing unintelligible conduct I can only perceive the motive of serving a warm friend and supporter . . . Mr Hack is the acknowledged partizan of Mr Fisher and of Col. Light, the Surveyor General, and . . . Mr Gouger.[92]

Hindmarsh also wrote to his patron Admiral Sir Pulteney Malcolm, protesting about his dismissal.[93] Once again he mentioned the payment for the canal, and after criticising John Morphett, he went on: 'The next to speak of is a Mr. Hack, a rich Quaker, and a Man of Education and more like a gentleman than any one of the party, but unfortunately and notwithstanding his riches etc, he is the most avaricious person I ever knew . . .'

Barton knew nothing about these letters, but it didn't matter, because Hindmarsh was finished. He sailed for London, leaving in charge George Milner Stephen as Acting Governor, the man who was about to become his son-in-law.

The merchant business

By the middle of 1838 the Hack brothers' merchant business was going well. Captain Devlin was bringing goods down on the *Lady Wellington*, Captain Hart on the *Hope*, and they chartered other vessels as well. Stephen reported that Barton had 'sold several thousand pounds of goods on commission as well as what we have purchased'.

The third trip of the *Lady Wellington* was however its last. In August she ran onto the bar at the entrance to the harbour and was damaged. She was sold to a merchant named Neale, who afterwards sold her to Governor Gawler for use as a government store ship. The loss was not disastrous, as Devlin sold the hulls, sails and rigging for nearly £1000,[94] and in addition they had insured her well.

With the Hacks, Hart and Devlin now needing another vessel, Devlin purchased the 258-ton brig *Adelaide* for £2800. In December the *Adelaide* left Sydney for Port Phillip under Captain Devlin with extensive cargo and passengers. They ran into a gale lasting twenty days, and Devlin was later praised for his skill as commander. Devlin made several voyages in the *Adelaide*, including one that involved Barton in another unhappy lawsuit with Henry Jones.

Gates Darton – correspondence in England

During 1838 relations between the Hack brothers and their brother-in-law Gates Darton deteriorated rapidly. At the beginning of 1838 Gates was faced with bills for the brothers' expenditure totalling about £1800. This was for the purchase of the *Lady Wellington* and merchandise on the *William*. Gates accepted the bills, as he could not 'ruin B & S's credit and standing for ever in Australia', but he had to borrow heavily to do so.

Gates's problems increased when his father Samuel Darton retired from Darton and Harvey, the family publishing business in London. Gates joined as a junior partner and the business name was changed to Harvey and Darton. Gates was not happy about his position in the firm, telling Barton later that because all his capital was advanced to meet bills from Australia, he could only go into a business where he had some connection, and on 'very disadvantageous terms'. Nor could he emigrate, 'because you had tied me to England'.

Shortly after becoming a partner, Gates received another bill from Barton, this time for £100. Maria Hack was shocked, and urged Gates to refuse it. In a letter of 27 April 1838 she wrote to him:

> I am fortunately £100 ahead ... this I will lend thee for <u>thy own</u> purposes until some remittances come from B & S ... I do feel very anxious about <u>thy</u> affairs. To be riding dead horses at first starting in business must be so discouraging.

Maria's offer of a loan of £100 was accepted by Gates, but he said he would have to use it to pay Barton's bill. He then explained in detail the 'foolish and imprudent conduct of poor dear B & S in drawing upon me as they have done'. Barton and Stephen had sent the bills for £1800 thinking they would be covered by the next division of the family property. In fact, each of them received just over £300 from the family estate in 1838. Gates had sold the South Australian country acres for £500, but was still short.

Gates said he had written to Barton and Stephen by every ship, explaining how their 'mad conduct' had placed him. The next day Maria wrote to Gates: 'If this does not make a <u>deep</u> impression, poor dear Barton will ruin himself in some other mad scheme. Oh, if he would but settle down quietly on a small grazing farm'.

Soon after Gates paid Barton's bill of £100, he received the two bills for cattle in Sydney, for £200 each. This time Gates's patience had run out, and he decided to send the bills back. Maria agreed entirely and said she had reduced her income by £100 per annum and lived in strict economy, but had been forced to draw on the principal of her husband's estate to assist Barton and Gates.

Barton and Stephen's reply to Gates

By April 1838 Barton was aware of the problems in England, having received several ledgers and letters from Gates, full of complaints. Now for the first time, Barton learned that his calculations about the family inheritance were wrong. Maria may have wished that Barton would settle down quietly, but he had no intention of doing so. He wrote to his brother Tom that he was overly busy and hoped that his brothers-in-law Henry Watson and Gates Darton would join him.

'I fear that I shall have put dear Gates to some inconvenience by my drafts having exceeded the amounts received', he wrote, 'but it can cause only temporary inconvenience, for I shall of course, if I find it to be an inconvenience, remit the balance immediately. It will be merely retaining the sums borrowed at interest for a longer period'. In this rather airy way Barton dismissed the problems at home. Instead of sending money back to Gates, Barton thought he could pay interest on these 'loans' until he was well established.

In May 1838 a new issue arose that further increased the rift between Barton and Gates. In South Australia the rural acres were slowly being surveyed, and a meeting was called of those who had purchased preliminary land holdings to enable them to choose their rural sections.

The Hacks' three preliminary land orders represented 134 rural acres each, or 402 acres in total. Barton had earlier swapped Gates's rural acres for thirteen town acres, so all the rural acres now belonged to Barton and Stephen. They nominated the district of Yankalilla, which had not yet been surveyed.

Not long afterwards, Barton received the news that Gates had already sold *all* the rural acres to pay debts. Barton was shocked, especially since all the rural acres belonged to himself and Stephen – the year before he had given Gates thirteen town acres in exchange for Gates' rural acres. After some thought, Barton decided that if none of them now held any rural land, then his gift of thirteen town acres to Gates had been pointless. Having reached this conclusion, Barton took back the thirteen town acres for himself.

Barton may have felt this was reasonable, given that the thirteen town acres had been roughly the same value as the rural acres, but he was only seeing it from his own point of view. In fact it was unfair to Gates, particularly in light of all the struggles Gates was having in England as a result of Barton and Stephen's debts. Barton now left Gates with just the one town acre selected in 1837 from Gates' preliminary land order. This was acre 345 in the centre of town, in Wakefield Street.

Months later, when Gates received this information, he felt even more aggrieved. He thought this was shabby treatment, as

Barton had kept all the future profit-making investments and left Gates with just one town acre. Later on, when Barton sold some town acres at a high profit, Gates felt he should have had a share in those profits, in compensation for having had been forced to sell his rural acres and being left to bail out Barton in England.

Sometime in September Barton learned that the two bills for £200 had been refused, on 30 September 1838 writing to his mother:

> These bills which have formed the subject of Gates's letters for some time will now soon be at an end and we shall at length escape from the disheartening and chilling feeling of opening letters from home and finding nothing but bitter complaints of ill-usage and reproaches for imprudence. If an attempt to form a mercantile [trading] concern which should afford occupation to two or three of my brothers is imprudent, I suppose we must plead guilty . . . We bore the first few letters pretty well, but these last have almost worn out our patience and our temper which is worse.

Barton defended himself by saying that Gates had promised to join them when they were established, and had let them down by settling in England. Barton said he had felt able to draw on Gates because Gates had money in the family estate (through his wife's inheritance) and had spoken of doing something with Barton and Stephen in Australia. As for the bills for £200 each, Barton said he would pay them himself, and added 'We are doing business to such an extent in Sydney that an amount such as this could not do us any injury, and I hope we shall never again have occasion to trouble our relations in England for any assistance'.

Barton explained to his mother that he had received a setback with the wreck of the *Isabella*. The case had been referred to arbitration, the result being that the Hacks had to pay for the cargo, but not for the stock. Henry Jones and John Hart were awarded £1400 but Hart said the claim was unjust, and refused to accept his half. Barton however had to pay £700 to Jones.[95]

At the end of the year Stephen Hack asked his mother why he had not received any letters from her or Tom since April. 'What I am afraid of is that it is caused by Gates, whose letters have latterly, especially the last two, been nothing but a tissue of insults ... Barton will tell thee we ship our first oil by the *Goshawk* and that will free us from Gates's dunning at all events'.

The money from the sale of oil and whalebone could have helped Gates, but it did not arrive in England until May the following year. Worse still, the *Goshawk* carried less than half the oil, the remainder being taken by Devlin to Sydney in the *Hope* in October 1838 and used to buy the brig *Adelaide*.

The balance sheet – 1838

Throughout the year Barton and Stephen felt their efforts to build a family business were not sufficiently appreciated by those at home. They tried to explain how well things were going.

First there was the dairy, which had brought in £500 in the past quarter. Then there was the carrying business with five teams of bullocks, which had also realised £500 in the past quarter. The flock of sheep was quite small and the Hacks were selling them. The cattle speculation was huge, and by the end of the year Stephen had sold about 300 cattle for £4601, at good prices. But there were still several hundred more to sell, including those Hart was bringing overland.

Then there was the whaling station at Encounter Bay. In July the Hacks, Hart and Devlin purchased a little cutter forty feet long, the *Hero*, for the whaling business. Later that year it was the first vessel registered at Port Adelaide. The *Hero*'s certificate, No. 1, was for many years hanging on the wall of the Customs Office.[96]

The Hacks had invested a great deal of money into the fishery and it had been profitable, but there were management problems. For this reason, they decided to go into a joint venture with the South Australian Company's fisheries, with Captain Hart as manager for both. The new company was called the United Fishing Company of Adelaide, with four stations – at Cape Hind and Rosetta Cove – and two at the mouth of Spencer Gulf – Thistle Island and Sleaford Bay.

Barton would be involved in the whaling industry from 1838 to 1841, and would find the risks involved in this industry to be high.[97] But in December 1838 he reported: 'The fisheries are the source from which I anticipate the best return; we have £2500 invested in this department'. This was a substantial commitment by the Hacks, Hart and Devlin in a business, which to date had been unreliable. But Barton was his usual optimistic self and believed that the joint venture with Hart as manager would fix any problems.

Stephen knew his mother liked hard facts and in September sent her a long letter listing their assets. He set these out in a column in the middle of the page showing a grand total of £21,100. The main item was the increase in the value of their town acres, which he valued at £10,000. Stephen valued the remaining cattle at £9000 and their twenty-two horses at £1100. He mentioned the whale fishery, of which they owned two-fifths and he said they had been offered £1000 for a one-sixth share. In summing up he wrote: 'We may consider that we began the world with four thousand pounds, so we have done pretty well for one year'. The four thousand pounds referred to the money Barton got from the sale of the currier business and Stephen's inheritance.

In December there was still no letter from Maria or Tom, with Stephen writing anxiously that he feared she now regarded him and Barton as swindlers. To convince her otherwise, he gave an updated list of their assets with a grand total of £25,500. He said they had valued their stock and had the books balanced and found they had made £16,000 profit since landing in South Australia. He said the only debt was to the bank, and it was constantly shifting as they paid money in and took money out.

A letter from Maria finally arrived on 21 December. Barton replied on 30 December that it was wonderful to see her handwriting and they had finished stocktaking and were very pleased with the result. His estimate of their property was more modest than Stephen's. He said it was worth about £18,000 and they had 900 cattle, 'the only individuals in the colony who have a herd', by which he meant other than the South Australian Company.

By the end of 1838 then, everything was going well for the two brothers and their future prospects were good. In addition, there was another exciting development they had not yet reported to their relatives in England. They were squatting with cattle near Mount Barker, and hoped very soon to purchase the land.

John Barton Hack's journal (1836–1837, 1839) and the first page, 18–20 June 1836. Original in State Library of South Australia (PRG 456/6).

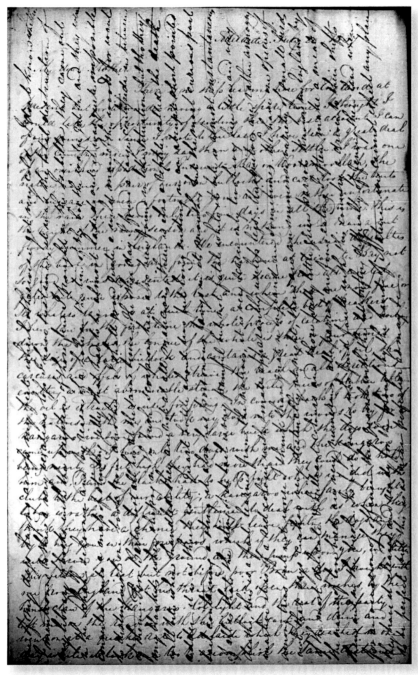

Letter from Stephen Hack to his mother Maria Hack, 29 October 1836, showing 'crossed' lines.
Original in possession of Iola Mathews.

Clockwise from top left:

John Barton Hack (1805–1884), in about 1850, aged 45. Courtesy of Nicholas and Caroline Darton.

Bridget Hack, in about 1860, aged 54. Courtesy of the State Library of South Australia (SLSA: B 10506).

Stephen Hack as a young man. Courtesy of Julia Hedley.

John Barton Hack (1911–1996), great-grandson of John Barton Hack.

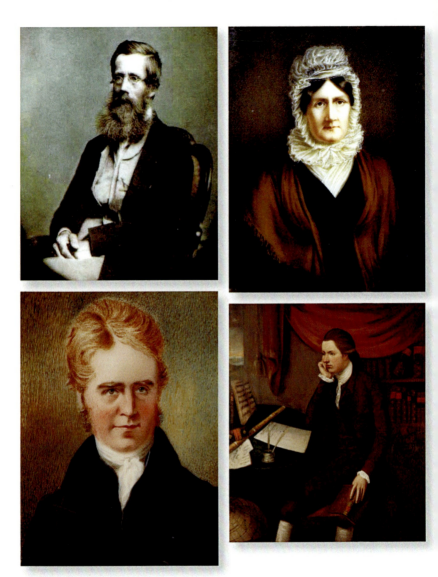

Clockwise from top left:

Stephen Hack, aged about 46. Courtesy of Julia Hedley.

Maria Hack, née Barton, mother of John Barton Hack, painting possibly by her daughter Elizabeth. Original in the Cotsen Collection, Princeton, USA, (C A.28).

John Barton, Maria Hack's father in 1774, aged about 20. Courtesy of Dr David Barton.

John Barton, Maria Hack's half brother. Courtesy of Dr David Barton.

Thomas Gates Darton in old age, and Margaret Darton, sister of John Barton Hack, perhaps a wedding portrait around 1834. Courtesy of Nicholas and Caroline Darton.

Chichester, 29 Little London, the former currier business of the Hacks, until lately the Chichester Museum, and the family home next door at no. 30 (pink building).

Children of John Barton Hack, mostly ca 1868.

Photographs SLSA and Iola Mathews. Note: there are no photographs of Edward, Louisa, George or Jessie.

Left to right: 1st row: William Hack. (Also SLSA: B 7759/4.) Alfred Hack. (Also SLSA: B 7759/1.) Bedford Hack. (Also SLSA B 7759/4.) *2nd row:* Emily and her husband Cornelius Mitchell. (Also SLSA: B 7759/3 and 7759/2.) *3rd row:* Theodore Hack and his wife Elvira, ca 1880. *4th row:* Charles Hack and his wife Annie. (Also SLSA: B 7759/4.) Francis Hack. (Also SLSA: B 7759/1.)

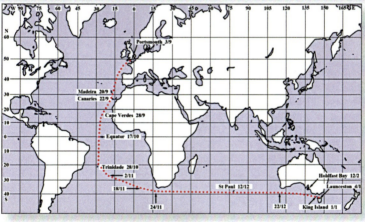

From top:

Quaker Meeting House at St Helens near Liverpool, where Barton Hack and Bridget Watson were married in 1827. Courtesy of St Helen's Meeting House.

Voyage of the *Isabella*, 1836–1837.

A barque similar to the *Isabella*. Photograph of signboard at Point Nelson where the Isabella was wrecked in 1837.

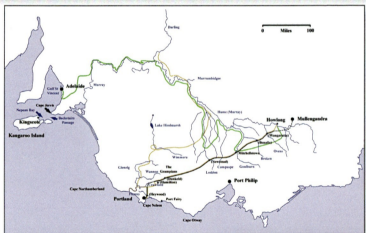

Top: 'Holdfast Bay, South Australia 1836' by John Michael Skipper (Australia, 1815–1883), watercolour on paper, 16.0 x 24.0 cm, Morgan Thomas Bequest Fund 1942, Art Gallery of South Australia, Adelaide. Actually painted in March 1837, it shows the flagstaff with the Red Ensign and the mouth of the Patawalonga Creek. The bullock team on the right could only have been the Hacks'.

Above: South-eastern Australia 1838, showing overland routes taken by Major Mitchell in brown, by Stephen Hack in black, and by Hawdon and Bonney in green.

A Manning cottage today. The Hacks had two joined together on North Terrace, with three rooms added on. Courtesy of the Pioneers Association of South Australia.

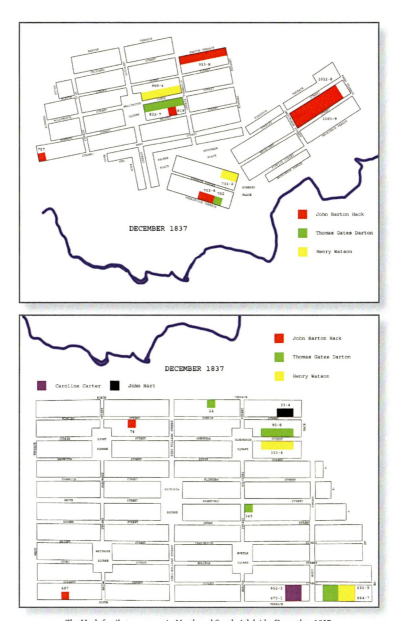

The Hack family town acres in North and South Adelaide, December 1837.

Top: 'A view of the Country and of the Temporary Erections Near the Site for the proposed town of Adelaide in South Australia', by William Light, early 1837, engraved by Robert Havell. Courtesy of the State Library of South Australia (SLSA: B 10079).

Above: 'North Terrace 1841', by E.A. Opie, engraved by J. Hitchen. Image courtesy of the State Library of South Australia (SLSA: B 7070), reproduced with the permission of Francis Edwards Ltd. The Hacks' Manning cottages were no longer on the left, but the small building with pointed roof was one of his outbuildings, then used as the police station. The bridge on the left replaced, on the same spot, the first bridge over the Torrens built by the Hacks in 1837.

Left: The 'Three Brothers Survey' in 1840, after the surveyor Nixon, showing the 3,000 acres owned by the Hack brothers and the location of neighbours. Roads are shown as brown lines, tracks as dotted lines. The three stars are the Three Brothers Hills. E is the location of the current town of Echunga. (Based on SLSA: C 235.)

Below: 'No 1 built by J. Walker Lieut, R.N. 1838', Hindley Street, Adelaide 1838, by the surveyor Frederick Nixon. Courtesy of the State Library of NSW (a128077). John Walker, a merchant, had the two storey house on the left with a verandah, Barton Hack's two storey house is on the right with a separate store behind and a cottage on the left. The two storey building next to the Hacks' was the Victoria Hotel (later the South Australia Club).

Top: 'Echunga Springs', by Governor Gawler, a watercolour sketch of John Barton Hack's house, June 1841. Image courtesy of the State Library of South Australia (SLSA: PRG 50/34), reproduced with the permission of Mrs J. Chesterton.

Above: Echunga Springs in 2013, the site painted by Gawler. The house on the right between the cypress trees is roughly where Barton Hack's house stood. Echunga Creek is below the trees in the foreground. Hack's vineyard was on the hill at the back.

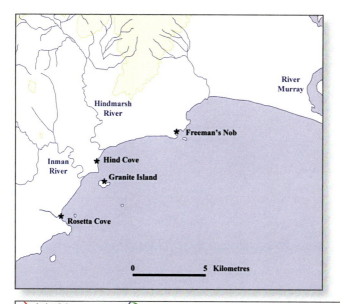

Top: Whaling stations on Encounter Bay in 1840.

Above: The Coorong and the Ninety-mile Desert, early 1860s.

'Panorama of sheep station at Coonalpyn, South Australia', by Charles Babbage, May 1862. Courtesy of the National Library of Australia (an11432433-s89).

Jacob Hagen, the Quaker merchant who took possession of the Echunga estate. Courtesy of the State Library of South Australia (SLSA: B 6288).

Quaker Meeting House in Pennington Terrace, exterior and interior of building in 1959. Courtesy of the family of Colin Ballantyne, great-grandson of John Barton Hack.

'Parnka', by Charles Babbage, June 1862. Courtesy of the National Library of Australia (an11432433-s92).

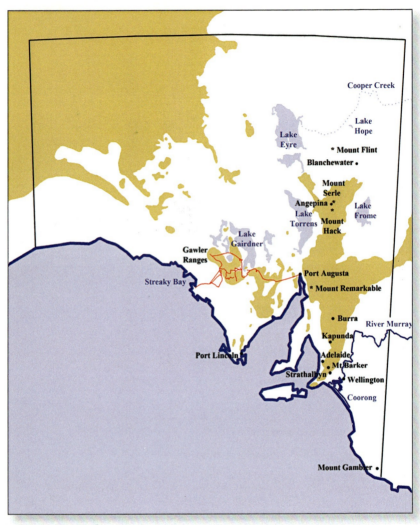

Stephen Hack's explorations. His expedition of 1857 is marked with a red line, places explored in 1859–1860 are named.

Chapter 12

Landed gentry

At the end of 1838, the Hack brothers squatted on a large area of land near Mount Barker. When Governor Gawler arrived in the colony, he introduced a system of special surveys to open up large areas of land for grazing or agriculture. In 1839 the Hacks purchased one at Mount Barker with the Joint Stock Cattle Company, and one at the Sources of the Para with Governor Gawler. The Hacks established dairies on both their surveys. Later on they rented land at Yankalilla, so they had three stations, the main one being the Three Brothers survey near Mount Barker, later known as Echunga.

The Joint Stock Cattle Company

By 1838 there were thousands of sheep in the colony, but very few cattle, and the price of dairy products was high. Barton Hack and others saw the opportunity and set up the 'Joint Stock Cattle Company', to 'supply the Colonists with the purest and most appropriate breeds of cattle, as well as butter and cheese at a moderate price'. They raised capital by offering eighty shares for sale at £25 a share. The first directors were Barton Hack and four others. John Shepherdson, formerly the teacher for the South Australian School Society, was appointed Secretary.

By July 1838 the Cattle Company was setting up a station over the Mount Lofty hills. Barton wrote, 'We, the Company, have 150 or more cows, and are going to establish a dairy on a large scale. We are now fencing in a bend of the Onkaparinga River as a stock yard'. This was near Balhannah, some 23 miles from town, towards Mount Barker.

Stephen's cattle were arriving overland from Portland in relays, and he and Barton established a temporary station for them by squatting about four miles from Adelaide, near Fourth Creek, probably where the village of Klemzig was established the following year by Lutheran refugees escaping religious persecution in Germany. The Hacks sold fifty dairy cows to the Cattle Company and looked after them at Fourth Creek for £2 a week while the company's station was being established.

Goodwood

In August 1838 Captain Charles Sturt appeared in Adelaide. Sturt was famous for having explored the Murray in 1830 and had settled in New South Wales. Now, with a party of eleven, including Captain John Finnis and Giles Strangways (brother of Thomas Strangways, the Colonial Secretary), he brought 400 head of cattle overland from New South Wales following Hawdon's route down the Murray. They squatted on land under Mount Barker to allow the cattle to recover condition.

Barton and Stephen were aware of the good pastures in the Mount Barker area, and a few days after Sturt's arrival in Adelaide they rode over, choosing a site for themselves about three miles west of Mount Barker. They were jubilant about their find, and agreed to call it Goodwood because of its resemblance to Goodwood Park, the seat of the Duke of Richmond near Chichester. Barton later claimed it was where the town of Mount Barker was eventually established.

In early October Stephen took his friend Charles Stuart to visit the new station. The road up to Crafers and Mount Barker today is the start of the M1 freeway to Victoria, and is so steep that on the way down to Adelaide there are safety tracks for trucks to take in the event of brake failure. In 1838 the track followed a somewhat different route and was even steeper. Climbing on horseback was extremely difficult, and at times travellers had to dismount and lead their horses. Taking bullock carts down was even more hazardous and they often overturned.

On 5 October Stephen and Charles left the Crafers inn and rode on to Balhannah on the Onkaparinga River, where they visited the Cattle Company's station. They arrived at the Hacks' new station in the early evening. Stuart noted in his diary that it was 'a beautiful spot, a hill side on beautiful grassy bottom with large waterholes'.[98] The following day they rode over to the station established by Captains Sturt and Finnis, about a mile away.

By December Stephen had moved all his cattle from Fourth Creek to Mount Barker and was planning to live on the station. He wrote to his mother from his hut in Pennington Terrace, saying he was still missing Julia, but for company had some pets: 'There is a tame cockatoo that I have reared from the nest, on the tie beam of my hut over my head, a native puppy in one corner of the yard, a tame wallaby . . . in the stable, and two young pet kangaroos at the cattle station'.

Gawler's visit to Mount Barker

Governor George Gawler, his wife and five children arrived in the colony in October 1838, and he came with instructions to bring some order to affairs in South Australia.[99] The first problem he had to confront was the delay in the land surveys. Colonel Light had resigned as Surveyor-General in July. Kingston was in charge, but he was handicapped by inadequate resources and impractical instructions from London. Urgent action was needed. The settlers were trapped in Adelaide, many without employment. The delay in releasing rural land was also holding up the development of agricultural production. Gawler needed to move swiftly, and his first act was to assess the possibilities himself.

On 14 December he set out with a large party which included his private secretary George Hall, the deputy surveyor Boyle Travers Finniss[100] and the Superintendent of Police Henry Inman. They visited Mount Barker and Gawler went hunting with Stephen Hack, Charles Stuart and John Finnis. Gawler and his men then explored around the Mount Barker area and reached Encounter Bay on Christmas Day, returning to Adelaide via the Inman Valley and Yankalilla.

1839 – the special surveys

The rich land Gawler had seen convinced him to invoke the South Australian Act for 'special surveys'. As Barton Hack explained later, the 'plan was originally called the special survey system, by which on £4000 being lodged with the Colonial Treasurer . . . the applicant might select 4000 acres'.[101]

The Hacks were desperate to obtain a special survey in the Mount Barker region where they were squatting. They planned to acquire 3000 acres for themselves and 1000 for the Cattle Company, of which Barton was a director. He approached his bank manager, Edward Stephens of the Bank of South Australia, 'for discounts to cover £3000'. (Barton had been paid this amount for goods, but in bills with a later maturity date, so the bank would discount the amount by ten per cent.) Stephens however, 'declined to move in the matter'.

So in early January 1839, Barton turned to another bank manager. This was Richard Newland, who had just arrived on the *Parland* to manage a new branch of the Bank of Australasia. Newland was the son of a Chichester banker, a family that Barton knew well. Newland agreed to Barton's proposition, so Barton transferred his account to Newland, a move which did not please his former bank manager.

Newland had arrived in Adelaide with friends from Sydney – Duncan McFarlane and William Dutton – from whom Stephen had earlier purchased cattle. They had brought with them 1500 sheep and cattle. Barton invited Newland and his friends to see the Hacks' Goodwood station at Mount Barker, where Barton and Stephen had marked out their paddocks and laid out a large number of posts and rails.

Barton soon regretted his invitation, because a day or two later when he went to pay his £4000 for the land, the Treasurer, Osmond Gilles, informed him that the survey had already been taken by Dutton, McFarlane, and Barton's neighbour John Finnis, who was related to Dutton. They had not yet paid the money, but Gilles had given them a receipt for the full amount and had taken a section in the survey for himself. Barton wrote later, 'I was very indignant, and applied to Colonel Gawler for redress. He, however, said the Treasurer's receipt was his authority and he could not go behind it'.

The money was paid by Dutton on 11 January 1839, and the following day the *Gazette and Register*, whose editor was no friend of Barton's, heartily congratulated Dutton and his friends. The survey was gazetted as being 'In the District of Mount Barker, including the Cattle Stations of Messrs. Hack and Finnis'.

Barton was probably right in suspecting collusion between William Dutton and the treasurer, Osmond Gilles. On 22 January an agreement was drawn up between Dutton and his partners that they would set aside 250 acres for Gilles, and divide the rest amongst themselves. Dutton also promised an area to Captain Dirk Meinerts Hahn for what would become the town of Hahndorf on behalf of the 189 German immigrants Hahn had brought out on the *Zebra*. Dutton later sold them 240 acres at £7 an acre.[102]

Also outwitted by Dutton was David McLaren, the manager of the South Australian Company, who applied on 14 January for two special surveys. The first was the Lyndoch Valley to the north of Adelaide, the second for a survey that would include the Cattle Company's station at Balhannah as well as those of several other squatters nearby. But McLaren did not realise that the boundaries of the surveys were fixed in order of application. William Dutton had priority, and immediately made it known that he would include in his selection all the stations between Mount Barker and the Onkaparinga. McLaren was forced to amend his survey to 'Northward of the Joint Stock Cattle Company's Station'. Dutton and his partners thus acquired all the best pasture land then known in the hills region.

The Sources of the Para

Osmond Gilles was not the only colonial official interested in obtaining land in a special survey, with numerous of them speculating in land; in fact their masters in London justified their low salaries by the expectation that they would benefit from the development of the colony. Governor Gawler was no exception and joined Barton in another special survey. On 16 January Barton lodged an application for land known as 'the Sources of the Para River'.[103] This was a region about fourteen miles east of Adelaide, at the headwaters of the Little Para River.

In his memoirs, Barton said that of the 4000 acres available, he took 1000, Gawler the same number, with another settler taking 2000. Gawler purchased his land anonymously, using his private secretary, Lieutenant Hall, as his agent. Barton paid the £4000 upfront with the bills he had obtained to purchase Goodwood.

The boundaries of the Sources of the Para were established by the end of January. Barton took his 1000 acres in an area which includes modern-day Paracombe, Inglewood and Houghton. The Hacks' station was in the Strangways Valley, through which flowed Raymond's Creek, one of the headwaters of the Little Para.

Those sections of the survey not claimed by Hack, Gawler and Williams were soon offered for sale, some purchased by John Richardson, a merchant in Hindley Street. Richardson later took his family to live on the Little Para estate. Barton, however, had different plans for his land: he would farm there only on a temporary basis since his purchase was mainly for the purposes of speculation. As soon as he had purchased the land, he moved thirty cows to the run.

The Three Brothers Survey

Barton's real interest lay in the Mount Barker area. After losing Goodwood to Dutton and his friends, it was essential for Barton to find new pastures for his cattle and he eventually chose a site to the south of Dutton's known as the 'Three Brothers' after three hills in the area.[104]

On 23 January, Barton paid the Colonial Treasurer the required £4000, presumably once again with the help of the Bank of Australasia, which meant that he was then able to select 3000 acres for himself and 1000 acres for the Cattle Company. The limits of the Three Brothers survey were fixed by the Survey Office on 31 January, after Dutton's had been determined.

A good supply of water, preferably year round, was the main consideration in choosing a special survey. Applicants were allowed to secure the watercourses for themselves, much to the annoyance of those who could not afford a special survey. The Hacks' new property was ideal, with its chain of deep waterholes and ponds and springs close to the surface.[105] Another attraction was the climate in the Mount Barker district, which is milder than in Adelaide, although much colder in winter.

Barton and Stephen must have been jubilant. They were now landowners like their father, but whereas their father's farm had been 134 acres, they had 3000 acres at the Three Brothers and 1000 acres at the Para. Stephen Hack and his men quickly moved the 400 cattle from Goodwood to the Three Brothers survey. They began to fence their land and build a dairy. On the first day of March in 1839 Captain Hart arrived at the station with the remaining 500 cattle from Portland Bay, making a total of about 900. Soon the Hacks had two dairies at work, one at the Three Brothers and one at the Little Para, each with seventy cows.

The Hacks needed a place to which they could transfer several hundred cattle and calves for fattening and breeding. They chose a large area of land at Yankalilla and squatted there on unsurveyed land. A year or two later they leased this land from the South Australian Company. It was a long way from Mount Barker, but it was the land Barton had chosen earlier and lost when he learned that Gates had sold the country acres. This cattle station was at Dairy Flat, now Torrens Vale, at the head of the Yankalilla River.[106]

Other special surveys

The Sources of the Para and the Three Brothers were not the only surveys Barton was interested in. He was a trustee of the Adelaide Survey Association, and on behalf of the association he and John Russell, a Rundle Street merchant, secured two more surveys. The first was on the eastern side of Spencer Gulf, around Point Victoria. The second was on the western side of Gulf St Vincent, around Port Vincent. They soon realised, however, that there was little hope of these regions being settled and changed their location. They nominated Rivoli Bay in the south-east of the province, and an area called the Sources of the Upper Torrens and Bremer.

South Australia was opening up.

Chapter 13

The estate at Mount Barker

In 1839, the third year of the colony, the Hacks were joined by Bridget's brother, Henry Watson, and his family. Henry became a partner with Barton in the mercantile and whaling business, while Stephen took over the rural properties and built up the Three Brothers estate near Mount Barker.

The Watsons arrive

At the beginning of 1839, Stephen attended to their new properties, while Barton remained in Adelaide to oversee the mercantile business. He also needed to be near home because several of the children were seriously ill. All seemed to recover, except for the eldest daughter, Annie, who died of typhoid fever on 17 February.[107] She was Edward's twin and was only nine years old. The Hacks' five-month-old baby Gulielma was also unwell, mainly suffering from teething problems. A few days later Barton wrote to Gates Darton:

> We have just had the sad trial of laying our poor dear little Annie in the grave. I scarcely yet dare to recall to mind all the engaging & endearing qualities of our precious little girl. She had almost the discretion and industry of one many years older & promised to be such a companion & assistant to dear Bbe . . . This has been the first trial we have had in our happy little family & it could scarcely have been a more bitter one . . .

The Hacks, as Quakers, could not bury their daughter in church ground, so they buried her on a small corner of their land in Pennington Terrace. This became known as the Friends Burial Ground and was used by the Quakers until 1855, when the graves were moved to the West Terrace Cemetery.[108]

Little Guli continued to be unwell, but Bbe had something to look forward to, the arrival of her brother Henry Watson and his wife Charlotte and two children, and Henry and Bbe's parents, William and Martha Watson. They arrived in Adelaide on 22 March. Henry kept a diary of the voyage and continued it for a few months afterwards.[109] Barton Hack had ceased regular entries in his diary in 1837 and his letters home had become infrequent, so it is mainly from Henry Watson's letters that the family's fortunes can be gleaned.

The Watsons, who had been met on their arrival at Glenelg by Barton and the children, travelled to Adelaide, where Henry was astonished to find it had a very town-like appearance. 'A large stone church was nearly finished, excellent brick and stone houses, large warehouses and shops ... Our dearest Bbe welcomed us most joyfully, she was looking quite as well as we could have expected'. The Watsons moved straight into the Hacks' large residence in Hindley Street.

The Hacks showed the Watsons around the town, Charlotte a month later writing that they liked Adelaide very much and their children were thriving. The Watsons heard that Barton's mother and brother Tom wanted to come out, but that Tom's wife Lydia would not be able to manage 'without the comforts ... of civilised life'. Henry was astonished:

> I am writing in a room 20 ft square; on the floor is an elegant Brussels carpet; in a recess is a handsome sideboard of French-polished mahogany, a German sofa with spring cushions is on one side, a couch on the other, canary birds in cages are in the window, flowers such as roses, carnations &c are in vases, all about looks thoroughly English and I am at a loss to see wherein we poor savages are to be pitied.

On 14 April Henry wrote delightedly to Gates that Barton was 'a prosperous gentleman – no one in the colony is more universally respected, or more influential'. Henry attempted to be a peacemaker, and said he hoped the arrival of the whale oil on the *Goshawk* would put Gates mind at ease in money matters.

> It grieves me much to find that dear B and Bbe have felt hurt at you for not coming out, and have expressed themselves in such a way as may cause you pain. I feel sure that this has arisen from some

misunderstanding. They concluded that it was quite arranged that you should follow them, and that your money that was lying idle should be drawn as wanted . . . all this mess is merely owing to the unfortunate distance that separates us . . . Barton says to my astonishment that he has never had a statement of accounts from Gates and asked me with much anxiety if I could furnish him . . .

Henry's letter was unlikely to appease Gates, because Barton had in fact received several sets of accounts. Gates had sent the accounts and letters on three vessels in 1837 and on two vessels in 1838, and the family in Adelaide had acknowledged receipt of letters from all of these vessels. Barton may, however, have been referring to the accounts from the family trust, which his Uncle John had been handling: a division was expected, and Barton and Stephen were anticipating a substantial payment. Barton had received no news about this, since Uncle John had not yet attended to it. Even if Gates had understood this to be what Barton was referring to, Gates would not have enjoyed reading that his money (his wife Margaret's inheritance) was 'lying idle' and ready to be drawn on in Australia.

Henry had debts of his own in England, and wrote 'I much wish I could remit at once but town acres, though they keep their price . . . are not in such brisk demand now, there are so many new towns starting into existence'. Henry's sixteen acres which cost £100 in 1837 were now valued at £1700, but he could not find a buyer. Barton and Henry realised that land prices had reached their peak and set out to sell as many of their town acres as they could.

Henry and Charlotte Watson's happiness was shattered when their baby daughter Louisa died suddenly just before her first birthday. Henry wrote in his diary: 'Several of her teeth were pressing, we had her gums lanced, lest congestion came on and after two days illness we lost her . . . She was the darling of our hearts'. They buried her in the burial ground in Pennington Terrace, next to Barton and Bbe's daughter Annie.

The Hacks and the Watsons were still grieving for the loss of their children, when, on 22 May, Barton and Bbe's baby daughter Guli died, aged nine months. As Henry noted, 'There continues a great mortality among young children'. He said the houses were full of fleas, especially the rush houses with earth floors, and dysentery was prevalent among young children.

Fortunately, all the other children were happy and healthy. Henry wrote that the weather was perfect and the sunsets 'exquisitely beautiful', especially when he and Charlotte returned from a ride into the Mount Lofty hills. There were tensions though. Henry and Bbe's parents, William and Martha Watson, were miserable and compared everything unfavourably with England. Martha quarrelled with everyone, including Charlotte, her daughter-in-law. The problem was that three generations were too close for comfort in Hindley Street. A year earlier, when Caroline Carter married Dr John Woodforde, they moved into a cottage next to Barton's new house and store.[110] Things improved for the Watsons when the Woodfordes moved out of their cottage and Henry's parents moved in. Soon Henry could write that his parents were extremely well and contented.

Henry erected a Manning cottage on his acre at Pennington Terrace and planned to sell the cottage and the land together, to pay off his debts in England. In July Henry reported that his little daughter Charlotte Emily (Apetty), now aged two-and-a-half, was great friends with her two-year-old cousin Emily, but they had the occasional squabble. 'A frequent dispute is whether or not they have two mamas – Emily will insist upon it that she has, but Appety who is a few months older, takes great pains to explain, "Dis is my Mamma and dat is oos Mamma".'

He said Barton's eight-year-old daughter Louisa was a tomboy, who horrified Bbe by galloping off on Stephen's horse. Louisa clearly did not ride side-saddle, like the women in the family.

The family continued to grow. On 7 September 1839 Bbe gave birth to her ninth child, a baby girl, whom they called Lucy Barton, after Barton's cousin. On 15 December Charlotte gave birth to her third child, naming the baby Fanny Rogers.

The Three Brothers estate

Soon after the Watsons arrived, Barton took Henry and his father to Mount Barker to see the Three Brothers station. Henry reported:

> We ascended the 'tiers' with some difficulty, the road being very steep. The views down the different ravines became very grand . . . on looking back we obtained a fine view of the Gulf with the vessels at anchor . . . we passed through the stringy bark forest . . . then entered a very superior country consisting of rich well watered valleys beautifully wooded . . . We passed a little village of poor German emigrants [Hahndorf] . . . in a beautiful fertile situation.

The hills in those early days before clearing were covered in eucalypts with a thick layer of native grass underneath. Below the tall trees were smaller shrubs such as wattles, native cherry and banksias. Henry was visiting in late summer, when the grass would have been yellow and shimmering in the heat of the sun. They found Stephen branding cattle, and joined him in a meal of pork, damper and tea.

Stephen was doing well managing the rural properties, and in June he wrote to his mother that he had thirty-six men employed on the Three Brothers estate. In addition he had 1000 head of cattle, sixty working bullocks, thirty horses and thirty pigs. A few weeks later he planted twenty-five acres of wheat and commenced building a second dairy on the estate with a three-room hut, milking yard, cow-yard and a six-acre paddock. He was also selling fat cattle and bullocks and making a good profit from these activities.

Stephen's accommodation was a primitive slab hut consisting of two rooms, with a bedroom on top of one of them. Large gaps had been left between the slabs, but he'd been too busy to fill them in with mud. Although rain came in, the roof over his bookshelves and his gun rack was sufficiently waterproof to keep them dry. He had his notebook, filled with his favourite poems and songs,[111] which he would have read at night by the fire, thinking sadly of Julia. At the back he made notes on the cost of importing horses from England, and names for his bullocks.

Stephen hinted to his mother that he might pay her a visit, and wrote 'I wonder how I should like living in England . . . seeing a man or a horse every hundred yards. Only fancy calling Greyling Wells lonely, one whole mile off about [from] 10,000 people. Here I grumble if anyone comes within 8 or 10 miles of me'.

He was far from lonely though. Barton had let out two farms, one to Captain William Field, first officer on the *Rapid*, and the other to an emigrant named Oscar Lines. Field had recently overlanded 600 to 700 cattle along the Murray. Each took a section on Western Flat, which was a grass-covered valley, dissected by a chain of waterholes.

Stephen also had two 'house guests' in his slab hut. One was a young man named Alfred Barker from Chichester. He had some capital and twenty heifers, and Stephen planned to give him forty acres of land rent free for a year or two and two old bullocks to help with his fencing. The other guest was Stephen's friend and stockman Samuel Mason. A couple of weeks later Stephen added: 'I have just taken a young gent by the name of Easthope as a kind of pupil; he pays me £100 per one year ... and places himself wholly under my orders ... He is a quiet peaceable fellow and willing to help all he can and that is all I care about'.

Although Stephen was only twenty-three, he was employing a large number of people and seems to have done it well. He said that among his employees, 'I have hardly one troublesome one, which is saying more than most folks can in this country'.

During the year the Joint Stock Cattle Company took over its 1000 acres, which were to the north of the Hacks' station, between it and Hahndorf. A manager's house, huts for the men and a dairy were built, and the Cattle Company moved there. It might have been the transfer of these acres that prompted Barton to acquire more land. The Hacks purchased an additional 1225 acres for themselves and others in the district, including their brother-in-law Edward Philcox.

Joseph Barritt

In September 1839 more Quaker emigrants arrived in Adelaide. One of these was Joseph Barritt from Essex, who carried a letter of introduction to the Hacks. Within three days, Barton offered to put him in charge of thirty cows on the Little Para survey, in return for a percentage of the butter sold.[112] Barritt soon set off for the Little Para, where on his arrival he found 'two very good huts, a man and his wife, two sons and a daughter'. He employed them and began to build a dairy for himself, completed at the end of October. On his return to Strangways Valley after collecting his cows from Stephen, he received a surprise visit from Barton, Bbe and three of the children in an open carriage:

> As he [Barton] left, he said to me, 'Joseph, if at any time thee want anything, send me a note and thee shall have it', which was very kind of him; indeed, he has behaved more like a brother to me than a stranger. I have several times been to his house to dinner or supper; he is spoken of very highly by almost all here, it would be a very good thing for the colony if there were a few more like him.

The May family

Other Quaker emigrants included the May family, who were distant relatives of the Hacks. This was a large family from Oxfordshire who soon became neighbours at Mount Barker. Joseph May had travelled with his wife Hannah and eleven children and Joseph's brother Henry. While in town, the Mays reported that Quaker meetings were held on Sundays in the dining room at Barton's house in Hindley Street. The meetings were at 11 am and 6 pm and attended by about twenty to thirty people.

'We have been much pleased with the Mays', Henry Watson wrote, 'they pull well together and ... are sure to prosper.' The Mays were a close-knit family, bound by strict adherence to traditional Quakerism. Their letters tell us quite a lot about life at Echunga and the fortunes of the Hack family.[113]

Soon after their arrival, Barton advised the Mays to look at the Three Brothers special survey. Two of the older boys, William and Fred May, travelled to the survey and were shown around by Stephen Hack and his tenant Oscar Lines, who was planning to leave. The Mays agreed to take over Lines' farm, agreeing to pay Barton rent of 12s per acre, but they also had the right to run 100 head of cattle on the Hacks' land. They paid Lines £108 for the buildings and fences and purchased ten of his cows for the dairy. Stephen offered them as many heifers as they wanted, if they would break them in for milking.

The May family moved up in November, travelling with a wagon and three bullock drays lent by Stephen. Hannah May wrote that the family moved into three detached buildings on the farm, and 'thus we shall shift till we can get our own house built on our own land, which we hope we will accomplish before winter, as this is not wind and water tight'. She said it was a pretty spot with a stream of water running about 100 yards from the front of the house.

> We have many advantages in being so near such influential neighbours as the Hacks. We are pleased with Barton and his wife; they are much more friendly in their manner and appearance than we expected to find them. There seems a great stability about the former and he seems to be highly, and I have no doubt deservedly, respected by his fellow citizens. Stephen has mixed so much more with others that he has thrown off the Friend more, but he is very candid and good-natured . . . They [Barton and Bbe] are having a nice slab house built just by Stephen's.

Stephen wrote to his mother that the more prosperous he became, the more he regretted the death of Julia. He was ready to settle down, and it seems that later in the year he proposed to one of the May daughters, twenty-year-old Maria. The story was told some eighty years later by Lucy Coleman, one of the May sisters:[114]

> In those early days he was a very frequent visitor . . . and I can picture him now as he used to stand by the hour talking to my sisters Maria and Margaret. Perhaps I have never heard that he wanted my sister Maria for his wife but her parents would not consent. (I do not know of what her feelings were on the subject) but I know that his visits stopped so suddenly, as to make my brothers remark what can have offended Stephen Hack that he does not come near us now. I knew nothing of all this till many years later.

Lucy was eight in 1840 and she was remembering this at nearly ninety; but if it was true, Stephen can hardly have been surprised. The Mays were very strict Quakers, whereas Stephen had only the loosest attachment. Through his mother he was interested in the Beaconite controversy in England and agreed with her criticism of traditional Quaker ways. Besides, he had never liked going to 'Meeting' even as a child.

Stephen would not have brooded for long though; he had already decided to return to England for a visit. He planned to travel on the *Katherine Stewart Forbes*, which was expected to load oil at Encounter Bay in October.

Division of the family business

When Henry Watson arrived in 1839, Barton and Stephen took him straight away into the family business. It soon became apparent, however, that they needed to divide up their responsibilities. At first Barton suggested to Stephen that they make Henry a third partner in the family business. Stephen was not happy with this. He was responsible for the agricultural and grazing part of the business, but had no involvement in the mercantile side, and did not want to be in partnership with anyone other than Barton. As he wrote to his mother:

> Now only consider that in case of anything happening to Barton, HW would be the managing partner on shore, and Hart and Devlin at sea, of a most extensive business, which I had neither any accurate knowledge of or control over, this . . . I would not consent to . . . The matter was then settled in this way; I gave up my share of the store and half acre in Hindley street, and 14 acres of town land, on condition that I retained under the firm of JB and S Hack all the cattle, land and property of every description belonging to us in the country and the acres on Pennington Terrace.

Stephen was jubilant about the arrangement. The firm of J.B. and S. Hack, of which he was half-owner, retained all the rural properties and activities, while the mercantile and whaling interests were shifted into a new firm, later called Hack, Watson & Co. Stephen said the advantage for him was that he came out clear of debt and with half of all the rural holdings. He calculated that his share consisted of 2000 acres of land and improvements worth about £7 an acre, 500 head of cattle, 15 horses and 30 bullocks. He also had five acres of land on Pennington Terrace worth £300 an acre. The total value of all this, he told his mother proudly, was £23,000. 'Now this is clear and free from a single expense of debt or encumbrance, and is what I call a very creditable three years' work, considering I began with about £2000', he wrote. He was now 'master of an independent fortune and . . . not four and twenty yet'.

Stephen's statement that he was free of debt is surprising, but true. When the two businesses were separated, the country business 'sold' its debts to the town business, in exchange for land and property of equal value to the debts. Stephen gave up his half-stake in Hindley Street and fourteen acres of town land. It seemed fair to the three men at the time, but it would later cause Henry Watson a great deal of concern.[115]

Stephen said his Uncle John Barton had called him a foolish boy for comparing their land in Australia to Petworth Park near Chichester, but their Three Brothers estate was proving Uncle John to be mistaken. Stephen went on to explain his philosophy of life:

> I have made it a rule throughout never to bother about a thing after I was once satisfied there was no help for it, and never to give up a thing while there was a chance left. In landing the cattle, one cow laid down in the surf so weak she could not move, but I and Hart mustered all the hands and carried her bodily above high water mark and two months afterwards I sold her for twenty pounds. <u>Don't give up the ship</u> is the finest maxim ever was.

By the end of the year Stephen was very busy with the rural side of the business. The cattle speculation was paying off with the sale of many of the cows and bullocks he had purchased in New South Wales. He had three dairies and was growing wheat. Meanwhile, the mercantile and whaling ventures were in the hands of Barton and Henry Watson. Stephen felt very confident about how things were going and began to plan his visit to England.

Chapter 14
Hack, Watson & Co.

When Governor Gawler arrived in South Australia, he opened up land outside Adelaide and introduced an ambitious program of public works. It was in this new era of optimism that Henry Watson reported that Barton had the best house in town, a large business as a merchant, a whaling station at Encounter Bay and a splendid estate at Mount Barker. Barton was also on numerous committees: he was the first Chairman of the Adelaide Chamber of Commerce and first Chairman of the South Australian Agricultural and Horticultural Society.

Gawler and public works

Governor Gawler's instructions were to bring order to South Australian affairs, but his expenditure was limited to £8000 a year with only a small extra amount for contingencies.[116] When he arrived in Adelaide in October 1838, he found conditions much worse than expected. The annual allowance had all been spent and the records were in disarray. The population at the end of 1838 was 6000,[117] with some 4000 people living in temporary shelters, waiting for the country land to become available.

There was a central flaw in the British Government's plan for the colony and that was that it should proceed without incurring expense to the British Treasury, the underpinning principle being that the sale of land in South Australia would provide money for the free transport of labourers and artisans. The colony was thus to have capital and labour, but there was no money for infrastructure.

The early success of the colony prompted a stream of emigrants. As Resident Commissioner as well as Governor, Gawler had to house, feed and employ these settlers if they could not be absorbed by the labour market. The emigrants who had capital were stuck in Adelaide, where they were building houses and buying up town land for speculation, rather than investing in businesses and agriculture. This meant the price of the town acres soared and unemployment increased.

Gawler was a deeply religious man and committed to reform. Within a short time he decided that he had to ignore his instructions and treat the situation as an emergency. The first task was to speed up the rural surveys and he did this by establishing the special survey system.

The next task was to provide employment and he commenced an ambitious program of public works by drawing bills on the London Commissioners. Over the next two years this program included constructing roads into the country, building a new government house (worth £10,000 alone) as well as police barracks, customs house, hospital, wharf, jail and houses for public officials.

The mercantile business

We saw that as soon as Henry Watson arrived, he began to assist Barton in the mercantile business. Early on there was a setback when a transaction with Henry Jones ended badly. Despite having been sued by Jones the year before over the loss of the *Isabella*, Barton had agreed to import some sheep for him from Van Diemen's Land. Jones chartered the *Adelaide* under Captain Devlin. But on leaving Launceston it grounded, and by the time it was lifted off, only 200 of the original 1500 were alive.

When the vessel arrived in Adelaide, Jones took possession of the remaining sheep. Barton asked for £200 payment for shipping them, but Jones made a counter claim for damages. As Barton recalled later, 'The case was tried in court and we obtained a verdict for the freight and Mr Jones the same for damages. The lawyer therefore had the oyster; and a shell each for myself and Jones'.

Despite this setback, the mercantile business was thriving. Gates had sent out a consignment of books for Barton to sell, which arrived on the *Planter* on 16 May. Henry reported that they had sold the invoices to a bookseller named Alexander Macdougall in Rundle Street. The amount was large, about £800 worth of goods, and Macdougall was allowed time to make his payments at six months and later intervals. They were not to know that this arrangement would collapse as economic conditions deteriorated.

In his letters Henry explained that although they were selling off their town acres fast, at an average of £200 an acre, they preferred to send remittances to England in wool and oil, because 'in a new colony people may have great wealth and little ready money'. That included Barton. Henry described the decision to split up the family business into the mercantile business, in which Barton and Henry were partners, and the rural business, in which Barton and Stephen were partners. Henry explained the mercantile business would be 'very valuable when we get consignments from the leading English houses, which we must have from the export of the oil'. They were using the sale of the oil in London to purchase goods to be sold in Australia.

The influx of emigrants into Adelaide soon created a shortage of food. Flour had to be imported from the other colonies, and the price increased to £10 a bag. This was unaffordable for many of the colonists. As Barton recalled later:

> A few of the leading men formed themselves into an association to import flour and sell it at cost price. I acted as secretary and custodian and the first shipment reduced the price to £6. The Government was also induced to buy a cargo of Lombok rice.

He was still importing flour in November.

Barton and Henry purchased cargo which had arrived in the *Hooghly*, and goods from the merchant firm of Jacob Hagen & Son in England that arrived on the *Seppings*. Captain Devlin went to New Zealand to get timber on commission for the South Australian Company; the *Adelaide* was chartered for the same purpose. The *Pleiades* arrived from India with a consignment of rice, coconut oil, tobacco and cedar, and Barton and Henry sold the whole cargo in two days, grossing £6000. Their merchant business, according to Henry, was second only to John Morphett's.

The whaling business

By 1839 the whale fisheries were being run jointly with the South Australian Company, with Hart as manager, and early in the year they chartered the brig *Rapid*, Colonel Light's old survey vessel, for the whaling business. They also built a rough wharf on Granite Island, opposite Hind Cove, to enable the ships to tie up.

By August the fishery at Granite Island had taken 140 tuns of oil, which was a reasonable amount (a tun was nearly 1000 litres), but then disaster struck.[118] As Barton recalled later:

> The chief headsman (John Dutton) was a fine whaler, but a hot-tempered man. On one occasion he had, for some insubordination, tied up a lot of the men to a boat cable stretched from one hut to another, and given them a flogging. One of the men got away and in crossing the reef to the main was drowned ... the Coroner ... called an inquest, and sent the chief headsman to town in custody, on a charge of manslaughter. Of course the charge could not be substantiated and after some time he was liberated. In the meantime the station, which was very successful at the time, was abandoned.[119]

The fishery at Rosetta Harbour was more successful and had taken in 176 tuns of oil. The two fisheries at Spencer Gulf had encountered problems and most of the men had deserted.

In December a further disaster struck. The *Katherine Stewart Forbes* had been chartered to arrive in Encounter Bay in October, but did not arrive until January 1840. In the meantime the oil that had been lying on the beach waiting to be collected was leaking away. In his memoirs Barton recalled, 'An attempt to make the ship liable was defeated by a legal error in suing the captain instead of the owner, and the law costs were added to the loss'. Once again Barton had unfortunately lost money while attempting to recoup his losses.

Local politics

Robert Gouger returned to the colony in June 1839, reinstated as Colonial Secretary. Henry and Barton were at Government House when he arrived. 'His coming caused no small sensation', Henry wrote. 'The Governor I have no doubt is heartily glad of his coming, as it will relieve him of this ugly dilemma about [G.M.] Stephen'. George Milner Stephen had been the acting Colonial Secretary (and before that the Acting Governor) and Henry described him as 'a scheming little fellow'. Henry's judgment was pretty accurate: later in the year George Milner Stephen was tried for land speculation and perjury.

Governor Gawler had been busy ordering special surveys. Henry commented that the results were electrifying; 'Gilles [the Colonial Treasurer] tells me £100,000 has been sent home already from the purchase of land. What we have seen of the prosperity of the colony is nothing to what a few years will produce'.

Other milestones in Gawler's time were the development of the port and the expansion of the South Australian Company under David McLaren, an able administrator. The Company had a successful bank, they were buying land and stocking it with sheep and cattle, and they were involved in whaling with Barton Hack, Hart and Devlin. The Company built a new port further down the river from the old one, and a new road to it (Port Road) at a cost of £30,000.[120]

Henry Watson, like Barton Hack, came from a Quaker background with an interest in community service. During the year he joined Barton on the committee of the South Australian School Society and the Literary and Scientific Association and Mechanics Institute.

At the beginning of the year the Adelaide Chamber of Commerce was formed, and Barton became its first Chairman.[121] He was also involved in the founding of the Botanical Gardens and on the first committee of management.[122] In October Barton helped establish the South Australian Agricultural and Horticultural Society,[123] and was one of the vice-presidents, with Stephen Hack and John Knott as committee members.[124] In December that year Barton was chairman of the committee that drew up the rules.

It is unlikely that Barton had much time to devote to all of these committees, but clearly he had the drive and initiative needed to set up the institutions so necessary in the new colony. These committees also helped his networking and business interests.

Aboriginal people

Early in 1839 after an old shepherd was killed and a number of sheep and cattle were speared, the fragile peace between the colonists and the natives was broken. The settlers were spreading out into the country, reducing the Aborigines' traditional hunting grounds. Barton Hack and Henry Watson, with their Quaker backgrounds, were very concerned for the welfare of the Aborigines. Henry noted in his diary that the Colonial Secretary distributed daily rations to the hundreds camped on the parkland between north and south Adelaide.

Henry wrote that there was great alarm and anxiety in the colony after the murder of the shepherd. Henry said the accused natives had:

> scarcely the consciousness that they are committing a crime . . . It is too late to discuss our right to usurp their territory; we have taken it for granted that we have the right, giving them in exchange food and protection, however they kill our sheep and our shepherds, what is to be done? The stockkeepers now look upon every Black as a foe and I fear will fire upon them all indiscriminately.

An inquest was held into the shepherd's death. Henry was foreman of the jury that brought down a verdict of murder. Another shepherd was subsequently killed and Superintendent Inman recruited fifteen Aboriginal trackers to find the culprits, the police returning with six black prisoners, three for each shepherd. They were examined at the jail and John Morphett, David McLaren and Henry Watson were summoned to the Executive Council to give their opinion on a speedy trial. Further incidents included a man being knocked off his horse and the horse speared, and an old woman, nursemaid to the Watson's baby, attacked because she refused to give money. This was all the more shocking because it was in the middle of the town.

A public meeting was scheduled, and one of the issues for discussion was the nature of the punishment if a native was convicted. Henry's remedy was to transport convicted natives to Kangaroo Island with their families, where there was an abundance of wild animals and they could be provided with food rations and a missionary. His suggestion was not, however, adopted.

The public meeting was held at the Court House, and the first motion put forward was by Barton Hack. It deplored the 'murders and outrages recently perpetrated', and claimed the right of protection of life and property, but 'we cheerfully and willingly admit the right of the Aborigines to equal protection and the fullest provision for their wants'. It was passed unanimously.[125]

The meeting suggested that the natives should be prevented from bringing their weapons when camped by the river and recommended that a larger number of mounted police and magistrates be employed for the protection of settlers in outlying areas. The Protector of Aborigines was strongly censured for inefficiency and a committee established with the dual roles of suggesting measures for the protection of both the settlers and the natives and for watching over the interests of the local Indigenous population. The members of the committee included David McLaren, John Morphett, Barton Hack and John Brown.[126]

In June, two of the Aborigines were convicted of murder and hanged.[127] The government and settlers hoped their fate would deter other Aborigines from attacking Europeans, but this was unrealistic. Clashes between the Aboriginal people and settlers were inevitable as the settlements extended out from Adelaide into other parts of South Australia.

Correspondence in England, 1839

During 1839 relations between Gates Darton and the Hack brothers continued to deteriorate. Barton had ceased sending bills after December 1837, but he did little to pay off his debts.

Back in England Maria Hack wrote to Gates in March 1839 about his pressing financial problems:

> I know not what to say, dear Gates, in apology for B. and S. not writing . . . it passes my comprehension . . . I am exceedingly afraid of Barton being tempted to accommodate himself by this sort of fictitious capital, and borrow more to pay interest . . . I wish he would be wise enough to have no designs upon this oil cargo beyond setting himself square again.

Gates replied that he needed £1000 and Maria suggested he apply to Halsey Janson for a temporary loan, which would be paid back on the sale of the oil from the *Goshawk*. She added, 'Don't fret thyself bilious dear G'.

The *Goshawk* arrived in England in May 1839, but the oil money was less than expected, because half of it had been used to purchase the *Adelaide* the year before. Gates now turned to his brother-in-law the Reverend George Bliss for assistance. Bliss agreed to send Gates some money, but Gates was still short. He then approached Barton's sister Priscilla and borrowed £1000 from her family inheritance. Priscilla had just married Edward Philcox in Chichester. They were soon to leave for Australia, and the arrangement was that Barton would pay her back the £1000 when she arrived.

In September the Philcoxes left England on the *John* with Edward's youngest brother, Henry Owen Philcox, aged about fifteen.[128] They travelled with Priscilla's sister Ellen Knott and her two small children, Ellen Maria and John Barton. John Knott had come to Adelaide ahead of his wife and was listed as a surgeon in North Adelaide, although he was engaged mainly in business. Stephen Hack reported to his mother:

> It certainly was quite right and judicious of JK to come himself first, as this is certainly not the place for a delicate female to rough it. For though Bbe got through it amazingly, yet it was the same high spirit which was *not wanted* in England but which, if she had not had [it] here ... she must have sunk under the real slavery of first settling.

Reply to Gates

In September 1839 Henry Watson wrote to Gates that they were selling the town land and intended to send more oil and enough remittances on the *Katherine Stewart Forbes* to pay off every debt in England.

Barton had not written to Gates in a long time, but added a note by way of apology. He explained that Stephen would travel on the *Katherine Stewart Forbes* and would 'discharge all obligations in money affairs ... We feel most deeply that we have not treated you either justly or kindly in the whole affair'.

Henry explained why it was taking time to repay Gates:

> The grand difficulty is the immense necessary outlay at Mount Barker. That is now almost at an end; the produce from the dairy now pays the expenses of the station, and we are doing everything to keep down expenditure. It has been next to impossible to withdraw capital so as to remit as we wished; our engagements were so many and so intricate.

Barton decided to sell his 1000 acres at the Little Para and most of the Hindley Street property. They would keep only the store, the counting house in the yard and a store at the port. He was putting up a house at Mount Barker, and Bbe was anxious to move there for the children's health. She was keen to see the new station, so Barton took her up to the Three Brothers in their open four-wheeled carriage. As he recalled later:

> The only way from Adelaide was up the face of Gleeson's Hill. Two of our men from Echunga met us at Crafers, and assisted us by removing the timber from the track. In crossing the bed of the Onkaparinga one of the shafts broke off, but we arrived at our station in about six hours from Adelaide. The carriage was so far damaged that it was for the time useless. However, the attractions of a baby [two month old Lucy] in Adelaide could not be overcome, and my wife had a side-saddle put on one of the stockhorses and we rode in to town, though long after dark. It was a serious matter for Mrs Hack to descend Gleeson's Hill in the dark.[129]

On their return from Mount Barker, Barton and Bbe started packing up their belongings in Hindley Street. They were about to start a new life in the country.

Chapter 15
Barton moves to Echunga

In 1840, the fourth year of the colony, Barton Hack and his family moved to their property near Mount Barker. They built a two-storey house and developed a twelve-acre orchard, garden and vineyard. The Quaker merchant Jacob Hagen arrived in the colony and purchased some of Barton's land at the Para and joined in the whaling business. A Quaker Meeting House was erected on Barton's land at Pennington Terrace, and Henry Watson moved into his Manning cottage next door.

Barton and Bbe move to the Three Brothers estate

At the beginning of 1840 the Hacks and Watsons were living together in Hindley Street, when both their babies succumbed to dysentery. Fever and dysentery were rife in Adelaide and especially bad in summer. The Hacks' baby, four-month-old Lucy, became ill in January and died shortly afterwards. Henry and Charlotte's baby Fanny, just a few weeks old, was also ill, but seemed to be recovering.

The death of little Lucy meant the fourth funeral in twelve months. Bbe was desperate to remove the rest of her children from the vicinity of Adelaide, where there was no sewerage or drainage. Mount Barker was healthier and several degrees cooler than Adelaide, and she decided to move there. Barton was building a two-storey wooden house on Echunga Creek, but it was not yet finished. Stephen had gone to the station at Yankalilla, so Barton and Bbe moved into his house.

The Hack family's journey up to Mount Barker was described by Henry Watson: 'The children and servants were packed in the wagon drawn by ten bullocks; they got up extremely well without any mishap. Bbe and Barton went in a gig, having a postilion on a leader as far as Crafer's [sic] at the top of the Mount Lofty range.' How the Hacks managed to fit themselves and the six children into Stephen's two-room slab house is not mentioned, but they must have used other buildings on the farm as well, especially for their servants.

The farm on the Three Brothers survey was flourishing, with two dairies milking 150 cows and sending butter and cheese into Adelaide. Barton procured fruit trees, shrubs and vines from Hobart, and Suter the gardener transplanted trees and plants from Chichester Gardens in North Adelaide. As soon as the family settled in, Barton began a strenuous routine of travelling the twenty miles (32 km) to town twice a week to attend to his various business and community interests. As he recalled in his memoirs:

> While resident at Echunga I was fully occupied. I left the station at 6 a.m. on Mondays, arrived in town before 10 a.m., attended to business all day and book-keeping till late at night. On Tuesdays I left town at any time between 4 and 9 p.m. Station business employed Wednesdays. On Thursday mornings, as on Mondays, I went to town, returning on Friday evenings. Saturdays I spent on the farm. When driving to Adelaide I carried an axe and chain, and, cutting down a small she-oak, attached it to the axle of the phaeton [as a brake].[130]

Barton maintained this routine for the next two years. Stephen was about to leave for England, with the day-to-day management of the farm left in the hands of Samuel Mason, Stephen's stockman friend.

Barton's letter to his mother reflects his pride in becoming a landed proprietor:

> I have . . . 3000 acres of land, 600 of them enclosed, and improvements to a great extent, plus on the estate 1000 head of cattle, 60 horses and mares, and all the comforts of civilized life about us, and as beautiful a garden of about 6 acres as I ever saw. Sutor [Suter] . . . brought me in this afternoon a water melon 14½ lbs weight, and 6 beautiful fruit melons . . . I am going to send a sample of our produce in this way to the Governor, who is a very kind and friendly person; he has been a very steady friend to me.

Barton also had a vineyard and planned later to make wine:

> We have at least 500 vines planted in circular rows in a warm aspect, and as many plums, apples, cherries, pears, peaches, nectarines, apricots, all growing most luxuriantly ... We have reaped about 25 acres of wheat and have a beautiful sample of grain, about 400 bushels ... We live now on our own flour ground in a steel mill and it tastes sweet indeed ... We have only nowhere to buy luxuries, tea, sugar, wines, ale etc. Beef of course we raise and kill every week, and salt down all not sold or consumed on the station.

Barton wrote later: 'I felt very proud when I sent my first basket of grapes to Colonel Gawler. Some bunches were very large'. At the end of the year the official government return showed that the estate had grown to 12 acres of gardens and orchard, 60 acres of wheat, 4 barley, 2 oats, and 6 potatoes.[131] It said the plantations contained 700 vines and 400 fruit trees.

The farm had a large number of employees:[132]

> In the workshop – a foreman, carpenter, blacksmith, and miller; farming hands – three ploughmen, two boys, two labourers, one gardener and assistant; stock department – one overseer, one groom, four stockmen for Echunga and Yankalilla; also a storeman and two pairs of fencers. With the dairy hands this staff meant an outlay for wages of about £2000 per annum.

In June the German settlers finished a bridge over the Onkaparinga, on the road used by the Hacks. The bridge was half-paid by the government, with the remainder by the local land owners, including the Hacks. This bridge today is at Mylor, and although it's a later replacement, it is still called Hack's bridge.

Barton had purchased more acres on the Three Brothers survey, but he had also sold some. By December 1840 he had 3091 acres, and they were held jointly with Stephen.[133]

Barton's sisters arrive

At the beginning of February 1840, Barton and Stephen's sisters Priscilla and Ellen arrived on the *John* from England. The trip must have been very uncomfortable for Priscilla, who was heavily pregnant on arrival. A month later Henry Watson wrote that Priscilla was nicely settled in, and that Philcox was a worthy fellow and his success certain. In April, Priscilla gave birth to a baby whom they named Anna Priscilla. Edward had an eighty-acre section at Mount Barker near the Hacks, with cattle and a dairy. In the 1841 returns his farm was called Burnwath, but it was probably Burwash, where he came from in Sussex.

Ellen Knott had not fared so well however. 'You will have heard how cruelly Ellen has been used by her worthless husband', Henry wrote. 'She has been in a hovel that is no shelter from the sun, rain, wind or dust. He treats her with the greatest neglect, 'making his lucky' as he calls it from early in the morning to late at night ... He seems to have been completely unsettled by his living about at public houses and to have no taste for home or home pleasures'. This 'hovel' was the timber cottage at Pennington Terrace that Knott had been renting from Barton. Ellen Knott's situation improved, however, when John Knott agreed to rent a stone house nearby with a nice garden.

At the time the Hacks moved to Mount Barker, the Watsons were also desperate to get their baby out of Adelaide. Charlotte and baby Fanny took lodgings with a family at Macgill (modern-day Magill) near Third Creek. Henry and little Apetty (Charlotte Emily) stayed on in Hindley Street. After two months at Magill, Charlotte Watson returned to Adelaide and Henry reported that baby Fanny was much improved. Apetty was 'so pretty that Stephen wonders how such an ugly fellow as I [Henry] should have such a child'. Henry said he and Stephen were excellent friends: 'There is a great deal that is honest and straight forward in him'.

Neighbours at Echunga

By the middle of 1840 Barton's two-storey timber house at Echunga was finally completed and the family moved in. It overlooked the springs which fed Echunga Creek, and was later called Echunga Springs and their vineyard and orchard Echunga Gardens. The following year it was painted by Governor Gawler as a watercolour.[134]

This sketch shows the two-storey house, with numerous out-buildings and yards for animals. The house was large enough to hold Barton's growing family and frequent visitors. It had a very large veranda where the children played on rainy days.

Nothing remains of this house today, but the location has been identified.[135] It was on the south side of the creek, overlooking the orchard. Today the spot is on the property of Mr Terry Rothe at the end of Marianna Street in Echunga. A few of the fruit trees from the Hacks' orchard are still there. Later the village of Echunga developed nearby and today is a small town with a population of about 800.[136] The name Echunga is said to come from the word 'Eechungga' meaning 'close' in the dialect of the Peramangk people.

There was quite a community now in the Mount Barker area. Apart from the Hacks and their large number of employees, there were several neighbours close by, including the tenant farmers Captain Field and Alfred Barker. To the east was the large May family: Joseph and Hannah and their eleven children. To the north was the Cattle Company with its 1000 acres, managed by John Shepherdson.

A new arrival was Daniel Kekwick, a Quaker relative of Gates Darton. He arrived in April 1840 with his nine children and his daughter's fiancé, Fred Hodding. The young couple were married in May and the whole family moved to Mount Barker. In July, Fred Hodding replaced Alfred Barker as one of Barton's tenant farmers. Another neighbour was Samuel Bond, a graduate of Cambridge University.[137] He was farming, but needed to supplement his income, and so was engaged to teach the Hack boys.

On 17 November Bbe gave birth to her tenth child, Theodore. Soon afterwards another Quaker family arrived near the Hacks – George and Sarah Sanders and their children, from Whitby. Their story is told in their daughter Jane's journal, written when she was nearly seventy.[138] They arrived in Adelaide at the end of 1839 and Barton encouraged them to use their land order for a section on Echunga Creek. They called at Barton's 'old dairy' on Echunga Creek, and Jane recalled that it was 'one of the finest in the colony'.

The Sanders lived at first in tents on a hill overlooking the creek, about a mile and a half from Hack's dairy. As Jane wrote later:

As I write, memory brings back the quiet hush and calm of the place, the glowing sunshine with the rippling shadows that ran across the waving grass, the silence broken now and then by the scream of the cockatoos as they flew in flocks over our heads. Then there was the chatter of numerous parrots, or a rushing, crashing sound as some monarch of the forest fell under the axes of the splitters . . . I never now smell the scent of withering gum leaves without recalling those happy days.

Jacob Hagen and the Little Para

Another new arrival in the colony was the merchant Jacob Hagen, who was to play a significant role in Barton's life. Hagen and Barton had several things in common. Both came from Quaker merchant families and had an eye for business opportunities. They had both attended Josiah Forster's school in Southgate, Middlesex, although Jacob was three years younger than Barton.[139] Hagen also knew Gates Darton in London. Soon after arriving, Hagen purchased land in town and settled in North Adelaide.[140] He became a prominent businessman and a shareholder in Barton's whaling business.

Barton had purchased 1000 acres at the Little Para as a speculative investment and was trying to sell it, as well his remaining town acres. Early in 1840, Jacob Hagen purchased 391 acres of the Little Para from Barton at £3 an acre, a sum of £1173.[141] As Barton had paid £1 an acre, this was a good profit. Hagen then purchased and installed sheep on the Para with Walter Duffield as his manager. Duffield came from Essex, as did Joseph Barritt, the young Quaker who was running the dairy for Barton on the Para, and the two men became close friends.

The Quaker Meeting House

At the beginning of 1840, the Quakers in Adelaide received a wooden Meeting House, made for the purpose by Manning of Holborn (London). It was paid for by a subscription of Friends in England.[142] Gates's father, Samuel Darton, was the clerk of the small committee appointed to look after this project. The prefabricated timber building and iron pillars arrived on 6 February

1840 on board the *Rajasthan*. The trustees also sent 3000 slates on the *John*.

With it was a letter from Samuel Darton to Barton and Stephen Hack, stating that the trustees would cover the expense of sending the packages to Adelaide and the erection of the building. The trustees were Samuel Gurney (a cousin of Edward Gibbon Wakefield and brother of Elizabeth Fry), Josiah Forster (Barton's former schoolmaster), George Stacey and Robert Forster. Samuel Darton wrote that, unless they could procure a piece of land free of charge, they should purchase some land and send the details to the trustees.

The idea for a meeting house had originated a year earlier, when Barton offered the South Australian Friends a third of his acre 704 on Pennington Terrace for this purpose. When the meeting house arrived, Barton offered this land for £200, which he felt was reasonable, given that a full acre was then worth £400, and there was a stone cottage on the land which had cost him £300 to build.

Samuel Darton died in January 1840, but news of his death did not reach Barton until some months later. In June Barton wrote to Gates Darton that the Meeting House was finished except for painting, and was a 'very handsome building'. He expressed his sympathy over Samuel Darton's death, and asked Gates to arrange with the trustees of the Meeting House to reimburse him for the cost of the land and the erection of the building.

Barton then sent a bill to Gates for £431 for the total costs, including £200 for the land. Once again, this caused tension between the brothers-in-law. When Gates received the bill, he refused to pay it. His father's letter was vague, and the trustees in England took the view that the South Australian Friends should pay for the setting-up of their meeting house.

Some months later, Barton learned that his request for reimbursement had been refused. In July the following year (1841) he wrote to two of the trustees, Samuel Gurney and Josiah Forster. He attached the original letter from Samuel Darton, which he believed authorised payment for the land and the erection of the building. Barton said the Friends in South Australia agreed to the price of £200 and he did not know why his draft on Gates for £431 was refused.

By the end of 1841, the amount had increased to £607 because of 'interest and the heavy bank charges against dishonoured cheques to England'.[143] Two South Australian Quakers, Jacob Hagen and Henry Phillips, came to Barton's aid and wrote to the trustees asking that the bill be accepted and the southern portion of the land sold.

In the end the trustees paid £307, allowing only £50 for the land, because they considered one-eighth of an acre sufficient. Hagen and Phillips protested, lending Barton £300 to clear his debt and maintain the good name of the Society. In February 1843 Samuel Gurney intervened and personally reimbursed Hagen and Phillips. Finally in August 1847, the English trustees agreed to the sale of the southern section in front of the Meeting House, which included the stone cottage, and it was sold for £80.[144]

The Quaker Meeting House is still there today, at 40a Pennington Terrace, up a laneway next to St Peter's Anglican Cathedral. When the Meeting House was erected, the land on the eastern side facing King William Street was occupied by stockyards. Twenty years later, in 1862, that land was purchased by the Anglican Church for £1052, with the foundation stone for the cathedral laid in 1869.[145]

The Friends Burial Ground remained behind the Meeting House until 1855, when the graves were moved to West Terrace Cemetery. The only gravestone behind the Meeting House today is that of Mary Ann Barritt, who died in 1848 aged 32, and her five-year-old son Joseph, who drowned in 1849. She was the wife of Joseph Barritt, who had once run the dairy on Barton's land on the Little Para and later farmed at Lyndoch.

The Meeting House is still in use and can be visited (www.sa.quakers.org.au). It has been restored to its original condition. The wooden benches are the same ones used by the Hacks and other early members. The Quaker Meeting House is probably the oldest building in Adelaide still in its original form.

Quaker meetings are held mostly in silence, a tradition that arose as a reaction against the opulence and power of the Church of England, avoiding even music. It is perhaps ironic therefore, that the Meeting House in Adelaide is towered over by the Anglican Cathedral, and the silent meditation is broken sometimes by the sound of the organ and hymn singing.

In the Mount Barker area there were about fifty people connected with Quakers, and this included Barton and Bbe and their children, the May family with eleven children, the large Kekwick family and Barton's cousin George Deane and his wife Rachel and three children. The Quakers at Mount Barker decided to hold a meeting for worship every Sunday and, as they were too far away from Adelaide to use the new Meeting House, Barton offered his stone dairy on the Western Flat for the purpose.[146]

Soon after the Quaker Meeting House was completed, Henry Watson and his family moved into their Manning cottage next door. Henry made the house more comfortable by surrounding it with a brick-paved veranda.[147]

At the end of the year the Watsons found the house too hot in summer and encased the whole house in brick. At the same time they extended some rooms and added a new veranda and attic rooms. The house has been owned by St Mark's College, part of Adelaide University, since 1928 and is now known as Walkley Cottage.[148] It is the oldest brick building in South Australia, and both it and the Meeting House have been classified by the National Trust.

Chapter 16

A cloud settles on the colony

During 1840 the Commissioners in London sent out another 3000 emigrants on free passages, all of whom expected to find work. By the end of the year the population was nearly 15,000.[149] In order to employ them, Gawler continued his ambitious program of public works, drawing bills on the Commissioners. But a crisis faced the colony when land sales in Adelaide dropped suddenly and the speculative bubble ended. This diminished the flow of badly needed capital and hastened a financial depression.[150]

The merchant business

During 1840, Barton rode into town twice a week to attend to his 'town' business. Now that he was no longer living in Hindley Street, he and Henry Watson tried to sell the property. They soon discovered it was hard to sell, as emigrants wanted land in the country now that it was available, not in the town.

In March 1840 Henry received letters from Gates, again complaining about the money he was owed by Barton. Gates wanted Barton and Henry to sell their town land immediately, including his acre in Wakefield Street. Henry wrote back that this was impossible since town land nominally retained its price, but it was unsaleable.

Henry's letter explained that the merchant firm was frequently turning over £1000 a week, but had large debts with the banks in Adelaide. All these borrowings had to be met. 'There was nothing for it, but to go on and struggle through', Henry wrote.

> A very anxious time of course it has been. We are now getting all straight. Part of the Para is sold to Jacob Hagen Jr. The rest there is good hope of selling . . . Extensive sales of cattle have been made. If we could but sell the Para and this house [Hindley Street], we should be free.

Henry had other concerns; his baby Fanny was ill again. Bbe rode down from Mount Barker and sat up until 2 am with her, as Charlotte was unwell. On 4 April, Fanny Watson died, aged three months.

With the merchant firm having a debt of £3000, Henry was fearful about their commercial prospects. Although he had been in business with Barton for a year, he had only just come to understand the true situation. Barton and Stephen had overall debts totalling £11,000 (in modern terms, over a million Australian dollars) and on the credit side they had recently sold some town acres and cattle, but this was nothing compared with the borrowings.

Henry came to the crux of the matter. Stephen owned half the country properties, but the merchant firm was saddled with the debt by which they were purchased. The agricultural firm also owed the merchant firm for stores and advances, but in the meantime Stephen had gone on buying cattle and horses 'in the most reckless way'. Henry did not blame Barton though, he said Barton had the kindest intentions to him and had not seen the unfairness until recently.

Two days later Henry wrote again to Gates, saying that Stephen had behaved in the most honourable way as soon as it was pointed out to him that the merchant firm was saddled with a debt of £3000, which was in fact the rural firm's responsibility. Stephen immediately agreed to give up his share of the Para, his five acres on Pennington Terrace, his horses and stock, and to the immediate sale of the herd at Echunga, in order to pay off the £3000. The valuations were worked out by Barton on current prices. Henry said that with this transfer of assets, the merchant firm would 'soon be out of hot water'.

Stephen was left with his half-share of the Three Brothers estate, roughly 1500 acres with improvements, and no liabilities, as those had been transferred to the merchant business. When he left the colony he was still, in his eyes, worth a considerable amount.

Henry told Gates he had done his best to keep the merchant firm from incurring any fresh liabilities. They had made no investments and had realised a considerable amount of sales.

They had not been able to sell the house at Hindley Street, but were trying to sell the store separately. They had built a wharf and warehouse at the new port, and this would change their way of doing business. They now sold all the goods to the storekeepers from the ship, and rarely had to take goods into the store.

The *Katherine Stewart Forbes* finally left Adelaide at the end of April 1840, and on board were Stephen Hack and the long-delayed cargo of oil from the previous year's season. Stephen would not return for two years. He travelled with Jack Foley, the bushranger turned stockman. In a letter to his mother Barton told her that he approved of Stephen's trip, and that Stephen was taking home documents and accounts about their situation. Barton said these would show that, if Tom were to join their rural business, it would 'almost ensure him a fortune'. Barton hoped his mother would join them too.

Barton wrote that the mercantile business was doing well, and the promise of business was very great. 'I find Henry a most valuable assistant as partner, he is an excellent salesman and a good collector, and Captain Hart in the whaling and shipping department is invaluable'.

Barton turned to the subject of money he owed Gates for the books. He said he had arranged payment of the first bill of £400, and had planned to pay the rest with the oil on the *Katherine Stewart Forbes*. Barton had received warnings about the money market in South Australia from his older relatives John Barton and Halsey Janson. He reassured his mother that he was aware of their opinion, but he had seen an immense advantage in raising the funds to buy the Three Brothers estate. He said he had been taking measures to pay off the loan, and the agricultural firm was nearly out of debt.

In June Barton sold the remaining 609 acres on the Little Para to John Richardson, a land agent in Hindley Street, who paid $2027.[151] This was a little over £3 per acre, another good profit for the sale of land.

The whaling business
The whaling season of 1839 had been fraught with problems, but Barton still believed they could make money from the industry.

His view was shared by John Morphett and Jacob Hagen, both canny businessmen; in 1840 each purchased a one-fifth share in the company for £1000.

David McLaren of the South Australian Company was more realistic, and in 1840 the directors in London decided to withdraw from whaling operations. They scaled down operations in 1840, sold half their gear, boats and stations to Hack & Company and closed their whaling and shipping operations.

At the end of 1840 the oil and whalebone was sent to London on two vessels, the *Lalla Rookh* and the *Guiana*. More oil was taken at Encounter Bay than in any previous year, but there were other problems. Many of the whalers had deserted, and the cost of provisions was exorbitant. A full account of the whaling industry, year by year, was made in a report later by Captain Hart.[152]

In 1840 the *Hero* withdrew from the whaling business and turned to coastal trading and carrying.[153] In October Captain Devlin bought the *Rapid* from the other partners. Barton was lucky he had sold out, because the *Rapid* was wrecked on its way to China a few months later. It was not insured and the loss ruined Devlin, although he recovered and later settled in Victoria.

The colony in trouble

In Barton Hack's memoirs, he wrote:

> In 1840 my brother left for England and remained away for two years. During this interval the cloud came over the colony, and difficulties began to accumulate. Banks refused accommodation and demanded the payment of overdrafts and in the two years ending February 1843 . . . terminated in the loss of all our property. In 1840 the balance sheet showed a credit [assets] of nearly £30,000.[154]

Barton's estimate of £30,000 (in modern terms over three million Australian dollars) was based on land values at the beginning of 1840 before prices slumped. He believed that with a bit more time he could pay off his debts. By July 1840, however, it was clear that the colony was in serious trouble. Henry Watson wrote to Gates:

> I suppose you will have heard we are in great commercial difficulties in Adelaide. The fact is that the banks have been putting on the screw and refusing discounts. There had been perhaps too great a facility in obtaining credit, and speculation had been too extensive. Persons without capital obtained credit, and if without principal, swindled their creditors. The result has been that a great deal of property is selling at sacrifice ... everyone looks with distrust on his neighbour and no one knows who is safe.

The banks were pressing for payment of loans, and Edward Stephens, the manager of the South Australian Company's bank, put pressure on the Hacks. Barton was forced to give him security on the premises in Hindley Street, which he was trying to sell.

Henry Watson visited Echunga Springs and said it looked magnificent, but the annual cost was about £1200, while the returns from the property were less than half that amount, not to mention the debt related to the purchase. Henry observed:

> I believe Barton would have been a richer man if he had never owned one rood of country land ... But it is delightful to see what has been effected by the intellect of one man. The more I see of Barton, the more I admire him. As Hart said the other day, 'He has head enough to be Chancellor of the Exchequer'.

Henry still thought highly of the commercial prospects of colony, and had recently visited the new port, where there was a brick customs house, spacious sheds, wharves and several vessels discharging goods. He described changes to the town and said, 'You sober jog-trot stay-at-home people cannot understand the rate at which ... we go ahead ... all this is the work of three short years ... never in the history of colonization was anything like it'.

Committees

Despite their business worries, Barton and Henry continued to be involved in public life. The Royal South Australian Almanack for 1840 shows Barton Hack's name on the boards of management or the committees of all the institutions listed, except one.

He was still Chairman of the Adelaide Chamber of Commerce

and President of the Literary and Scientific Association and Mechanics Institute. He was on the committee of the Botanic Gardens Board, a member of the Association for the Prosecution of Felons and a director of the Joint Stock Pastoral Company.[155] He was also a director of the Adelaide Auction Company, which he had helped establish in 1839 to sell land, stock and goods by public auction.[156] In 1840 the financier John Baker became Chairman and would play a significant part in Barton's later downfall.

Henry Watson was involved with Barton in the Literary and Scientific Association and Mechanics Institute, and during the year he stood for office when the first municipal elections took place in Adelaide and was elected an alderman. James Hurtle Fisher became mayor and John Morphett treasurer.[157] The council was handicapped by lack of funds, however, and was wound up a few years later.

Letters to Gates

At the end of the year Henry Watson wrote to Gates with some good news: they had finally sold the books sent out by Harvey and Darton, mostly at auction. It is unlikely that Gates was thrilled at this information, however, as the books were sold at a very low price, and Harvey and Darton were still owed several hundred pounds.

When Priscilla arrived in Adelaide at the beginning of 1840, her husband Edward Philcox asked Barton to repay the £1000. This was the money Priscilla had lent Gates before she left, to pay off Barton's debts. Barton paid Philcox the £1000, but sent Gates a letter saying he had only owed him £700, and the remaining £300 was for Harvey and Darton. In short, he was asking Gates to pay £300 of the money still owing for the books.

When Gates received this letter, he was astonished and had no intention of paying for the books. Gates believed Barton owed him more than £300 for a share of the profits on the sale of town land. Gates was also angry that Barton had not sold his town acre in Wakefield Street. In addition, Gates had never accepted the way in which Barton had taken back the thirteen town acres after learning that Gates had been forced to sell the rural acres. The dispute over payment for the books was to drag on for some years.

Meanwhile, Barton and Henry Watson struggled to keep afloat.

Chapter 17

Crisis in the colony

The financial crisis in the colony intensified in 1841 when the Commissioners in England refused to pay Governor Gawler's bills. The colony was bankrupt and Gawler was recalled. He left in June, but shortly before that, he and his family spent a few days at Barton Hack's house at Echunga Springs. Governor George Grey arrived with orders to rein in spending and the financial crisis further deepened. Barton sold Hindley Street and mortgaged his half of Echunga Springs. The mercantile firm became insolvent and Henry Watson fell out with Barton and Bbe. Stephen Hack was in England, where he married in June.

Gawler recalled

At the beginning of 1841, news arrived from London which caused shock and alarm in the young colony. Some of Governor Gawler's bills had been rejected, and he was to be replaced. In April, Gawler received formal instructions that he was to cease drawing on the Commissioners immediately.[158]

Gawler was shocked, since he believed he had approval for his program of public works, which had cost £200,000.[159] But the fall in land sales in Adelaide meant the land fund in London had shrunk, and the Commissioners were bankrupt. On 10 May the new Governor, Captain George Grey, arrived on the *Lord Glenelg*, carrying with him a letter for Gawler's recall.[160] Grey had been a military man and had spent some time as an explorer in Western Australia. He was only twenty-nine, but strong-minded.

Before leaving South Australia in June 1841, Gawler and his family paid a visit to the Hacks at Echunga Springs. This was when Gawler painted Barton's house and garden. As Barton explained to his mother:

> I invited Colonel, Mrs and Miss Gawler to come and spend a few days with us at the 'Springs' and very much did we enjoy their visit ... I drove the ladies ... nearly to the top of Mount Barker from which ... We could see the whole extent of Lake Alexandrina and trace the Murray for many miles.

Gawler's departure was lamented by the colony. As Barton wrote later:

> On Colonel Gawler's leaving for England he was accompanied to the Port by a large cavalcade of the leading colonists, who felt that we were losing a man more single-minded, honest and energetic than we could hope to see again. In parting with the Colonel I felt I had lost a valuable friend. He set an example of Christian life which was of incalculable benefit to the colony in the first struggles for existence.

Henry Watson wrote to Gates: 'there does not breathe a man whom I so highly venerate ... Never was man so vilely used as Gawler'. Henry said the commercial distress was extreme, and the labouring class was deserting to Sydney and Van Diemen's Land. The colony had lost its land fund and with it the end of free passages for emigrants. 'We all now devoutly pray to be relieved of the incubus of the Commissioners and to be placed under the responsible charge of the Colonial office', he wrote. In fact the Colonial Office had taken over already, and the following year the colony was placed under the sole control of the Crown.

Gawler returned to England to find he had been judged in his absence and he tried desperately to defend himself. George Grey had promoted the false idea that Gawler was responsible for the land speculation and the concentration of the population in Adelaide, and that he had prevented rural settlement. In fact before Gawler left, the rural population was over 5000, nearly 16,000 acres had been enclosed and 6700 acres put under crop, making possible the magnificent harvest of 1841 for which Governor Grey was able to claim the credit. Gawler could not get further appointments and retired into private life.[161]

Governor Grey takes over

George Grey arrived with strict instructions to rein in expenditure. Gawler had already begun making economies and Grey increased them. The merchants in Adelaide waited anxiously to see if their claims on the government were going to be paid. Soon after Grey took office, the Chamber of Commerce met with him to discuss the crisis. Barton Hack as chairman addressed Grey on the need to pay the government's debts to local merchants, which Barton estimated to be about £30,000.

Grey said he would sell what government property he could, and use that towards paying the debts. He agreed to grant certificates acknowledging the amount of each debt, so that the creditors could try to dispose of their claims at a discount. When Grey examined the debt to local businessmen more closely, he found it was nearly £54,000, but he drew bills on the Treasury in London for only £14,000. The British Government refused to pay even that, and Grey later had to convert the bills into government debentures, which were almost worthless. This led to many insolvencies and property changed hands at ruinous prices.[162]

Another matter which Barton discussed with Governor Grey was the 'Great Eastern Road' to Mount Barker. Begun under Gawler to provide work for the unemployed, it was designed to replace the difficult and dangerous tracks into the hills and would provide easier access to Echunga, Hahndorf and Mount Barker via Glen Osmond. When Gawler departed, it was announced that work on the road would be abandoned. Lobbying by Barton and others produced a compromise: Grey would allow them to raise a loan for a toll road, and in the meantime the government would continue the road.

Legislation was passed for the toll road and a committee of management set up to raise the sum of £1000, with Barton Hack as one of the trustees. In October 1841 a section of the road from Adelaide into the hills was opened, with a tollhouse at Glen Osmond. The tolls were very unpopular, however, and did not raise sufficient revenue and passage on the road eventually became free.[163] The old toll house at Glen Osmond remains to this day.

With the slump in land sales, the banks were pressing for the payment of mortgages and overdrafts. Edward Stephens urgently demanded the payment of Barton and Stephen's old debts. To meet this demand, in February 1841 Barton sold Hindley Street to the young Quaker merchants Henry and George Phillips for £4000, where they installed themselves as ironmongers.[164] Barton and Henry relocated to Morphett's old premises in North Terrace, Barton also selling his land at the port.

The bank continued to press him, and in March he mortgaged his half of the Echunga estate – 1508 acres – to his friends John Morphett, James Hurtle Fisher and John Brown for £2000, at an annual interest of 15 per cent.[165] The Echunga property was still in Barton's name and he was holding Stephen's half in trust until the mortgage was paid.[166] Stephen was in England and knew nothing of this.

A death in the family

Early in the year three women in the family gave birth. In February Charlotte Watson produced a son, whom they named William Woodman. Charlotte could not feed the baby herself and engaged a wet nurse. At first the baby thrived, but two months later he became extremely ill, developing inflammation of the lungs. The Watsons discovered the nurse was in the habit of 'stuffing him with bread and milk and dosing him with gin'. Fortunately, the baby survived.

In May Ellen Knott gave birth to a son, whom they named George Gawler, and in June Priscilla Philcox gave birth to another daughter, Margaret Esther. Priscilla had been strong and active up to the birth, but after the birth began to haemorrhage, which lasted for several days. The bleeding stopped, but her pulse was very high and she was very weak and on 5 July 1841 Henry Watson wrote to Gates and Margaret:

> I have the painful duty of informing you of Priscilla's departure, she expired early this morning. Poor Edward seems quite overwhelmed, poor fellow... My sister Bbe I hear has been unremitting in her attention to the poor sufferer.

Priscilla was buried on 8 July next to the Quaker meeting house. Barton wrote of Priscilla:

I have known few persons so free from the love of self and so solicitous to promote the happiness of those around her. My sister Ellen Knott feels the loss very keenly as the sisters have scarcely been separated from childhood, and have been much attached to each other.

Bbe Hack took in Priscilla's two babies and prepared to bring them up, in addition to her seven children. Theodore was just eight months old and William, her oldest, was thirteen. Bbe and Barton offered Edward Philcox a home for the time being, as he was in great distress.

One of their neighbours was the schoolteacher James Macgowan. Barton had built a house on the estate for him and Macgowan commenced a school, which the Hack boys attended. Macgowan had eleven children of his own, and these formed the nucleus of the school with the May and Hack children.[167]

Stephen Hack marries

Stephen Hack had been in England since January the year before, mainly in Gloucester where his mother and his brother Tom and wife Lydia lived, although they moved to Southampton in the middle of 1841. Around this time Margaret and Gates Darton came to live in Gloucester,[168] when Gates gave up his partnership in Harvey and Darton and replaced Tom in the ironmongery business.

It was a difficult time for Gates and Margaret. Just before they moved to Gloucester, their baby Margaret Elizabeth died a few weeks after the birth.[169] In addition, Gates was still liable for £1571 for the books he had sent to various people in Australia. The largest of these bills was for the books for Hack, Watson & Co.

On 3 June 1841 Stephen married Elizabeth Marsh Wilton, known as Bessie, from the hamlet of Littleworth St Michael near Gloucester. Bessie's father, John Wilton, was a surgeon, and they were Anglican. This would not have bothered Stephen, and they were married in the parish church of St Michael in Littleworth. They were both twenty-five.

News of the wedding would not reach Adelaide for months, but Barton was anxious that Stephen return as soon as possible.

Maria had advised Stephen to separate from Barton and take his share of the land and cattle, and this angered Barton. He reminded his mother that when Stephen left, there was a debt of £2000 on the farm which had been transferred to the mercantile firm, with a further debt of £2000 on the rural firm. Barton wrote aggrievedly:

> Stephen knew when he left me that I was passing sleepless nights and was in a bad state of health from excessive anxiety... The only great fault I had to find with Stephen was that I could scarcely get him to consent to make the sales of cattle necessary to keep the farm out of debt.

Turning then to the problem of the debts that Stephen had incurred during his eighteen months in England, Barton was hurt that Maria thought he had 'placed Stephen in a sad dilemma as respects funds'. Barton said he had given Stephen £200 for his passage and outfit and asked him to spend as little as possible while in England. Stephen wrote asking for money, and Barton asked Hagen & Son to assist. Stephen then drew on Hagens for £1000 as a loan.

Barton went on to explain the difficulties in the colony with Gawler's recall and the rejection of Gawler's bills. He explained that this, as well as the cessation of emigration, had 'rendered the colony so poor that individuals are unable in many instances to pay their debts. The shop keepers do not pay their acceptances, but bills are absolutely worthless, and no cash is to be procured'. It was time, Barton wrote, for Stephen to return and help out.

The whaling business

Barton was still involved in the whaling business, with the 1841 season commencing well. Provisions were purchased at a lower cost, and the economic downturn in the colony meant the whalers had no incentive to desert. In Encounter Bay oil and whalebone were procured, and after shipping expenses there was a profit of just over £1000. The station at Sleaford Bay was not as fortunate, making a loss.

By June Barton was writing to his mother that he wanted to free himself from the whaling business, but had to see the season out. He tried desperately to sell his share of the business, and in the meantime left it in the hands of Hart and Hagen.

The collapse of Hack, Watson & Co.

Once the financial crisis hit the colony, Henry Watson became desperate to disentangle himself from the mercantile company. It was encumbered with debts, mainly incurred before he arrived. The estate at Echunga was drawing off the income from the sale of goods, and owed the mercantile firm for stores and advances. In February 1841 Henry told Barton he would pay no more cheques for the Echunga estate.

The year before, Henry had been happy with the separation of the family business into two companies. Stephen had transferred debts from the rural company to the mercantile company, but in exchange he had given up an equivalent amount of property and cattle. Barton had estimated the worth of Stephen's property according to the values of the day, but since then economic conditions had deteriorated and Stephen's assets were now worth much less. The mercantile firm had debts they could not pay off.

Henry had put his trust in Barton's business acumen and knew very little about the whaling business or Barton's complex financial transactions. By August 1841 Barton agreed to wind up the affairs of Hack, Watson & Co., but was waiting for Stephen's return.

Towards the end of the year the mercantile business collapsed completely and the partnership was dissolved. In December Henry Watson wrote to Gates informing him that the firm was insolvent to the tune of about £4000. Some £3500 of this was owed to Hagen & Son in England. Barton had been sending them oil, but the price in London was low and Hagens had been sending goods to Adelaide, where they had sold at very low rates, meaning that Barton received little return.

Jacob Hagen insisted on a settlement of the debt, and in December he wound up the firm of Hack, Watson & Co. and sold the remaining consignments. Barton still owed money to Hagen, but was given time to settle. He hoped to sell his remaining town acres and the whaling business.

Henry Watson continued to pour out his grievances to Gates,

complaining that, in winding up the business, Barton 'took credit for £1400 of my own property, land purchased for me by JBH with money lent to him for the purpose'. Henry had earlier given Barton £100 to invest in town acres, which were now worth £1400 on paper. Henry's problem was that, as a partner in the mercantile business, his assets were counted along with Barton's.

Henry explained that when the mercantile firm was dissolved, he called in Captain Hart and Edward Philcox as arbitrators. They went through the books of Hack, Watson & Co., calculating half the profits and half the losses, but they still had to work through what Barton had siphoned off to the rural firm. 'When accounts are settled ... a considerable balance may be coming to me', Henry continued, '[but] I do not ... feel particularly grateful. I feel that nothing can compensate me for the irreparable loss that I must suffer from my name being mixed up with him'.

With the collapse of the company, Henry's cottage in Pennington Terrace was sold to Edmund Trimmer. Edward Philcox, alone on his farm since Priscilla's death, took in the Watsons and their two small children, and Barton supplied them with stores.

Henry reminded Gates that when he (Henry) had joined the business, he invested about £600 from the sale of some of his town land, and because of this, 'all the profits of the business were to be mine, and a very handsome thing it would have been, the commissions amounted to about £1000 a year'. He believed the collapse of the mercantile firm was because Barton kept the proceeds of the sale of goods. 'It is impossible for any commission business to exist under such circumstances and I feel almost a relief to get out on any terms'.

Henry was right. The revenue from the mercantile business had been used by Barton to pay interest on massive bank loans, invest in the whaling business and keep the Echunga estate going. But the main reason for the collapse was the financial crash in the colony. Barton's plan for paying off the loans with profits from land sales, the merchant business, cattle sales and whaling was no longer remotely possible.

As a result of the breakup, Barton and Bbe were no longer on friendly terms with Henry and Charlotte. Henry told Gates,

'They have shown... every possible disrespect to poor Charlotte. She has been nearly two months at Edward Philcox's and they have been once over to see her, the distance is a little more than a mile and they know Charlotte has no means of stirring out'. He said Barton and Bbe were indignant about the decision of the arbitrators.

Henry was broke and without a job, and wrote to Governor Grey hoping for a position in the public service. His sole income now was his wife's small inheritance and he added plaintively to Gates: 'I feel particularly thankful that dear Charlie's money was settled upon her or it would all have gone'.

Henry and Bbe's parents were living in a cottage in Barton's garden at Echunga, and only just surviving. By the end of 1841 one-sixth of the population were without work.[170] The colony was in crisis, and as far as Barton and Stephen's situation was concerned, things would only get worse.

Chapter 18
The crisis continues

By 1842, most of the merchants were becoming bankrupt. Emigration from England had ceased, capital had dried up and labourers had moved to other colonies. Property could not be sold and barter took the place of money. Barton owed money to the English merchants Hagen & Son, and was forced to give Jacob Hagen a second mortgage on his half of the Echunga property. Stephen Hack returned from England with his new wife and baby to find all in disarray. He had borrowed from Hagen & Son in England and therefore had to mortgage his share of Echunga to Jacob Hagen. Barton and Stephen kept the farm going, but debts threatened to overwhelm them.

Two births and a death
At the beginning of 1842, Stephen Hack was in Capetown, South Africa. He and Bessie had left England in October 1841 on the *Guiana*, and arrived at the Cape in January 1842. Bessie was heavily pregnant, so they stayed at the Cape instead of continuing on to Adelaide. On 6 March 1842 a daughter was born and they named her Julia Africaine. Three months later they took the *Lady Fitzherbert* for Adelaide. Stephen's family in Australia knew nothing of this change in plan and were surprised when the *Guiana* arrived in Adelaide without him.

Charlotte Watson was also expecting a baby and the family moved into a small cottage in front of the Quaker Meeting House. This must have been painful for them, as it was right next to their former home. On 9 January Charlotte gave birth to a son, Henry Edward.

At Echunga, Bbe Hack was pregnant, the birth expected in May. In addition to her seven children, she was still looking after Edward Philcox's two little girls. At the beginning of the year the baby, Margaret, aged six months, became ill with inflammation of the lungs, and died on 31 January. Bbe continued to look after Anna, who was nearly two. Edward Philcox's brother James and his wife Anne arrived from England and James began farming with Edward.

Henry Watson gets a job in Customs

The economic crisis continued, with Henry Watson writing to Gates that the colony seemed utterly forgotten. There were no more immigrants, no influx of capital, and many of the labourers were leaving for New Zealand. Prices were down and it was impossible to sell anything. Henry said his only property was some land, which was unsaleable. 'Until JBH's affairs are more settled, I may be sold up any day by his creditors . . . my position at the present is most deplorable.'

Things looked up a little when Governor Grey gave Henry a job as chief clerk in the Customs. The Watsons rented a house close to the harbour, where they could see ships at anchor, and the new job was not very arduous, being only six hours a day. 'On the whole I am pleased with my occupation', he wrote, 'and relieved from a load of anxiety which for the last few years has been almost intolerable'.

Henry's chief was Robert Richard Torrens, Collector of Customs, a son of Colonel Robert Torrens, former chair of the South Australia Commission in London. Torrens's period as a government official in South Australia was filled with controversy, but he later became famous for his system of land title registration and was knighted for it.[171]

Hagen takes a mortgage on Echunga

While Henry was settling into his new job, Barton was desperately trying to straighten out the affairs of the mercantile firm, which owed Jacob Hagen £3500. In March 1842 Hagen secured this debt with a second mortgage on Barton's half of the Echunga estate. The first was to Morphett, Fisher and Brown, on which Barton was paying interest.[172]

Hagen was a Quaker, but he was also a moneylender and a tough businessman. The mortgage document still exists, couched in the legal language of the time.[173] It shows that Hagen was ruthless, even to a friend and former business colleague. The mortgage document stated that the £3500 had to be paid in six months time, by 20 September 1842. Interest had to be calculated at 12½ per cent from 20 September the previous year (1841) and paid half-yearly on 20 March and 20 September 1842. If the principal was not paid by 20 September 1842, the interest would rise to 15 per cent.

Hagen could foreclose if Barton could not pay both the interest and the principal on the due date. Hagen could sell up the land six months later, but Barton had to pay the higher interest until the land was sold. Hagen appointed as trustees Captain Hart and the lawyer William James.

The mortgage further stated that, unless Hagen foreclosed, Barton could remain on the property and collect rent from his tenants. This implied that Barton was still the landlord. This paragraph was contradicted however by a strange last paragraph. It said that to assist Hagen to pursue a 'remedy of distress' (the seizure of goods for non-payment of rent) Barton admitted himself to be a tenant, at a yearly rent of £600, payable to Hagen on 20 March and 20 September. It seems that Barton had to pay rent as well as interest on the mortgage.

That Barton signed a document containing such extreme conditions gives an indication of his desperation. He faced the prospect of losing everything he had worked so hard for. But he was an eternal optimist and tried to buy time, in the hope that he could still find a way out of his problems. Meanwhile Hagen looked on, perhaps mercilessly. In the economic climate of the day, he must have known that Barton had virtually no hope of meeting these requirements.

Soon after the mortgage was signed, Barton wrote to Gates Darton about his 'cares and anxieties'. Echunga was a large property but in the current recession they could not sell any of it. If the loans were called in and there was a forced sale, they could be left with nothing. Barton was very worried about Stephen, who would arrive soon. Stephen seemed to think there was a large amount of income due to him, forgetting that the property was not free from debt.

Apart from the problems relating to the mercantile firm, there was pressure to pay off the debts on the rural firm. Barton delayed this until the *Guiana* arrived in March, but when Stephen was not on it, Barton had to present a statement of all the property belonging to himself and Stephen. As he told Gates:

> The Two Banks ... had the decision and they have behaved in a very handsome manner to me, and have left all in my hands being satisfied that I could work it through. I know Stephen's wife has come out intending to return almost directly and how she will take it all I cannot see.

The two banks were giving him time to pay off his debts. Barton's principal asset was the whaling station, but he could not find a buyer. 'It is a great vexation to me', he wrote, 'I have a deal of town land and many debts to collect, but such are realised very slowly'.

Gates was still asking for his share of the sale of town land, and Barton said this was impossible, explaining that the winding-up of the mercantile business would probably leave him worth less than when he began, but he hoped to be in a position to gain a living on the farm. 'I shall not be otherwise than a careworn, anxious man until I can see sufficient property realised to place me in an independent position.'

Making the farm profitable

By the beginning of 1842, Barton had abandoned all his businesses except the farm. He worked hard on the estate and hoped it would soon be profitable. Labour was much cheaper and he was clearing land and preparing crops for market. He described to Gates how the farm was prospering: they had grown 1500 bushels of wheat, making all of it into flour, and 600 bushels of oats. His grapes were 'very fine' and he had made £50 from them over the summer and sent several tons of melons into town. Barton said he had about forty foals and they would be valuable when grown, but whether there was time was the question.

'Our cheese is in great request and commands the market here', he wrote, and he was moving the dairy which had been two miles away, next to his garden, so that it would be under his eye and 'I shall save the wages of 2 men by making all the farm servants turn in to milk before breakfast'. Barton said his labourers now averaged more than two years' service with him and were a 'capital set'. The domestic servants were also excellent and had been with them a long time. His groom was going to marry the housemaid and, as they did not want to lose her, Barton would have to find them a cottage. Despite his adversity, Barton sounded optimistic and cheerful.

Bbe was eight months pregnant, but Barton said she was fully occupied with her needle, as she made all the family's clothes, even Barton's. The boys and Louisa were being taught by Macgowan, who paid rent for the schoolhouse Barton had built him, and this covered the Hack children's fees. Barton also supplied him with beef and flour towards the fees.

Governor Grey breakfasted with the Hacks at Echunga Springs and Barton commented:

> I wish I could like him, but he is much too young and common-minded a man for so responsible a post. He appears to me to square his conduct on what he thinks will advance his interest at home rather than on any fixed principle. He is very civil to me though, so I ought not say anything to his disadvantage.

Barton had a kind letter from his mother, who was living with Tom and Lydia in Southampton. Thomas had trained as an architect as a young man, and was now practising as an architect and surveyor.[174] Maria Hack was mourning the loss of her daughter Priscilla, and worried about Ellen, whose husband John Knott had lost money. Maria was sixty-four and feeling her age. She hoped that Ellen might return to England with Stephen, but added, 'at my age life is so very precarious that I dare not look forward to any plans'.

Barton replied that he was concerned that Stephen's wife thought they only needed to stay a few months in Australia. He wondered how Bessie would manage:

> She must cling to us for she will have no other friends, and if she is but reasonable and disposed to 'put her hand to the plough' dear Bbe will do anything for her, but thou knows my good wife can

tolerate nothing like fine ladyism and I am full of fears til I can see if they are well founded or not.

Barton wished his mother could see his children, 'a finer family could not be seen and I hope on the whole, one more united and well inclined'. William, the oldest, had just turned fourteen and was very advanced in Latin and Arithmetic and very steady. Edward, twelve, was more volatile:

> His mind is full of horses and stock, and with a natural propensity to show off, he requires a good deal of care and check, but I think I can see my way with him, he is a universal favourite with our friends.

Louisa, ten, was a very bold rider 'and certainly does not know what fear means'. Alfred, at eight, was the cleverest of the children, while Bedford, aged six, a 'fine open-hearted lad'. Four-year-old Emily was a dark-eyed merry little one, and Theodore, the youngest, 'a most beautiful child'. The family was about to expand. Bbe, aged thirty-five, gave birth on 29 May 1842 to a son, whom they named Charles.

Barton's letters do not tell us much about Bbe, but she seems to have been remarkably strong and resilient. She recovered quickly from her frequent child-bearing, and was a loving mother. Marrying Bbe was probably one of the most sensible and rewarding things Barton ever did. She had to endure considerable hardships at times, but she was very capable, and always loyal and supportive to her husband, despite all the ups and downs of his 'chequered' life.

Barton proudly told his mother that his garden was the showplace of the colony. The orchard consisted of nearly 800 trees of all sorts and the apples were particularly fine. In the vineyard 1200 vines had been planted. He was about to send six hundredweight (300 kg) of grapes to market and had sold 10,000 cuttings for the season. Dray loads of melons, fruit and vegetables were loaded and sent into town for sale.

As for the dairy, in the past year it had realised a profit of £400 on 100 cows. Although his family were large, they had never lived so economically. They raised their own beef and poultry and had ample supplies of flour, milk and butter. Four of the workmen lived in the household and there were often visitors as well. Being Quakers, they rarely drank alcohol, as Barton explained to Maria:

> Wine and beer are unknown except as medicine, huge jugs of water and milk grace the dinner table and appear to give as much satisfaction as the more potent beverages. Our water is splendid, pure and clear, from the garden springs. It is a great blessing as well as a luxury having ample supplies of vegetables and fruit . . . Our roses are most beautiful and we are getting up sweet briar hedges in great perfection.

And, wrote Barton, the view from the house was beautiful, overlooking the undulating ground of the garden.

The Hacks and the Watsons were still not on speaking terms. Henry Watson indicated in a letter to Gates that he was not sure Barton would overcome his financial difficulties: 'I do not see any mode of escape, but Barton possesses such extraordinary talents, and his splendid estate is a prize so well worth struggling to preserve, that he may get through yet'.

Stephen returns

Stephen Hack left Cape Town in early June 1842. As he sailed across the Indian Ocean, he wrote to his mother that little Julia, three months old, was doing well. 'She is the sweetest child that ever was born, with such deliciously large, dark blue eyes'. He and Bessie were getting on splendidly: 'We have now been married more than a year and we can both of us say with truth that there has not been a hasty word, look or even thought between us during that time'.

Life on board was cramped however: 'only think mother, child and servant in a box six feet every way for bed, nursery, clothes drying, washing &c, and sometimes with me for a spectator – it's just the size of a large packing case'.

Stephen was angry with Barton however, and anxious about their impending meeting.

> He has broken every agreement and arrangement we made previous to my leaving . . . and if I am not perfectly satisfied I shall dissolve

the partnership ... Though I received 5 sheets from Barton, I have no certain information except that he has swelled the debts of the [rural] firm from £4500 to £7500. The former amount we had decided was to be met by certain stock ... the greater part of which appears to be sold, but not a penny paid as we agreed. I don't like the looks of it a bit.

Stephen finally arrived in Adelaide in mid-July and introduced Bessie and baby Julia to the family, along with Bessie's nephew George Henry Wilton, who had travelled with them. George was the son of Bessie's brother John Wilton. He suffered from asthma and they hoped the warmer climate would be beneficial to his health.

What Stephen and Barton said to each other is not recorded, but Stephen must have quickly observed the effects of the financial depression. Money was so scarce that it was replaced by barter: even tailors were offering to take cheese in exchange for clothes. Stephen soon realised he had no choice but to work on the farm and hope for the best. He and Bessie stayed with Barton and Bbe in Echunga Springs, while Stephen began building his own house nearby. Bessie must have settled in well, because Barton later wrote about her in glowing terms.

On 1 and 2 August 1842, soon after Stephen's arrival, Barton transferred his half of the estate (which Barton had held in trust) to Stephen.[175] Stephen could then make a separate arrangement with Jacob Hagen.

Stephen owed Hagen £600, and as soon as the land was divided, he asked Hagen for a further advance of £400. Hagen agreed and secured the £1000 with a mortgage on Stephen's half of the property, at 12½ per cent interest. The land of both brothers was now mortgaged to Hagen. As with Barton's mortgage, there was a clause about Stephen renting the sections he occupied, in his case at £200 a year.[176]

William Bartley helps the Hacks

Barton still had large overdrafts with the banks and in August 1842 Richard Newland of the Bank of South Australia asked Sheriff Newenham to enter Barton's premises and seize his property. Barton turned to his solicitor William Bartley for help, saying that he would pay him back when bills which were owed to him, became due. Bartley, who claimed later he had 'great confidence in the Messrs Hack', stepped in and made an arrangement with the banks and the bailiffs were avoided.[177]

In his memoirs, Barton wrote that Newland told Barton that if he needed money he should apply to John Baker, the manager of the Auction Company.[178] This was all very cosy, since Baker was Jacob Hagen's business partner and the sole director of Newland's bank. Barton had helped set up the Auction Company and Baker was Chairman. Now it was used by Hagen and Baker for money-lending at very high interest. But Barton had no alternative and obtained a mortgage from the Auction Company for £1000 for the Hacks' cattle at Yankalilla, and also mortgaged the cattle at Echunga. Barton may have started to feel apprehensive about the close relationship between Newland, Hagen and Baker, perhaps recognising that he was now in their power.

Barton was struggling to pay off debts, and he was not alone. As the historian Douglas Pike has noted, by the end of 1842 most people had been forced into the country, one-third of houses in Adelaide were empty, and only seven merchants were left standing out of the thirty who had set themselves up during the boom.[179]

A good harvest

Henry Watson was still estranged from Barton and Bbe, but early in 1843 he sent Gates news about the family at Mount Barker. Henry said Edward Philcox had given up Burwash Farm and was practising as a surgeon at Mount Barker. His little daughter Anna was still with Barton and Bbe, and his brother James Philcox had taken a house in Adelaide. Stephen's wife Bessie was 'universally admired' and little Julia was 'a paragon'. His letter also said the harvest had been good and the colony had passed the crisis, although many were ruined, sadly commenting:

> They who now come will benefit by the ruin and errors of their predecessors – will have cheap food, labour and stock, roads, wharfs and all the comfort of life ready to hand: alas! for the poor pioneers.

Stephen and his family were moving into their house, on the opposite side of the garden, and Bessie was expecting another child in the autumn. Barton Hack reported to his mother:

> I am glad to say we have lived comfortably together and that Stephen has given his mind to the farm ... and has become reconciled to the prospect of working for some years, instead of retiring on his property. Bessie, like a woman of good sense and feeling, as she is in a greater degree than is common, also seems to feel disposed to buckle to and make the best of everything. Bbe and Bessie have been very comfortable together and have mutually endeavoured to make the long visit with us as little trying as could be.

Unfortunately, wrote Barton, the colony was still in trouble. The price of cattle and horses was down 100 per cent and business was conducted by barter, with stores only available if produce was sent for exchange. Barton was in the middle of harvesting and the crops were excellent, but the price of wheat and oats was low. The grapes in the vineyard were 'a noble show' and there would be tons for sale.

Barton reported proudly that the four older boys had been very useful with the harvest, and were 'as good as men'. William and Edward each had a team of six bullocks, which they took to and from the fields. William helped out in the milking yard every morning before his lessons or before taking his bullock team out, and had been given a calf as a reward. There were 100 cows in the dairy and Alfred could almost assign the calves to their respective mothers. Alfred and Bedford managed a flock of around sixty goats. Barton said if his boys turned out to be lazy, it would not be for lack of work or having too much time on their hands.

Barton was still trying to wind up the affairs of the mercantile firm. He had reduced the debts considerably, but was not able to sell his shares in the whaling concern, or collect money owing to the mercantile firm. The price of oil was high, by contrast with the previous five years when he was sending oil home:

> I have sent about 500 tuns, and if the prices had been as they ... are now, I should have been £5000 richer than I am. There would have been no fisheries in South Australia if I had not gone on, although

every year I did all I could to shake the burden off. I found no-one who would undertake it.

Barton had withdrawn from the whaling business in 1841 and it was now in the hands of Hart, Hagen and Baker. The price of oil in London fluctuated, and after a few more years those men also left the whaling business.

Barton was planning to formally separate from Stephen, in the hope of protecting Stephen's half of the farm from the mercantile creditors. He wrote to his mother in January 1843:

> We shall have a fair prospect of doing comfortably in time, and Stephen is disposed, when all is settled, to consider me or rather my family, as entitled to a share in the farming property which will fall to him. I think he has acted in a very kind and honourable manner to me . . . and I shall not forget it. The debts of Hack Watson and Co are about £5000. The assets ought to have covered the amount, but [not] in these times.

'Thou wilt, dear Mother, now understand my position', Barton wrote. 'As it is, if I can secure my family a home and comfort I shall be thankful.'

Chapter 19
Ruin

In February 1843 Barton was woken in the middle of the night by sheriff's officers entering his yard, and soon afterwards, everything was auctioned. Jacob Hagen seized the Echunga estate and forced the Hack brothers into insolvency. Barton arranged to stay temporarily in his two-storey house, but Stephen was evicted and went to jail for two weeks for debt. While there, his wife gave birth to a son, and bailiffs seized his furniture. Stephen blamed Barton for his downfall and the brothers fell out. Both brothers made arrangements to continue farming at Echunga, but they struggled to support themselves.

The bailiffs arrive

At the beginning of 1843, Barton had reached accommodation with the banks and believed he had time to pay his creditors. As he explained in his memoirs:[180]

> The difficulties in which I became involved took their rise from the desire to make a landed property. The purchase of the land was only a small matter, a large amount of capital was required to make this property produce anything, and [required] advances from the Bank, very readily granted when the colony was flourishing, but as summarily called in when bad times came.

Jacob Hagen had not moved against the Hacks at this stage, although Barton and Stephen had defaulted on their payments to him four months earlier. On 5 February Barton attended the first Quaker 'business' meeting at Echunga, along with Bbe's parents, the Sanders, the Deanes, the Phillips brothers, the Mays, Joseph Barritt and Mary Ann Harrison. (Business meetings were separate from meetings for worship, and from 1844 onwards the Friends met every two months for business, alternating the meetings between Mount Barker and Adelaide.[181]) The meeting was held to arrange the marriage of Joseph and Mary Ann the following month. Barton had no idea that two of his friends there – Jacob Hagen and Henry Phillips – were about to bring him down.

Two days later Richard Newland lodged an 'execution' against the Hacks for £500, which meant the seizure and sale of goods. As Barton explained:

> I was awakened about two in the morning by two men riding into the yard at Echunga, and on my asking their business, was informed that they were bailiffs, come to take possession on behalf of the Bank.[182]

The bank was owed £5140, of which £4000 was Barton's mortgage of his horses, which the bank could sell, so this was entirely unexpected. Barton believed Hagen was acting in tandem with his business partner John Baker, who was the bank's director. (Hagen, who was a widower, married Baker's sister Mary in January the following year.) Barton explained:

> At the time there was only one director of the Bank [John Baker], and an English friend of mine [Jacob Hagen] . . . who held as security for advances a mortgage on a portion of the Echunga land, married a sister of the said director, and determined to obtain this property, and I presume the reason of the action of the Bank was intended to carry out my friend's views. This could only be done by my being compelled to an insolvency, and step by step this object was carried out, and the whole of the Echunga estate passed for a small amount over [above] the mortgage to my English friend and school-fellow.

By seizing all the moveable assets of the Hack brothers, Hagen was making it impossible for them to pursue their 'equity of redemption' and repossess the Echunga estate. Hagen and the bank had moved in concert. On 9 February without warning, Hagen put in a 'warrant of distress', for rent owed. Hagen claimed rent had not been paid on his two mortgages – £597 10s for Barton and £62 10s for Stephen. Hagen notified the sheriff that he was the landlord and had a claim of over £600 for rent.[183] Hagen was relying on the curious last paragraph of the mortgage which referred to the Hacks as tenants, which enabled Hagen to claim for rent owing.

The bailiffs' late-night visit took place around 10 February for the purpose of making an inventory of the brothers' property. By law, the Hacks had five days to pay Hagen for the 'rent', or the goods would be forfeited, except £30 worth of bedding, clothes and tools.[184] Barton requested a delay and paid the expense of keeping possession of his goods.[185]

The sheriff was required to sell the goods, with Barton standing to lose everything. At this point Hagen stepped in. He told Barton he would purchase the furniture and some bullocks at the forthcoming sheriff's sale, if Barton paid him £100 by drawing a bill on the Hack family in England, payable to Hagen. The furniture and bullocks would belong to Hagen, but Barton could use them. Barton agreed and wrote to his mother asking for the money to pay Hagen.

The sale was advertised in the *Southern Australian*,[186] which stated that it would consist of stock, cows, crops, stacks of wheat and oats, ploughs, grindstones, saddlery and furniture – sofas, sideboards, tables, chairs, bookcases, books, pictures, beds, an iron bedstead, bed linen, plate (silver cutlery), glass, and earthenware.

Directly beneath this advertisement was one for the sale of goods belonging to Barton's cousin George Deane, who lived on the Meadows Survey, about four miles from Echunga Springs. This sale was to commence immediately after the Hacks'. Deane was also in debt to John Baker of the Auction Company, who had forced the sale.

Sale at Echunga

The sales under distress (for Hagen) and execution (for the bank) took place at Echunga on 20 February. The auctioneer was Bentham Neales, acting for the sheriff. Neales later said he had 'never had such an assemblage of people in the country'.

Commencing at 11 am, the sale turned out to be a dramatic affair. Barton's solicitor William Bartley had been owed £407 and in January had received security from the Hacks in the form of one stack of wheat and two stacks of oats from the recent harvest.[187] He had advertised these for sale at the 20 February auction and brought his own auctioneer, William Lambert. Bartley explained to Bentham Neales that the wheat and oats belonged to him and not to sell them, but Neales ignored him.

Neales conducted the sale for Hagen first, selling the wheat and oats for £152. This enraged Bartley, who believed they were worth £400. After the sale, Bartley took legal action against Hagen for damages. The case opened later in the year and it is the proceedings and documents from Barton's insolvency cases that enable events at the auction to be explained.

When the sale of furniture began, the onlookers noticed Hagen conferring with the auctioneer and a Mr William Robinson. Hagen then took various people aside and told them not to bid, because Robinson was buying the furniture and other things for Barton's family. Of 100 lots, eighty were purchased by Robinson. People were even prevented from going into some of the rooms, and as James Hurtle Fisher said later, 'If Mr Robinson gave a nod, down went the hammer'. Robinson was bidding, but Hagen was paying with money drawn on Barton's family in England.

Hagen interfered with his own auction – and with the bank's. People later complained about the way the sale had been conducted and one onlooker was so dissatisfied that he did not purchase at all. People said the sale was too hasty; it was over in a few hours. In one room the contents were sold in two or three minutes.

Another complaint was that none of the goods fetched anything like their value. Under the sale for Hagen, Bartley's grain stacks and a variety of articles were sold for a total of £217. The sheriff's sale for the bank produced £256. One witness said the grapes were worth £250 but only fetched £20, which they considered was unfair. Hagen was not only helping Barton with furniture; he also gave Barton some of the grapes.

Stephen Hack was also taken care of, but once again Hagen was not using his own money. Hagen bought goods to the amount of £100 with money drawn on Bessie's brother-in-law, Russell Skey in England, as a way of making them available for Stephen. One witness said all of Stephen Hack's furniture had been bought for only £7. The witness later seized it because of money due to him, and sold it in Adelaide for between £60 and £80.

After the sale, the sheriff's office seized everything else on the Hacks' property, except those items purchased for the family. The bank took the horses mortgaged to them and the Auction Company took the bullocks and stallions mortgaged to them.

On the same day, George Deane's property was sold up, realising less than he had paid for it. He was another casualty of the financial crisis and the Auction Company.

Hagen takes the estate

Now that the brothers had no means of paying off Hagen's mortgages and no assets with which to raise more loans, Hagen foreclosed. As a preliminary, on 9 March the Hack brothers had to execute a 'deed of partition', no doubt at Hagen's behest.[188] The partition divided up the thirty-five sections of the Three Brothers Survey, giving Barton twenty sections and Stephen fifteen. This was to apportion the debts in terms of the various mortgages. Barton's twenty sections included all those mortgaged to Fisher, Brown and Morphett. They were unimproved sections, mostly along the Western Creek. Stephen's fifteen sections were the more valuable land, including Echunga Springs, Echunga Gardens and the dairy on Echunga Creek.

Hagen immediately foreclosed, acting before the brothers declared themselves legally insolvent. He did this because, once they were insolvent, their property would be surrendered and sold on behalf of all their creditors. Barton's sections were of little value to Hagen as they were encumbered by the first mortgage to Fisher, Brown and Morphett. Since Hagen's London business was a creditor, it is likely that Hagen did not want to be in possession of land that was of interest to Barton's other creditors. So Hagen had Barton's land transferred to Peter Peachy, an Adelaide land agent.[189]

The valuable land was in Stephen's name and on 10 March, Hagen took possession. First, Stephen conveyed an 'equity of redemption' in relation to his £1000 mortgage with Hagen. This meant Stephen could not redeem his land, even if he paid the mortgage. Next, Stephen worked out an arrangement relating to his brother-in-law Russell Skey. At the auction, Hagen had purchased goods for Stephen with money drawn on Skey and payable to Hagen. Hagen now agreed to convey four sections of Stephen's land to Skey, the four sections being to the west of Echunga Springs and including the dairy on Echunga Creek. As Skey was not planning to come to Australia, this was a way of allowing Stephen and Bessie to have some land to farm on. Barton later said that about forty goats and a plough purchased for Skey at the auction were for Stephen's use.

Stephen had fifteen sections, so Hagen now stood to get the remaining eleven prize sections, including Echunga Springs, for the mortgage of £1000. Barton in his memoirs claimed that the Echunga estate by that time had cost about £17,000, presumably counting the land, stock, orchard, vineyard, crops, wages and improvements, so Hagen got an amazing bargain.

Barton was now at Hagen's mercy. Hagen agreed that Barton could rent a small, unimproved section of the estate and stay in the two-storey house for a while, but only until he could build something on the land he was renting. Hagen was not acting out of kindness. He would get rent from Barton for this small area of land, plus the benefit of any improvements Barton made to it. Also, Hagen knew he could remove Barton at any time. Barton was hoping to grow wheat and sell this to pay the rent, but this was a forlorn hope. Hagen now owned everything that Barton and Stephen had built up on the Echunga Springs estate over the years. As Barton explained later:

> Time was the thing required, but this luxury was unobtainable. The people who were around me at Echunga could never be convinced that the property was lost to me irrecoverably, but believed that I should someday possess my own again. Judge Cooper was sometimes a guest at Echunga, and little thought when he talked over with me the new Insolvency Law he was meditating for the colony that I should be one its victims.[190]

On 9 March a new settler named Samuel Davenport passed by Echunga Springs and reported that John Barton Hack and his family were living there, also Stephen Hack and his wife and the Watson parents. Davenport was on his way to Watergate, where he was to purchase George Deane's property and call it Battunga.[191] This is the last reference to the Hacks all living at Echunga Springs.

In the midst of all this upheaval, Barton must have recognised the irony of the situation when on 17 March he won numerous prizes for his produce at the annual Agricultural and Horticultural Show in Adelaide. His oats won a silver medal, value two guineas. It was awarded to Messrs Stocks and Co., who had purchased the oats in February, but the judges acknowledged that the oats were grown by Mr J.B. Hack. Barton won prizes in his own name – for the best peas (one sovereign), grapes (£1), giant rhubarb (10s) and apples (10s).[192]

In April Walter Duffield moved onto the estate with his family, as manager for Hagen. Duffield had been Hagen's manager on the Little Para property and would now take over Barton and Stephen's farm with its orchard and vineyard, the 'showpiece of the colony'.

Insolvency

Barton waited until he had divided the estate with Stephen, and then on 25 March he made a 'Declaration of Insolvency' in the Supreme Court.[193] This was announced in the Government Gazette for all to see. On 29 March Stephen also declared himself insolvent.[194] He was described as a 'farmer and cattle dealer' and his address as Echunga Springs.[195]

The story can now be followed through the eyes of a twenty-year old neighbour, Margaret May, writing to her aunt Maria Morris in England. Barton rented land to Joseph and Hannah May on Western Creek, where they lived with their eleven children in five slab cottages grouped together like a little village.[196] The Mays were strict Quakers and had survived the financial crash by being scrupulously careful. Their children worked the farm instead of paid labour; they did not indulge in land speculation, and consequently were thriving.

Margaret May wrote regularly to her aunt until the aunt's death in 1880, but only two years of the letters have survived, 1843–1845.[197] Margaret's letters show that by April 1843, Hagen had possession of the Hack brothers' property and was often up at Echunga. On 12 April Margaret's sister Maria married Henry Phillips in the Quaker meeting house, which was Barton Hack's former dairy on Western Creek. The day before the wedding,

Margaret's brothers took a horse and cart and went to Barton's former property to get fruit and flowers for the wedding, 'J. Hagen having kindly given us leave to have what we liked'.

Later in the day the couple drove off to Stephen Hack's house, which 'J. Hagen had kindly offered them for a week'. This was Stephen's house in the garden at Echunga Springs. He and Bessie had been evicted, and Barton and Bbe, although part of the small Quaker community, were not invited to the wedding.

Henry Phillips was one of Barton's other creditors, and as soon as he returned from his honeymoon he submitted his claim to the Insolvency Court. Henry and his brother George had an ironmongery business in Barton's old property in Hindley Street and Barton owed them for hardware supplies. On 27 April Henry Phillips lodged a claim for £47 8s 10d for the firm of Hack, Watson & Company, and £38 14s 1d for the firm of J.B. and S. Hack, a total of £86 2s 11d. This allowed Henry Phillips to start proceedings against Barton, which meant that Barton would go to court rather than be imprisoned for debt. Barton went before the Insolvency Court and asked for time to disclose his full estate and effects, and was given until 9 June.

Stephen Hack goes to jail

When Stephen was evicted in March 1843, Bessie was heavily pregnant and their daughter Julia was only two years old. Stephen took up the land purchased for Russell Skey and started farming. He and Bessie moved into a small house, probably the wooden dairy on Echunga Creek, as Stephen's address a year later was Echunga Dairy.[198]

A few weeks after declaring himself insolvent, Stephen was thrown into jail for debt, as no creditor had come forward to start the proceedings. Margaret May claimed he was there for two weeks. He was still there on 21 May when Bessie gave birth to a son, Wilton, and three days later when bailiffs arrived at his home and seized his furniture. The story was told later by Stephen's son Wilton in his autobiography:[199]

> Father had been away from home with cattle somewhere, and when he returned to Adelaide he found the Hack Brothers were utterly

ruined. He was seized for debt and put in prison, and when I was only 3 days old the bailiffs came to our house at Echunga; they took <u>all the furniture</u> out of the house; all the cooking utensils, pictures, and turned out the boxes and drawers, heaped all the clothes on the floor and carted them off. Two men took hold of the mattress Mother and I were lying on, lifted us off the bedstead on to the floor and carried <u>that</u> away also . . . As there was nothing to be gained by keeping Father in prison, he was liberated.

Wilton said Stephen blamed Barton for this and the two brothers fell out.

Uncle Barton managed to protect his own home and personal belongings and this was the cause of the coolness that lasted between them the rest of their lives. Father had always allowed Barton to manage everything, and until the crash came knew nothing as to how the firm stood. And he argued that if Barton could manage to protect his own house, he should have protected my Mother in the state she was. After this Uncle Barton did what he could and in later years was always kind to me, but I could never forget.

Margaret May and her mother had visited Bessie two days after the bailiffs called, and were shocked:

[We] found the poor woman in as forlorn a place as you can well conceive, it was a wooden house that let the wind in all directions. She was sitting in the bedroom which contained a bed laid on the ground at one end, two of a kind of chest – with drawers . . . a trunk and a rocking chair. She . . . looked very sadly and the children looked very delicate. Her nephew [George Wilton] who came out with them on account of his health, has been confined to his bed for two or three weeks and is still very ill, he is consumptive, they have no bedroom for the poor boy who has been obliged to lie in the sitting room, which is used as a kitchen, and the noise has kept him back very much. We had not since we left England seen a house that bore such marks of such poverty.

The bitterness between Barton and Stephen lasted many years – and perhaps Stephen never really forgave Barton for the misfortune they endured. Over a year later, Margaret reported a conversation in which Bessie explained why she and Stephen had not moved back with Barton and Bbe after they were evicted:

> She [Bessie] says the most miserable part of her life, was the time she lived with the [Hacks] after she landed. Their £1800 of goods and money were seized, and they were left without a shilling and no means of getting one ... J[ohn] B[arton] and B[be] considered S[tephen] and herself as interlopers and treated them as such, though well aware they had not the means of getting a single meal out of their house. No one could tell what she suffered from being in such humiliating dependence; and the sight of her husband treated by his brother as if he were a child and not capable of judging for himself was almost beyond endurance. Yet poor S. owing to the peculiar state of affairs then, was obliged to bear it ... her wretched sojourn in J.B.H.'s family made her prize a house of her own, though it was almost without furniture and dismally forlorn.

Stephen was now destitute and wrote to England for assistance. He turned to 'carrying' with a bullock team he drove himself, and farming on a small scale with 150 cattle, some horses, pigs and goats and he planted some crops.[200] Bessie was unused to domestic concerns, but tried to do her best.

Barton's 160-acre farm

Hagen allowed Barton to stay on for a while in Echunga Springs but Barton had to establish a new farm on the 160 acres he rented from Hagen. Barton took up two sections of land, each of eighty acres, which were completely unimproved, later giving his address as the Three Brothers Farm. This must have been south of Echunga Springs, because the Mays visited it on their way to Stephen's at the Echunga dairy. He set out to build a house on this land, and for the beginnings of a farm he had twenty-five cattle (mostly belonging to his sons), one horse and two pigs.[201]

Margaret May and her mother visited Bbe at Echunga Springs, and found her with Rachel Deane and her daughter Ellen. The Deanes had lost everything and young Ellen was staying to help Bbe, along with twelve-year-old Louisa Hack. Bbe had always been resilient, but now she was really tested. Running a household in those days was very time-consuming, and Bbe had lost the four or five servants she was accustomed to. With no labour-saving devices, it took hours to prepare a meal, bake the bread, fetch the water, clean the house and make and mend clothes.

Barton said later Bbe and Louisa could not manage the washing, and 'often had to leave it for a long time with the washerwoman for want of the few shillings to fetch it home'. On top of all this there were the smaller children to look after. In May 1843 Charles, the youngest was only a year old, and Bbe was pregnant again. Margaret May noted:

> JB [Barton] and B[ridget] look ten years older than they did two years ago, the former has been very unwell lately, and it is no wonder, considering how he has been harassed, his examination [for insolvency] is not yet finished... Of what a great deal of misery J.B.H. has been the cause, he is the most unscrupulous man I ever knew...

Margaret May had a sharp tongue, and her attitude to Barton and Bbe was coloured by her fondness for Stephen, whose side she took firmly in this dispute. Margaret wrote to her aunt cryptically using only initials, and said the letters were 'not for the edification of the public'. Her aunt must have ignored this, however, because she made copies of the letters,[202] and when they reached England, Margaret's criticisms of Barton and his family came to the ears of other Quakers, including Gates Darton. This damaged the reputation of Barton and his family in Quaker circles, although later Henry Watson tried to correct some of the rumours spread by Margaret May.

Margaret May's behaviour was not in the spirit of Quakerism, but despite this Barton remained fond of her parents. The Quakers in South Australia were in general friendly and tolerant to Barton and his family, and relaxed the Quaker rules of behaviour. They could have expelled Barton for insolvency, but they did not. Nor did they expel Jacob Hagen when he married out, or when he behaved unethically in his business dealings.

Barton and Stephen's insolvency cases

Barton's insolvency case resumed on 19 May before Judge Cooper, Barton's friend who had written the new insolvency laws.

Richard Newland of the Bank of Australasia and John Baker of the Auction Company were appointed as assignees of Barton's estate and effects. Barton gave a full statement of his debts as well as money owed to him, and was examined about various items, mainly stock.

The examination resumed on 9 June. Barton stated that the balance of the whaling adventure was against him, and he had about seven acres in Chichester Gardens still unsold. Hagen had the deeds to that land. Barton said his interest in the Echunga property should be valued at £2000 'beyond the mortgages' and he had expected the crops at the sale to have realised at least £1000.

Barton had a long list of creditors, including his former servants and employees. One of the servants was given some silver before the sheriff's sale. Samuel Mason, Stephen's former overseer, sued the Hacks for unpaid wages. At the instigation of Mason, further sheriff's sales took place on 21 and 28 June.

At the end of the year Barton was listed as having debts of £24,156 and assets of £16,196, leaving a gap of £7960.[203] His insolvency case dragged on for years and was always hanging over his head. Any assets acquired later on, including his inheritance in England, were forfeited. According to the insolvency papers, the last payment to creditors was in 1859.

Stephen Hack also had to face the insolvency court, and while in prison he petitioned for relief. This was heard in the Supreme Court in July, and on 18 August there was a meeting of his creditors. At the end of the year Stephen was listed as having debts of £8956 and assets of £6876, a difference of £2080.[204] Stephen's case also dragged on, with the final payment made in 1849.

The final act in the Echunga drama took place in 1847. Barton still had an 'equity of redemption' in regard to the mortgage to Fisher, Brown and Morphett, which theoretically allowed him to repay the mortgage and regain the land. In December that year the Insolvency Court sold this right and Hagen snapped it up for £5. He then paid off the £2000 mortgage and Peachy's role ceased as his agent holding that land in trust for him. Hagen was then in possession of the whole of the Hack brothers' estate, in a process that smacks of cold-blooded calculation throughout and fully justifies the suspicions Barton expressed in his memoirs.

Even at the time, there was a general feeling that some of Hagen's actions were discreditable, as subsequent court cases show.

Bartley v. Hagen

In August 1843 another court case arose out of the Hack brothers' insolvency. William Bartley, Barton's solicitor, had seen his stacks of wheat and oats sold at the sheriff's sale on 20 February, and took action against Jacob Hagen. The case came to court on 21 and 22 August 1843 in the Supreme Court before Judge Cooper and a jury. A full account was later published in the *Southern Australian* and the *Register* and read by the colonists with great interest.

William Bartley accused Hagen of being collusive and deceitful in the sale and asked for damages of £1000. He was represented by James Hurtle Fisher. Charles Mann for Hagen responded that there had been no collusion and that Hagen had purchased goods for the Hacks to protect them from 'being turned out upon the world, shirtless, naked, and destitute as savages'. Judge Cooper, in summing up, suggested that Hagen's desire to buy furniture for the Hacks was praiseworthy, but he had no right to take the stacks. The jury gave a verdict for Bartley of £350 damages.

Hagen was not happy with this outcome and in October his lawyer asked for a retrial. Mann said Hagen was owed £400 rent from Barton and £100 from Stephen. The ground had now shifted from 'interest for rent' to the rent charged in the last clause of the mortgage. Even Judge Cooper seemed confused by now, saying it was a 'very difficult case', but granted a retrial.

The case opened again, with Judge Cooper and a new jury. Bartley and Hagen again called witnesses to support their cases. The jury said Hagen had been guilty of improper conduct and found for Bartley, with damages of £400. The trial was reported in full on 3 November 1843 in the *Southern Australian*, which said the case had 'formed quite a *cause célèbre* in South Australia'.

Barton in poverty

Towards the end of the year Barton was struggling to make his 160 acres into a farm, and did not expect a return from it for over a year. He had no labour except for his four sons, the eldest fifteen and the youngest eight. They had a small dairy and the boys were milking and managing the cows and driving the team of bullocks. They were making only ten to fifteen shillings a week from the dairy and barely subsisting.

In a letter to Gates, Barton said they were running short of clothing for the children and the family was often without meat, which on top of hard manual labour was a 'severe privation'. Barton's situation was so bad that he had to do something he now found 'painful and humiliating' – ask the family in England to send money to buy food until they could reap their first harvest. Barton hoped this could be an advance on his share of his father's estate when it was finally divided. He believed if he could get £100 it would last the 15 months until the harvest and after that they would be capable of supporting themselves easily.

On 4 December Bbe gave birth to Francis (later known as Frank). The Hacks' friend Dr John Woodforde attended her free of charge. Hagen had given the Hacks notice to quit Echunga Springs and had stopped giving them provisions, which Barton thought was an attempt to starve them out. They had stayed put until Bbe's confinement, and would have been forced out earlier if not for the intervention of Joseph May. 'We found in our sore distress Jos May and his wife very kind sympathising friends, and we shall always feel grateful to them', Barton wrote to Gates. Their new house was not finished, because Barton had run out of money, but Hagen insisted they move.

Chapter 20

Desperation

In the middle of 1843 Barton made some wine, the first in the colony. He tried to make a farm out of virgin bush, with only his young sons to help him. In the midst of his troubles he received an angry letter from Gates Darton about money owing, but this was put aside when Maria Hack died. Barton was forced out of Echunga Springs and moved into a half-finished house in the bush. He ran out of money for food, the children went barefoot and they all became ill. In June 1844 they were forced to leave Echunga and move back to Adelaide. Stephen Hack farmed his land and built a stone house near the old dairy on Echunga Creek. He took a partner, Thomas Corder, for his farm and carrying business.

Barton makes wine
In 1843 Barton Hack was the first person in the colony to make wine. At the beginning of the year, before Hagen took possession of his property, Barton wrote to his mother:

> We have a noble show of grapes in the vineyard and are likely to have some tons for sale. We have planted out about 3000 fresh vines this season and will in a few years have to begin making wine. Though till [until] fruit is cheap and plentiful it would pay better to sell it, or to make raisins.

Some of these vines were the first in the colony, having been acquired from Sydney in 1837, planted in Chichester Gardens, and later transplanted to Echunga. Other vines were brought in from Hobart and probably from South Africa. His grapes were Sweetwater (a white grape) and other varieties.

At the sheriff's auction on 20 February, Hagen had purchased some of the grapes for Barton, which were still unripe and on the vine. These were among those used later to make wine. Hagen took possession of the estate, but on 17 May the *Register* noted: 'A correspondent informs me that Mr John Barton Hack is now gathering grapes, of which he is about to make wine, an article destined ere long to be one of the staples of the colony'.[205]

Shortly after this report, Barton made a small quantity of wine, and in the bankruptcy proceedings in November he was credited with £20 for grapes made into wine.[206] This was confirmed by the horticulturist George McEwin, who wrote in December:[207]

> The plant was first introduced into South Australia by Mr John Barton Hack, in 1837, who brought a few cuttings from Van Diemen's Land [actually Sydney]. These have been propagated extensively at Mr Hack's garden at Echunga, in the Mount Barker district, and the rapidity of their growth has been the subject of general remark among all visitors to that beautiful place. There are now several thousand plants in full bearing, and Mr Hack, during the last season, in addition to a large supply of fruit to the Adelaide market, made a small quantity of wine.

McEwin was the gardener to Barton's rival horticulturist, George Stevenson, and he followed closely what people were growing in the colony. Barton's wine was white, later called a 'hock'. His vineyard was on the hill behind his two-storey house, and today a stone wall, which was part of a large above-ground wine cellar built after Barton left the property, is still there.[208] Two vineyards are now on Barton's former land, Argyle Estate, next to the old orchard, and further up the road sits Ironstone Estate, managed by Nepenthe.

Barton having made the wine, Jacob Hagen and his manager William Duffield rushed to take the credit. In January the following year, the *Register* reported: 'About 250 gallons of wine have, we understand been made at Mount Barker this season [i.e. Barton's 1843 wine], of the lateral shoots of the vine . . . several persons have tasted the wine and pronounced it very good'.[209]

Wine is usually made around May to June and in 1844 Duffield produced his first vintage, from Barton's vines. At the end of that year the *Register* reported: 'Duffield has we hear, some wine . . . on Mr Jacob Hagen's property . . . this wine is highly spoken of by competent judges, and in the course of a year or two, wine making in the colony will, we have no doubt, become general'.[210]

In February 1845 Duffield sent a case of 'Echunga Hock' (the 1844 wine) to Queen Victoria in England.[211] Duffield wrote to Lord Stanley, Secretary of State for the Colonies, suggesting that 'Her Majesty might graciously condescend to taste the first produce of this country'. Duffield was thereby implying that this was the first wine to be produced in South Australia, despite his knowing that Hack produced wine in 1843, and that he was using Hack's vines.

Jacob Hagen also wanted the glory. The *Register* reported: 'To Mr Hagen belongs the credit of the first successful attempt at South Australian wine-making, and from what we hear, his vineyard bids fair to return wines of first-rate excellence'.

This 1844 vintage was exhibited at the Agricultural and Horticultural Society Show in Adelaide in February 1845. Duffield labelled the wine 'Hock' but the *Register* disagreed, saying 'it has none of the character of a Rhenish wine; but it was pleasant in taste, and gives a pleasing promise of really good South Australian wine'.

Barton had earlier shared an interest in vine-growing with his brother-in-law Henry Watson, a chemist. Henry had given a lecture on the cultivation of the vine to the South Australian Literary and Scientific Association in October 1840.[212] Nobody had produced wine in South Australia at that time, and Henry urged the establishment of a wine industry to boost exports. A week after his talk, he set up the Association for the Introduction of Vines, and arranged the purchase of 57,000 vine cuttings from South Africa, which were delivered a year later. Barton almost certainly procured some of his Echunga vines from this source.

Gates loses patience

Barton's struggles following Hagen's seizure of the property meant little to Gates Darton, who by this time had run out of patience with his unlucky and at times unscrupulous brother-in-law. On 16 May 1843 he wrote a letter to Barton, in which he made his feelings more than clear. Gates's anger was triggered by the money Barton still owed for the books sent to Australia. 'I am unwilling to believe', Gates wrote, 'thou really considers thou has a claim upon me for a single penny, much less for £300'.

Gates said he had staked his property and credit to the utmost for Barton, and now needed to set out the facts of the case.

Gates reminded Barton that in 1835 he had provided money for the three preliminary land orders, on which Barton paid only interest. Then in 1836 Barton sailed, leaving large debts for Gates to pay, although these were unexpectedly repaid when the Smith brothers purchased Barton's share of the currier business.

In 1837 Gates received drafts for £3584, mainly from Launceston, which were partly paid by Stephen's inheritance, but still meant that, 'I was obliged <u>again</u> to advance ... every available farthing I possessed ... being at one time liable ... for £1800 to £2000, and I was also obliged to sell the rural acres'.

Gates then burst out: 'How on the other hand, hast thou served me!' In 1838, Gates wrote, all his available capital was advanced to meet bills from Australia, so that when he had to go into business on his own, he did so on disadvantageous terms. 'Emigrate I could not for <u>you</u> had bound me to England'.

Gates described in intricate detail all the problems Barton had given him, and the money owing for the books. Gates was particularly incensed about his one town acre: Barton had done nothing to rent, sell, or exchange it for something better, and this was 'cruel and unjust'. Gates believed he was entitled to a share in the profit Barton had made on the preliminary town acres, just as he had given Barton and Stephen a two-thirds share of the profit on the rural acres. 'I say ... that justice, to say nothing of gratitude, would accord me a sum considerably beyond the £300'.

Gates concluded by hoping there would come a time when there would be no cloud between them, and signed it 'thy affectionate brother'. He sent a copy to Uncle John Barton, and kept a copy for himself with the ledgers and other records of his transactions with Barton.

Barton wrote to his uncle acknowledging Gates's claim to the £300, but explained that he could do nothing, as he was insolvent. 'I am helpless in the matter', Barton wrote, 'I am truly grieved to be the occasion of embarrassment to Gates'. By December 1843 the family in England knew about Barton's desperate situation, but they had a more immediate concern – Maria Hack was dying. The £300 was now academic, because after Maria's death, the family trust could be distributed. Maria died on 4 January 1844 in Bevois Hill, Southampton. She was sixty-six and the cause of death was 'decay of nature'.

Maria's will had been made out in March 1842. It favoured Tom, who had financial difficulties, and left virtually nothing to Barton and Stephen, the two insolvents. Maria did not have much to leave, as most of her late husband's estate was still in the family trust. She left her shares and the copyright in her books to her three daughters Elizabeth Bliss, Ellen Knott and Margaret Darton. She left her furniture and household effects to Thomas. The residue of her estate was to be invested and the interest paid to Thomas during his life time.

With Maria's death, John Barton and Halsey Janson as trustees could now distribute the family trust. They did not move quickly however, and first they had to deal with Barton and Stephen's creditors in England and South Australia.

By the middle of 1844, Barton had learned of his mother's death and that she had left him nothing. He wrote to Gates:

> No one in England can judge correctly of our conduct here, for certainly there has been nothing in colonization to equal it, all even the most cautious of my contemporaries has failed, and only those who began after the crisis remain in business.

Barton evicted

In January 1844, at the time of Maria's death, Barton and his family moved out of Echunga Springs and onto the land they were renting. Their house was not finished, and Margaret May wrote that it was on the side of a hill and had only four rooms in which to house Barton and Bbe, their nine children and Ellen Deane.

Barton could only afford to put a roof over one room, and they put up carpets, bedspreads and oil cloths to keep out the rain. The rooms had only iron gratings for windows and the sitting room had no fireplace. They were cold and wet in winter, and in the hot weather they could hardly breathe as there was no ventilation.

The Deane family had moved to a little hut on Hagen's land. George Deane had entered into partnership with Stephen Hack in the 'bark trade', which entailed George stripping the bark off the trees and Stephen carting it to town where he sold it for tanning.

Margaret reported that Jacob Hagen had married Mary Baker on 23 January 1844, and they were spending their honeymoon in Stephen Hack's old house. Margaret said John Baker was a 'vulgar, disagreeable man, but we hear the sister is an amiable young lady and would do very well for a wife for him [Hagen] out here, but people smile at the idea of his taking her to England'. The implication was clear: Miss Baker would not be good enough for the folks back home.

In February Margaret reported that Barton's family had only enough wheat left to last three months, and so little milk that they had to give up cheese-making. Margaret said Louisa instead of running wild with her brothers was now a complete drudge, and with so many little children there was a great deal to do. Margaret's parents were kinder to the Hacks, and when the Quaker two-month meeting was held in their parlour on 3 March, Barton and Bbe with the two older boys, William and Edward, were amongst those attending.

Later that month Margaret reported that her parents had gone to visit the Hacks. She said Ellen Deane was about to go down to Adelaide with her family and then Louisa 'will have to do all that is done, her Mama [Bbe] says she has enough to do to take care of the little children and mend the clothes'.

Margaret said the Hacks' fifty goats had been taken away. The goats had been sold at the auction but not collected, and were being milked for the babies. Bessie's nephew George Wilton allowed the Hacks to use some of his, but when he went to collect them, Bbe was angry. 'That is the way they go on', Margaret wrote, 'the very few friends they have, they treat so oddly. Barton's troubles have made him so stern and severe that the poor children seem almost afraid of him'.

Margaret's parents then visited Stephen and Bessie.

> She and S.H. were as usual in very good spirits, though the latter was lying on the bed completely knocked up with a 200 mile journey to the North, during most of the way he could only get brackish water ... and it has made him quite ill, but he sticks to his carrying

and is spoken well of by everyone. He has just had a little money from England, so altogether they live pretty comfortably.

Stephen and Bessie had been living in the old dairy on Echunga Creek, but at some stage during 1843–1844 Stephen built a stone house nearby, perhaps with money from Bessie's family in England. Stephen's address was the Echunga Dairy and the land he farmed (which belonged to Skey) was known as The Old Dairy Farm. When Russell Skey died in 1844, the farm was advertised as having 'an excellent new and substantially built stone house' with thatched roof and wooden floors, a large living room and two bedrooms. It also had a detached kitchen with two servants' bedrooms, a wooden dairy, stockyards, cow-house and stables.[213]

The farm was later purchased by Edward Kavanagh, who arrived in the colony in 1846.[214] Decades later a letter in the *Advertiser* said 'The Old Dairy' was Barton Hack's house, and this error has been repeated by local historians.[215] Ed Kavanagh's grandson Pat Kavanagh said the house was a stone and lime construction and they carted marble from Macclesfield and burnt the lime on the property.[216] The Kavanagh family still owns this land, and in 1984, at the anniversary of the death of John Barton Hack, the house was still intact, but today only the walls are standing.

Stephen was more comfortable in this house, and Barton's struggles also eased slightly when he received £50 from his sister Elizabeth Bliss and her husband in England. Another relief was that he and Bbe had been reconciled with Henry and Charlotte Watson. Henry wrote to Gates Darton that Barton and Bbe had spent a few days with them at Port Adelaide and were 'tolerably well in health and spirits'.

Henry said the Hacks' farm was unfenced and 'how they are to exist til it becomes productive is to me a mystery'. Henry could not help them financially and was having trouble getting Charlotte's inheritance sent from England.

In March Barton had no money left at all. He stopped work on the farm and used his bullock team to carry wheat to Adelaide, which brought in 16s to 20s a week. With his bullock team tied up, he could not plough for crops and was so worried that he could not rest or digest his food, and developed an ulcerated leg. In April 1844 Margaret May reported that all the farmers were as 'poor as church mice'. Stephen was busy with his carrying business and William helped him drive the bullock drays. Barton's house was so cold that Bbe had developed rheumatism.

Stephen Hack regularly visited the Mays and told them he was going to continue farming on Skey's land, having made an arrangement with Thomas Corder, one of the Quakers in the district. Stephen would continue to drive the bullock dray to town, and Corder would work the farm and have a share in the crops, the carrying business and the goats.

On 12 April the Mays called on Bbe and found that Barton's leg had become an 'ugly, large wound' and he was confined to bed for a week. Barton later told Gates that when the bad weather came, the house was flooded except for the room with a roof over it. 'The boys had no shoes and got sadly lame', he wrote, 'I could not bear to see them go into the milking yard on cold mornings nearly to their knees in mud and in short we got all into a sickly way, and no wonder'. (Those 'cold mornings' were about 5°C.)[217]

At the end of April Henry Watson came up to Mount Barker and tried to persuade Barton to give up the land. On 5 May the Quaker two-monthly meeting was held at the Mays' house and the only attendees apart from the May family were William Hack and George Sanders and two of his sons. They stayed to dinner afterwards and Margaret reported to her aunt that they quite enjoyed William's company.

> He used to be a very stupid, awkward boy, owing in great measure to his being very tall for his age, he has gradually transformed into a sensible, agreeable and well-behaved lad; he is by far the most quiet of the whole batch and is much improved by the change in their circumstances, so indeed are all the children; they have now neither time nor opportunity for associating with the men [farm employees] as formerly.

On 16 June Barton and Bbe came to the Mays for the Quaker meeting and stayed for dinner, but it was a farewell visit. Barton did not want to give up the farm, but told Gates later:

> We ... could not continue to exist without some present help and I went to town as soon as I was able, to see Hagen and Hart. After much consideration I determined to give up Mount Barker ... Hart and Hagen had raised among some who had wished to assist us £65 which was expended by our friend Woodforde as trustee for the time in buying a team and drays to add to our other team.

Barton wrote that from the time of the auction in February 1843 until he left the farm, he had managed to raise about £170 and spent £120 on the farm, so he had kept his large family for more than a year on only £50, 'no easy task'. They left the farm about 18 June. William and Edward drove the two bullock drays; Alfred and Bedford drove the cows, Louisa rode the pony, and Barton and Bbe rode in a borrowed cart with the four younger children.

It must have been humiliating for the Hacks to leave their beloved Echunga in this way, stripped of their former wealth. Margaret May wrote to her aunt that the Hacks had been living in a little valley where no one could see them, which suited them better than living in Adelaide in such reduced circumstances. Now they had no choice, but they must have been grateful to their real friends like John Hart and John Woodforde, who had stood by them.

Barton and Stephen were now back where they started in 1837, earning their living as carriers with bullock teams, a rough occupation. Stephen was not going to stay however. He was making plans to return to England.

Chapter 21

Burra, Kapunda and gold

Barton Hack returned to Adelaide in June 1844 and found work carting ore by bullock teams from the newly discovered mines to the port. A few years later he was employed as a mine manager at Kapunda and then as a builder in Adelaide. In 1852, he visited the gold diggings in Victoria with his four older sons, and returned to Adelaide with 40 lbs of gold. He then commenced work as an accountant, firstly, for a lawyer and later for John Hart at his Port Adelaide mills. Stephen Hack and Bessie blamed Barton for their misfortunes, and in 1844 gave up their farm and returned to England.

Barton returns to Adelaide

In 1844 South Australia was still in a state of stagnation. The mother country seemed to have lost faith in the colony and was no longer sending out labourers and capital.[218] On the other hand, the production of wool and wheat was expanding and there were exciting new mineral discoveries. In 1842 silver was discovered at Glen Osmond in the Adelaide foothills and copper at Kapunda, forty-two miles north of Adelaide. By 1844 these minerals were being shipped to England.

Then in 1845 a shepherd discovered copper at Burra Burra, ninety miles north of Adelaide. This was an important find, and for the next two years revenue from the mines was enough to sustain the colony's economy.[219] By 1846, when the colony celebrated its tenth anniversary, the population was nearly 26,000.[220]

In his earlier life Barton would have been an enthusiastic investor in these mines, but in 1844 he was just a carrier with two bullock teams, transporting ore from the Glen Osmond silver mines to the port for export. He rented a house on the south side of town with a paddock for the children's cows, and wrote to Gates in August that they were living more comfortably than they had for a long time. Each bullock team made from eight to ten shillings a day and he planned to buy a third team with the £50 he had been sent by his sister Elizabeth and her husband George Bliss.

Bullock-driving was a 'sadly rough employment' and Barton regretted it for his boys. He wanted Alfred and Bedford to have some schooling, but they were such valuable helpers that this was impossible. Bbe Hack wrote to Margaret Darton that sixteen-year-old William looked like a man and was a steady character, while Louisa at thirteen had the figure of a woman, but her character was still unpolished. Louisa was no longer the household drudge, since Bbe had taken on a young servant and hoped to employ another as soon as there was enough money.

Stephen leaves for England

Stephen Hack was busy on the Old Dairy Farm, but he was planning to leave the colony, probably because Bessie was not cut out to be the wife of a poor farmer and perhaps also because Stephen and Bessie were still angry with Barton, whom they blamed for their situation. This is understandable, but Barton was not solely responsible: the 'crash' of 1841–1842 had also contributed to their downfall. Stephen should perhaps have accepted some responsibility too. He had been naive and in some ways compliant, because he left all the business decisions to Barton, and did not question them. Henry Watson made the same mistake. Stephen had also run up substantial debts of his own when in England, which forced him to mortgage his half of the Echunga estate to Hagen.

Barton claimed later that Stephen had contributed to their problems by spending too much on cattle when he went to New South Wales with Hart in 1837, but this was a statement made in hindsight. At the time the cattle were purchased, Barton did not complain, and he used the profits from the cattle speculation to fund other ventures.

Margaret May wrote to her aunt that Bessie 'is always in good spirits, [but] she does not know how to do anything and would consequently be best near her friends. Stephen is, I think, less fitted for living in England; he is a bushman all over'. Margaret was very fond of Stephen and loved to hear him laugh: 'It is a most extraordinary noise, and resembles the noise of the laughing jackass more than anything else . . . thoughtless he used to be, but is no longer. His jokes and amusing tales . . . keep you laughing incessantly. I do hope we shall hear of his getting on well for he does deserve it'.

Stephen estimated he would have only £40 left when he arrived in England, while Bessie feared some of her former acquaintances in England would look down on her now she was poor. She was very concerned about her nephew George Wilton, who was staying behind and was frequently ill. The farm belonged to Russell Skey, but Thomas Corder and another partner took over running the farm, keeping a half share in its profits, with Stephen then passing his share in the farm and some cows to George Wilton. George later returned to England and died in 1848 of asthma and consumption.[221]

Margaret May wrote that Barton's boys were getting out of hand, reporting that William and Edward had travelled up to Echunga to help Stephen and were sent out with three bullocks, 'but the boys went to Duffields, got intoxicated and lost the bullocks . . . Those young Hacks seem bad enough for anything . . . S. longs to give each one a good thrashing as a legacy just before he leaves, I think it would be the best thing for them'.

On 14 August 1844, Stephen and Bessie, their two children and a servant, left for England on the *Augustus*, captained by their old friend John Hart. Edward Philcox, who was the ship's surgeon, travelled with his little daughter Anna. His presence was important for Bessie, who expected to be confined while on board. Stephen and Barton parted on bad terms, and Barton wrote to Gates: 'I hope you may be more fortunate in your intercourse with him than I have been', but added, 'Bessie has behaved nobly in their many troubles and has won our love and esteem'.

Back in England

Barton's sister Ellen, her husband John Knott and their four children returned to England not long after Stephen, with her fifth child, Charlotte, born on the voyage. Unfortunately the return to England didn't mend what was obviously a shaky marriage because soon after the couple separated. Ellen remained in England while John Knott returned to Australia. Uncle John Barton wrote to Gates in relation to winding up the family trust, informing him that John Knott had agreed to leave £1000 in Ellen's account. At the time, a married woman's property belonged to her husband, so Knott kept most of her inheritance.

Although Maria Hack had died in 1844, it was some time before the family trust was wound up and distributed. The trust was worth £23,736, with Barton and Stephen set to inherit £3341 each. In the event they received nothing: their inheritance was paid to the agent in Adelaide dealing with their insolvencies. At the end of his life, Barton noted sadly in his memoirs that had this sum come to him and Stephen two years earlier, it would have saved their Echunga estate.

Everyone in the family was waiting for their share of the property. Gates Darton was struggling with his ironmongery business and asked for a loan to tide him over. Uncle John refused the loan, but enclosed a cheque for £300, representing the money Gates was owed by Barton.

Adelaide and Echunga

Back in Adelaide, Barton and his sons were busy working as carriers. Henry Watson was still employed at the Customs Office, but in December 1844 he was forced to declare himself insolvent, as a consequence of the debts incurred earlier by Hack, Watson & Co. In May 1845 Henry and Charlotte moved from Port Adelaide to North Adelaide and Charlotte gave birth to a girl, Eliza Maria. A week later Bbe gave birth to a boy and named him George Bliss.

Margaret May's gossip about the wayward Hack children found its way to England – and returned. The following year Henry Watson wrote to Gates defending the family, pointing out that the gossip was malicious and that William was now the only son working as a bullock driver, and that Edward was at school in the country and Louisa was a fine young woman.

Barton heard that Joseph May had labelled him as dishonourable, but Joseph had forgotten ever using such an expression. 'I have and do love Joseph May and his wife in spite of the injuries

I think they have done us', Barton wrote Gates, 'for I do think they are well intentioned and pious people, but in respect to us, mistaken'. Barton said he did not like the young people in the May family, who kept aloof in a self-righteous way. In February 1847 Margaret May married the merchant George Phillips, whose brother Henry was married to her sister Maria. Barton told Gates her marrying 'that little whippersnapper George Phillips' and in a church rather than with the Quakers, would be trying for her parents.

Jacob Hagen continued to prosper. In 1845 Governor Grey established the Legislative Council and appointed Hagen as one of its members, although Grey ultimately regretted the appointment. In 1844 Hagen and his brother-in-law John Baker accused Grey of corruption, and their complaints to London resulted in Grey's transfer to New Zealand and his replacement by Governor Robe in 1845.[222]

Hagen was also one of the proprietors of the Adelaide Mining Company and in the Legislative Council supported private enterprise and opposed government interference for the duration of his term of office, until 1851. According to one historian, 'he helped his pastoral friends to retain their leases, yet as a member of the Destitute Board inveighed against the dependence of the poor on official charity'.[223]

In 1848 Hagen sold off subdivisions of two sections of the Hacks' old estate to establish the little town of Echunga. He also erected an inn (behind the present Hagen Arms Hotel), gave land for St Mary's Church of England, and in 1853 formed the district council, serving as chairman and clerk. In 1854 he sailed for England and did not return. Echunga Springs was left in charge of his agent, the Quaker George Sanders, who had been Barton's neighbour. Sanders's letter books were filled with grim stories of penny pinching, and on one occasion Hagen threatened Sanders himself with foreclosure for failing to evict the widow and six children of a deceased tenant whose payments had not faltered for twelve years.[224]

Hagen died in 1870 and his daughter Marianna inherited the Echunga estate. The land around Barton's old house was purchased by William Smith, who sold it in 1902 to G.V. Rothe. A descendant, Alan Rothe, married Smith's granddaughter Peg, and they still live close to Hack's old estate, while their son Terry Rothe lives on the spot where Barton had his house.

Kapunda

When the mining boom hit South Australia, Barton Hack knew most of the mine owners, including John Hart, John Baker, Jacob Hagen, Osmond and Lewis Gilles, John Brown and Edward Stephens, and this was to his advantage. In late 1845 the Burra mine opened and Barton was engaged to bring the first dray loads of copper down to the port. He had three bullock teams and worked with his sons but later with hired drivers. Early in the year he and Bbe moved close to Henry and Charlotte Watson in North Adelaide.

The following year, Barton was offered a job at the copper mine at Kapunda, moving up there but leaving his family in North Adelaide. Appointed as a manager, his role was to oversee the exploration of the lode immediately north of the Kapunda mine. Mining methods were primitive compared with those of today – men crawled through underground galleries carrying a candle held in a piece of clay, and hacked into the rocks.[225] In February 1847 Barton wrote to Gates from North Kapunda complaining that living in Kapunda was dull and that returning to his home in Adelaide for a visit felt like a holiday. He explained that his income from the mine and the carrying business would be about £300 for the year, and all his bullock drivers were hired men, as his sons were employed in other jobs, no longer working for their father.

By April 1847 the project in North Kapunda had failed to find copper, with Barton then employed by a London company to sink shafts on a promising lode on Allen's Creek, about two miles from Kapunda. This was not successful either, and the lode was abandoned.

Barton becomes a Methodist

At the age of forty-two, while at Kapunda, Barton became a Wesleyan Methodist and remained active in the Methodist church for the rest of his life. As he wrote later, 'I had all my previous life been attached to the Society of Friends, but my residence among the Wesleyan Cornish miners caused me to long for a more active and useful religious life'. Barton used experienced tin miners from Cornwall, who had arrived in South Australia during the mining boom. He continued: 'There were one or two local preachers whom I much esteemed ... and I became a member'. The Wesleyans were one of four branches of the Methodist church, which combined in 1900.[226]

Barton's conversion to Methodism was described many years later at his funeral.[227] The story was that while working at Allen's Creek mines, he met and became friends with the Reverend John Harcourt. Harcourt, who was looking for somewhere to hold his services, asked if the Methodists could use Barton's house. Barton agreed and soon after became a convert. The funeral service was told that:

> He saw now that the foundation of Christianity was not duty but love ... from that time onward, according to the testimony of those who knew him, a marked change came over his whole life ... there was a thoughtfulness, a gentleness, an almost unmanly tenderness quite unknown before.[228]

On his return to North Adelaide, Barton became associated with the Methodists there and became friendly with the Rev. Daniel James Draper, whom he regarded as one of the most valuable acquaintances of his life. In December 1849 Barton formally resigned from the Society of Friends.[229] In an eloquent letter of resignation he expressed his grief at parting. He said the Wesleyan meetings had been for him a means of religious rejuvenation and he had seen their good effect on himself and his family. The Friends noted his letter, and on 3 March 1850 the Hack family's names were 'erased'.

Barton remained an active Methodist, and was an original trustee of the Plympton North Methodist church, which opened in June 1856.[230]

Barton's partnership with Breeze

When his job as a mine manager ended in 1847, Barton joined a timber business in North Adelaide with Robert Breeze, a builder.

Barton lived in Melbourne Street and Breeze lived in nearby Pennington Terrace, where the timber yard was located. Barton and Breeze built Christ Church, in Palmer Place, North Adelaide, which was used as the cathedral until St Peter's was finished.[231] In May 1849, Robert Breeze died and Barton continued the business alone, but in 1851, 'the diggings [goldfields] took away most of the male population and I had to wind up at a great loss'. Once again, Barton had to face defeat, but he was not one to dwell on disappointments and began to consider the idea of going to the goldfields himself.

During this time Bbe gave birth to another baby, Jessie Maria, on 29 July 1848. It was her fourteenth child, the eleventh living, and it would be her last. She was forty-two. From 1850 on, the Hacks owned a house on the corner of Lefevre Terrace and Archer Street, North Adelaide. The rate assessment book in 1852 described it as a stone house with seven rooms. A few years later it was described as having 'a fine view of the hills' with eight rooms as well as a washhouse, outhouses, stable and an underground tank.[232]

Barton's children were growing up and some were at an age to marry. In 1849 seventeen-year-old Louisa married Patrick James Tod, a merchant, in Barton's house in North Kapunda. Tod had property in North Kapunda, but lived in Gawler.

Barton was living in Adelaide, but William aged twenty-one was also married in Kapunda, on 16 April 1850 to seventeen-year-old Grace Stanlake. Barton's fourth son, Bedford, left home in 1850 and went with the Kelling and Kirkman families to Finniss Flat (later called Ashbourne) to learn dairying.[233] That left about seven children at home in Adelaide. Around September 1851, Edward, twenty-one, married Elizabeth Hackett, a twenty-seven-year-old widow with a five-year-old daughter.[234]

Watson v. Torrens

Henry Watson was still employed in the Customs office, but struggled financially after becoming insolvent. In 1849 Henry lost his job in the Customs office after a dispute with his chief, the argumentative Robert Richard Torrens.

In May 1848 Torrens made complaints against James Laffer,

the warehouse keeper in the customs department. Henry Watson supported Laffer, with his suspension following some months later. Henry had to defend himself, and revealed that Torrens was often absent from his office and neglected his duties. The dispute raged on for months, with the population avidly following the details in the local papers. The press supported Henry Watson and described him as 'a gentleman sustaining the highest reputation for honour and integrity'. The *Gazette*, edited by George Stevenson, lampooned Torrens, who sued for libel, struck Stevenson and was charged with assault.[235]

Henry Watson's case was referred to the English authorities and a board of inquiry established, but he was not reinstated. He reverted to his original profession of chemist and druggist and opened a shop on the corner of Hindley and King William streets. The *Adelaide Times* reported that he 'has obtained in no common degree the general sympathy of all classes'.

Gold fever

At the end of 1851 gold was discovered in Victoria, and thousands left South Australia. Barton, determined to follow, left in February 1852 with his four oldest sons. Louisa was married, so Bbe was left alone in North Adelaide with the six younger children to fend for herself for most of that year.

Barton and his sons took with them three horses and a dray loaded with food and the equipment needed for surface mining. In his memoirs Barton described the journey, which took several weeks, as 'toilsome'. The route at the time was via Wellington on the River Murray, south along the coast, then inland to Victoria.

Although Barton took the coastal route, a new inland route was soon established across the Ninety Mile Desert with wells every twelve miles or so between Wellington and Bordertown. In February a gold escort, led by Police Commissioner Alexander Tolmer, followed this route and returned in March with over 5000 ounces of gold.[236] These two routes, along the coast and inland, would expose Barton to land in the south-east, which he would later take up for farming.

Barton and his sons arrived at the diggings in Bendigo on 1 April. In his reminiscences he wrote:[237]

We worked principally on Ironbark and Long Gully, and were more successful than many. Our permanent camp was on Bendigo Creek, near Golden Point [present-day Bullock St, Bendigo[238]]. In September, I returned overland with one of my sons [William] on horseback, following the track of the gold escort which had preceded us. In a few days we overtook them at Wellington on the Murray. We were able to secure about 40 pounds of gold as the result of our expedition.

As gold was valued then at about £3 8s an ounce in Adelaide,[239] forty pounds meant nearly £2000. Barton probably split this five ways with his sons, and while he was away he sent some gold back with the escort to Bbe, to support the family at home. The remainder may have been used to pay off any debts from the business with Breeze, and to re-establish himself.

While they were away, Edward's wife Elizabeth gave birth to a daughter in Adelaide. Barton and Bbe were now grandparents of a baby named baby Annie Mary. On their return from the diggings, Barton's older sons went their own way. William took up farming at Finniss Flats (now Ashbourne) near Strathalbyn. Edward and Bedford went to work for their uncle Stephen, who had returned to Australia and was running a large dairy property on the Murray near Albury, called Brocklesbury.[240] Alfred served an apprenticeship as a chemist with Messrs F.H. Faulding and Co., but later took up farming like his brothers, and in 1858 was in Strathalbyn with William.

As for the rest of the family, Louisa and her husband Patrick James Tod left South Australia around 1853[241] and returned to England. Barton's younger sons, Theodore, Charles and later Francis, went to John L. Young's school just off North Terrace, whose playground was where the State Library now stands.

Barton the accountant, 1852–1857

After returning from the goldfields, Barton found work as an accountant and loan broker with Alfred Atkinson, a rising lawyer in King William Street. He was living in Lefevre Terrace and still friends with John Hart, who owned the vacant acre next door. Captain Hart had taken the *Augustus* to England in

1844, married an Irish woman, Margaret Todd, and returned to Adelaide in 1845, after which he became involved in mining and other business activities. Hart was a member of the Legislative Council from 1851 to 1852 for the seat of Victoria, in the south-east of the province. In 1853 he stood for the seat again and in July 1854 Barton spoke in his support at the nomination meeting at Robe on the south-east coast, and Hart was re-elected.

In March 1855 Hart opened a flour mill at Port Adelaide and offered Barton the position of accountant at a salary of £500 a year.[242] The mill was just off St Vincent Street, next to the harbour at Port Adelaide, and is still there today. The following year John Hart built a mansion at 8 Park Avenue, Semaphore South, which he named Glanville Hall. It is now owned by the city of Port Adelaide-Enfield. In 1857 Hart became the member for Port Adelaide in the House of Assembly, subsequently becoming premier on three occasions.

Barton continued at Hart's Port Mills until the end of 1857, when he became ill and his eyesight was impaired, forcing him to abandon office work. Barton's house on Lefevre Terrace was offered for private sale in December 1857,[243] but it did not sell and was rented to Abraham Salom and his son Maurice for £100 a year. By then Barton had left for the Coorong, where he was joined by Stephen, who had returned from his trips to the north.

Chapter 22
Stephen the explorer

Stephen Hack left the colony in 1844 and went to the Cape of Good Hope for seven years. He returned to South Australia in 1853 and worked as a manager on outback stations for John Baker. In 1857 Bessie returned to England and Stephen led an expedition for the government into the Gawler Ranges and around Lake Gairdner. He also explored in the North Flinders Ranges, and Mount Hack was named after him.

Stephen returns

Stephen Hack, Bessie and the two children had left Adelaide in September 1844, and while at sea Bessie gave birth to a baby whom they named Alice Owen. They arrived in London on 9 February 1845, visited Uncle John Barton and then set off for Southampton to see Stephen's brother Tom. Later they went to Gloucester, where Bessie's family lived, as did Gates and Margaret Darton. While in Gloucester their baby became ill, and died there on 5 December 1845, aged ten months.[244]

Stephen could not find suitable employment in England, and he and Edward Philcox set out for South Africa. In April 1846 Barton's sister Elizabeth wrote to her sister Margaret that Stephen was going to start trekking with bullock wagons. 'It may keep him from starving', Elizabeth wrote, 'but what provision can it offer for a family? Poor fellow, he is so set upon life in the wilds that I doubt his ever settling down here. What can poor Bessie look forward to?'

Stephen's son Wilton provided some details in his memoir:

> After remaining in England for some time ... [Father] left by himself for the Cape of Good Hope. He made a start there trekking into the interior and dealing with the natives and Boers. Fancying all was well, he sent for Mother and Julia and I ... We lived there

for about seven years; when failure after failure dogged the poor old Dad's steps, and he started off by himself again back to South Australia.

This was the period of the Frontier wars between the Xhosa people and the European settlers,[245] which would have been difficult for Stephen and his family. Edward Philcox stayed on in South Africa and married a Dutch woman and had two more children, but Stephen returned alone to Australia around 1853, leaving Bessie and the children in Capetown for several months. Bessie sent eleven-year-old Julia back to Bessie's sister Vittoria Milnes in Dover, to be brought up and educated with Vittoria's daughter Marian.

Bessie and Wilton left Capetown on the *Fortitude* in 1854 and arrived in Adelaide in November. Stephen was by then running a large dairy property on the Murray near Albury called Brocklesbury. He and Barton had made up their differences, and Stephen had Barton's sons Bedford and Edward working for him.[246] Wilton's memoir said he and his mother lived with Uncle Barton, so Bessie must also have made peace with Barton. Wilton went to John L. Young's school with his cousins Charles and Theodore.

By 1854 John Baker was established in the North Flinders Ranges with two cattle runs – Pernana and Angepena. Stephen Hack began work there as superintendent of the runs. He was accompanied by Barton's son, Bedford, who became manager of Pernana.[247] Around this time the highest peak in the North Flinders Ranges was named Mount Hack, after Stephen Hack.[248]

In 1856 Benjamin Herschel Babbage, exploring for the government, discovered Blanchewater in the Northern Flinders Ranges, roughly halfway between Lake Torrens and Lake Eyre. Bedford Hack in later life said that he and his uncle Stephen spent a couple of months 'in the desolate country up there' looking for springs in the Lake Torrens district. 'We visited Babbage's Blanchewater station which had just been discovered', Bedford said. 'On returning to Adelaide, I persuaded Mr [John] Baker to purchase the blocks which had been set out by Mr Babbage'.

In 1857 Stephen went south, but Bedford stayed on at Pernana. In August 1857 the Surveyor-General, Captain Freeling, on his way north to explore Lake Torrens, ran into difficulties just south of Mount Hack. Here he was supplied 'in the most liberal manner with bullocks and drays by Mr Hack'. This must have been twenty-two year-old Bedford.[249]

In April 1857 as one of the most experienced bushmen in the colony, Stephen was appointed by the government to lead an exploration into the north-west of the province. He was to be paid £300, with a bonus of up to £300 depending on the value of his discoveries.[250]

Bessie must have despaired of her wandering husband ever returning to civilisation, and a month later, she and fourteen-year-old Wilton sailed for London on the *Salacia*.[251] Her sister Vittoria Milnes had died and Bessie went to keep house for her brother-in-law Henry Milnes and to look after Julia and Marian. Wilton went to board at Sandbach Grammar school in Cheshire, remaining there for almost five years.

1857, Stephen explores for the government

In 1839 the explorer John Eyre became the first white man to travel over the country from Streaky Bay to Port Augusta, naming the area the Gawler Ranges, which he described as 'singularly barren'. Nothing more was known of this country until Stephen was employed in 1857 to explore it and report on its possibilities for pastoral country.[252]

Stephen's expedition set out on 14 May 1857 for Port Lincoln. The party consisted of eight men, including a surveyor named Harris and an Aboriginal man named Billy Grant. They were well armed in case of hostile natives and had thirteen horses and provisions for six months. At the time Stephen set out, the western boundary of South Australia was 132° longitude, while the border of Western Australia was 129°, and the land in between was part of New South Wales. Stephen's orders were to travel north from Streaky Bay and explore the land within South Australia, but if possible to travel west and cross the boundary line if the land there looked superior. (As 132° was 180 miles west of Streaky Bay and the border of Western Australia another 180 miles further west, the government's commission was next to impossible to fulfil.)

The party reached Streaky Bay on 1 June and established a depot. On 22 June they set out with seven pack horses laden with supplies, and travelled east looking for grass and water. Billy Grant became ill and died, and Stephen spent several days looking for Aboriginal people who could show him where to find water in the Gawler Ranges. His long experience in working with Indigenous people served him well, and he relied heavily on their advice during the expedition, recording the Aboriginal names whenever he found good springs.

The expedition then travelled north-west and on 29 July reached a place called Yarlbrinda at the end of the Gawler Ranges. Stephen climbed a hill and saw good land, but beyond that, to the west and the north, lay only black scrub, with no likelihood of water. His Indigenous informants told him he would only find water to the north-east and spoke of a 'Great Salt Lake', prompting Stephen to travel in that direction. Three days later he reached a place called Warrea, and saw that there was still only scrub to the west and north, so continued east.

The party travelled on through scrub until reaching the edge of a huge salt lake, which Stephen described as 'a vast expanse of dazzling salt, here and there studded with islands'.[253] This had been sighted earlier by Major Peter Warburton, the Police Commissioner. Stephen wanted to name it Lake MacDonnell, after the Governor, but by the time he returned to Adelaide it had been named Lake Gairdner. It was a vast ocean of salt, ninety-six miles long and up to twenty-four miles wide. Stephen went south around the lake, with a side trip west to examine the Gawler Ranges. He found good country and seemingly permanent water and concluded this was country with valuable pastoral possibilities. He travelled around the lake to the east and found more good country and water.

By now Stephen was running out of horseshoes and provisions. To explore the interior further, he would have to return to the depot at Streaky Bay for supplies, but, as he had only been allocated six months, there was no time. Setting out for home, he travelled across the southern part of Lake Gairdner, where he named Mount Ive,[254] and on to Lake Gilles. He reached Mount Remarkable on 19 September, and wrote a report to

Francis Dutton, Commissioner of Crown Lands. Stephen knew the Dutton brothers; Francis was the brother of William and Frederick Dutton. Stephen travelled on to Adelaide and he completed his report on 10 October 1857.[255]

Stephen's reports along the way were printed in the *Gazette* and aroused great interest. He wrote that he had found 4500 square miles suitable for pastoral purposes, and many springs of permanent water. He concluded (correctly) that the true route into the interior was between Lake Gairdner and Lake Torrens, where he saw good country 'seemingly without end',[256] and he proposed a new expedition to the north under his own leadership.

Stephen's resourcefulness and good judgment did not, however, find much favour with the government. He was criticised for not exploring to the west, across the border into the area the government wanted to annex. Others were more appreciative, and within a week of his return, squatters had applied for about 2000 square miles of the land he had surveyed. On 24 November an anonymous letter published in the *Register* praised his expedition and criticised the government's appointment of Babbage to lead the next expedition instead of Stephen. But the criticism continued, and in February 1858 Stephen had to issue a public vindication of his actions.[257]

In June 1858 Major Warburton travelled to the Gawler Ranges and Lake Gairdner, traversing similar country to Stephen, but took a more gloomy view. He said the land was dry and salty, and the water supply was in rock waterholes, which were full in winter, but vanished in summer. Stephen's 4500 square miles, he suggested, would sustain at most 5000 sheep in total. The area near Yarlbrinda, which had been marked into runs as a result of Stephen's information, was in Warburton's view, fit only for the rock wallaby.

The conflicting reports by Hack and Warburton aroused much discussion. The government was determined to have its three degrees, however, and by 1861 the disputed land to the west was annexed from New South Wales. South Australia also acquired all land south of 26° latitude, which later became the border with the Northern Territory.

1859–1860, Stephen explores in the far north

The payment of £300 must have been very useful to Stephen, and when Barton was offered a run on the Coorong, Stephen went south to investigate it. This was at the end of 1857 and Stephen stayed there until Barton was established on the run, after which Stephen travelled north again.

The land in the North Flinders Ranges is dry, hot and desolate, but has some of the largest cattle runs in Australia. Stephen and Bedford seemed to like it, because early in 1858 Bedford was up there again on Baker's runs and the following year stocking Blanchewater with 1500 head of cattle.[258] Stephen joined him in late 1858. In March 1859 a report in the *Gazette* said Stephen had been exploring around Blanchewater with an Aboriginal man.[259]

In March 1860 the *Gazette* reported that Stephen had made important discoveries in the far north.[260] He had explored north from Blanchewater up to Lake Pando (Lake Hope), claiming that much of the land in between was inhospitable, but beyond that there was 'fine country, richly grassed and well watered', all the way up to Cooper's Creek. On this journey Stephen named Mount Flint, 114 miles north of Mount Hack, and placed a beacon on it for future travellers.

Stephen found fertile country to the east of Mount Flint, where he met a large tribe of about 300 Aboriginal people, who lived on fish in freshwater lakes and wild animals. They had scarcely seen white men, but were friendly. The *Gazette* said Stephen had penetrated 'almost to Sturt's Stony Desert'[261] in the north-east corner of the province and his discoveries were 'an exceedingly valuable addition' to the knowledge of the interior.

Stephen must have travelled in an unusually wet period, as did most of the explorers at the time, who spoke of fresh water lakes and running streams of water.[262] Normally most of the north is dry, and the creeks, lakes and waterholes are only full after heavy rains, or after floods in Queensland, when the waters make their way south. Stephen's nephew Bedford Hack was to stay up north for several years more, but in the end he was 'droughted' out.[263]

By July 1860 Stephen had gone to the south-east again, and was planning to farm near Barton and his family.

Chapter 23

The Coorong

In 1858 Barton Hack took his family to the Coorong on the south-east coast of South Australia. They established a dairy farm at Parnka Point, on the sand dunes between the lagoons and the ocean, and were the first white people to live there. They had very few neighbours, apart from the local Ngarrindjeri people, who had lived there for thousands of years. The Hacks befriended the Aboriginal people and employed some in the house and as stockmen. The dairy made excellent cheese, but it was expensive to get to market, by boat up the lagoons to Goolwa and then to Adelaide.

Parnka

At the end of 1857 Barton gave up working as an accountant in Adelaide. 'I now had the offer of a run on the Coorong', he wrote in his memoirs, 'opposite MacGrath's Flat [Magrath Flat], which I purchased for £200, and leaving North Adelaide we removed there and commenced dairy operations'.[264] Stephen had journeyed to the south-east to assist Barton in investigating the offer of land. Relatively inexpensive to lease, it seemed a good idea because they had experience in dairy farming and had been successful at it. Barton knew the area already, having passed through on his way to the goldfields five years earlier.

The name Coorong is an Aboriginal word meaning narrow neck.[265] The Coorong starts at the mouth of the River Murray, next to Lakes Alexandrina and Albert. Below this is a line of salty lagoons that extend south for more than a 100 kilometres. Between the lagoons and the ocean lies a narrow strip of high sand dunes known as the Younghusband Peninsula. It's a wild and empty place, known for being the setting for the 1976 film *Storm Boy*, based on the classic Australian novel by Colin Thiele, about a boy and his pelican. The Coorong lies at the end of the great River Murray, and in times of drought, the health of the Coorong and the lower lakes is a vital indicator of environmental flows in the Murray-Darling Basin.

The site the Hacks chose was at Parnka Point, opposite Magrath Flat. Consisting of a strip of land on the peninsula, half a mile wide and eleven miles in length,[266] it was part of an earlier lease of twenty-two square miles that was being subdivided. Barton and Stephen purchased the lease jointly, although Stephen relinquished his part in the venture a few months later.[267]

The property was remote, but it had several advantages. It had good waterholes with fresh water and plenty of native grass where sheep and cattle could graze and it was close to transport, either by bullock dray up the track to Wellington, or by boat up the lagoons to Goolwa. The telegraph had opened in April 1857, connecting it with Adelaide and Melbourne. There was an inn and a telegraph office at Magrath Flat.

The site chosen on the sand dunes could only be reached by crossing the lagoon. Crossing at Parnka Point, which had a deep channel known as 'Hell's Gates', was dangerous.[268] Barton used a shallower point further south, which became known as Hack's Crossing. Although not the first person to graze stock on the peninsula, his station was the first permanent residence there.[269]

At the end of 1857 Barton and Stephen were busy preparing the run and erecting a temporary camp.[270] They investigated land further south, and in January 1858 Barton made a claim for twenty square miles to the east of the Coorong, an area called Bonney's Camp.[271]

Arrival and settling in

While Stephen stayed on to prepare the site, Barton returned to Adelaide to help pack up all the goods and equipment needed for his new home. He left Adelaide on 2 February with Bbe and their twenty-year-old daughter Emily and arrived at Parnka five days later. Barton was filled with great hopes for this new venture, but he and Bbe were in their fifties, twenty years older than when they first began to farm.

Only one personal letter from this period has survived, but it tells a great deal about how the two women must have felt. It was written by Emily just after they arrived, to her cousin Minnie in Adelaide.[272] Minnie was Charlotte Emily, the twenty-one year old daughter of Henry Watson married to John Sanderson Lloyd. Emily wrote that that they started their journey in a horse-drawn carriage.

> We started from North Adelaide at half past eleven and ... about three passed through Mount Barker, wished very much I was not going any further than there ... Mamma has borne the journey wonderfully well so far, she is lying on the sofa talking to Papa and I am lying on the other writing my journal. I feel tonight as if I shall go to bed to cry but still I know it will do no good.

At Langhorne Creek they were visited by two of Emily's older brothers, Alfred and Bedford, both in their early twenties, who had come over from nearby Strathalbyn. Alfred was also moving to the Coorong, as was Theodore, aged seventeen. It was the last time Emily would see Bedford 'for a long time', as he was returning to work on John Baker's properties in the North Flinders Ranges.

Barton, Bbe and Emily travelled on to the River Murray, where they stayed in the 'Wellington Inn'. Emily could not sleep because of the 'B flats and F sharps' (bugs and fleas) and the noise made by young men in the room next door.

> Minnie dear you never in your life saw such a horrid place as this Wellington, there is so much sand (in fact, the place is nothing but sand), there is also a high wind blowing, that just stepping from the carriage to the Public House we were almost blinded ... I was lying on the sofa this afternoon an immense B flat crawled up my dress, <u>pleasant, was it not</u>? I have suffered from faceache all the way up, and tonight I have a bad headache and my face is a good deal scorched with the wind ... Mamma is very tired tonight and I feel very weary.

The next morning they crossed the Murray on the ferry, transferring to a bullock dray, which was very slow and bumpy. That night was spent at Lake Alexandrina. The following day Emily wrote, 'Who would have thought it, here we are going to Camp out in the Wild Bush. Mamma and I are lying on top of the drey whilst they are rigging the tent, and making the fire to boil the kettle, it is miserable country to travel in – flat low land and sand'. The next day she continued:

> We . . . got here [Magrath Flat] . . . at half past five and all I can say is save me from crossing the Desert in a Bullock Drey again. O how weary Mamma and I are, Hills, Bush and Sand for twelve miles. We are staying tonight at a miserable public house . . . We are only five miles from our 'Home'. I feel so wretched tonight I can scarcely keep the tears from rolling down my eyes but for Mamma's sake I try to keep up.

On 7 February they were met by Stephen Hack and Emily's brothers William and Charles, who escorted the weary travellers to Hack's Crossing and across the lagoons. 'Home' was a piece of flat land covered in low bushes and native grasses and had a good waterhole for their domestic use. Most of the family were gathered there to help, and Stephen went out mustering cattle with a neighbour.

Emily completed the letter on 19 February when she'd been at Parnka nearly two weeks.

> You wish to know how I like the place – I do not like it at all, tho' I must say since I visited the sea I like it better . . . the surf is very loud, and we have had a great deal of thunder and lightning lately. I went a ride on horseback the other day and enjoyed it very much . . . The greatest nuisance here is the flies. We can scarcely do anything for them . . . Please write again as soon as you possibly can, my heart longs to hear of you all . . . We have seen no snakes as yet.

The station

The first task was to build a house and dairy and fence some of the land. In his memoir, Barton recalled:

> There was no sort of improvements on the run; everything had to be done. I took with me doors and windows for a house, and managed by degrees to make a home. A part of the deck of a vessel was washed ashore near our camp, and we broke it up and found deal battens enough for the framework of a house of five or six rooms, filled in with bush materials, and thatched with long grass.

Over time they constructed a series of buildings. A sketch made four years later by Charles Babbage shows the main house facing the lagoons and a smaller house beside it, probably William's. Stockyards and fencing are also shown in the sketch. Barton's sailing boat is on the lagoon, although they relied mostly on the Milang boatman, Captain Kruse, whose boat the *Burra Burra* made regular visits to places like Magrath Flat, Hacks' Station and Salt Creek.[273]

More information is contained in a report by George Goyder, the Surveyor-General, in 1864. Barton had left Parnka by then and his homestead was no longer occupied, but Goyder's sketch map shows several buildings constructed mainly from local materials, with thatched roofs, comprising a main house of five to six rooms and a separate kitchen and outdoor toilet, also a three-room house, stables, a woolshed, a dairy with yards attached, a well and fences for a garden and paddocks.[274]

More recently, an archaeological survey of Hacks' Station was conducted by Roger Luebbers for the South Australian Government in 1982.[275] Luebbers's excavation unearthed some timber and parts of the foundations, as well as the remains of lime-rich plaster rendered over mud and wattle walls. They found fragments of: 'fancy chamber pots, etched glass lantern shades, a tureen and ... A distinctive set of plates and cups with a black background, and several examples of hand finished ceramic vessels ... quality chinaware ... consistent with an affluent family residency on the site'.

Once the accommodation was ready, the younger children arrived from Adelaide and William Hack moved his family down from Finniss Flats. William and his wife Grace had four young children – Mary Louisa, Annie Catherine, Barton John and Julia Emily, just a baby. There were now about seventeen family members at Parnka, including small children.

The family ate well. They grew vegetables as well as purchasing bulk provisions like flour, sugar, rice and tea from Milang. Their farm provided dairy products and fresh meat from their cattle and pigs, while the lagoons and the sea were the source of a wide range of fish, crabs and birds. The Aboriginal people knew how to trap the fish in the lagoons and spear wild ducks near Magrath Flat,[276] and the family may have relied on these as well.

The Hacks had visitors, and continued their connection with the Methodist church. A friend later said that during the five years Barton lived on the Coorong, a 'religious ceremony was held every Sunday in his home, all the station hands being called together for that purpose. When Mr Hack was absent or unable to officiate, Mrs Hack invariably conducted the service herself'.[277]

The dairy farm

Barton ceased writing in his journal in 1839, but he took it to the Coorong and used the blank pages at the back to write copies of his business letters. The letters span the period from May 1861 until the end of 1862, and provide a snapshot of Barton's farming activities and his financial situation. Barton and his sons started the dairy farm at Parnka with about sixty-six cattle, the number increasing to 150. In addition to the cows they had some bulls, eighteen bullocks and numerous horses. Large paddocks were established for their dairy herd, as well as a system of wells at regular intervals along the shoreline.[278]

Dairying was the main venture, and since it was impossible to get milk to market without its going off, the family concentrated on cheese-making. They had twenty-three vats large enough to produce cheeses weighing up to thirty pounds. Likely to have been a hard variety, the cheeses were packed in salt to ensure their preservation and then transported to Goolwa, for sale there and in Adelaide.

The Parnka lease was formally purchased for the Hack brothers in Adelaide, and on 1 July the annual rent was paid. But Stephen did not plan to stay on at Parnka, and a notice appeared in the *Advertiser* in August, stating that the partnership of John Barton Hack and Stephen Hack, stock farmers at the Coorong, 'was dissolved by mutual consent on the first day of June, 1858' and that any claims on the partnership would be paid by Barton.[279] Stephen went back to the far north, again working for John Baker.[280]

By the middle of 1858 the dairy was established. Barton's next step was to stock his lease at Bonney's Camp, near Salt Creek.

In this venture he was joined by Alfred and Bedford, the latter returning after Stephen had left. 'Alf's Flat', named after Alfred, is still on the map today, and there was once a 'Bedford's Well' nearby.[281] At some stage Barton arranged for Archibald Cooke to take over the lease and be responsible for its rent, with Alfred Hack as overseer.[282] Archibald and his brother James owned grazing land further south near Maria Creek.

Barton was running short of money and mortgaged his run at Bonney's Camp to David Bayne, an Adelaide agent, for £300 at 12½ per cent interest per year. As was his custom, Barton paid the interest but not the principal.[283] In December 1858 Stephen sold his half share in Parnka to Barton. Barton paid him £400, an amount twice that paid at the beginning of the year, so perhaps Barton was paying for stock as well as Stephen's share of the lease. Being unable to pay the entire amount, Barton took a mortgage (loan) from Stephen for £180, with Parnka as security.[284]

Barton's letters reveal that he had several loans from Archibald Cooke. It seems that Barton had learned very little from his insolvency in 1843. He now had mortgages on his two leases, as well as debts to Stephen and the Cooke brothers. Once again he was borrowing heavily, and optimistic that all would turn out well.

In August 1859 a baby was born at Parnka: William's wife Grace gave birth to their fifth child, Arthur William. The following year Emily turned twenty-three, and she must have fled the isolation of the Coorong to visit her relatives in Adelaide, because on 29 August 1860 she married Cornelius Butler Mitchell. The wedding took place in the family home on the Coorong, and the minister was the Reverend Charles Henry Goldsmith. Cornelius was thirty-six and his father, Thomas Mitchell, was a draper in Rundle Street, Adelaide. Emily soon moved in respectable Adelaide society, even attending a 'drawing room' held at Government House by the wife of the newly appointed Governor, Lady Daly, in March 1862.[285]

The happy event of Emily's wedding was followed by a shocking tragedy a month later. In September 1860, William's wife Grace died. There is no death certificate, but her descendants relate that she died in childbirth, following complications while being rowed across the Coorong in an attempt to get help from a doctor.[286] The baby must have died too, as there is no record of a sixth child surviving. William, thirty-two, was left with five small children. With Emily gone, it must have fallen to Bbe, now aged fifty-four and a grandmother, to care for William's children, with the assistance of twelve-year-old Jessie and the household help.

The Aborigines

The Hacks had at least one female servant living with the family, as well as some Aboriginal helpers. Barton said that he used only Aboriginal labour,[287] meaning in addition to his sons. Barton established close relations with his Aboriginal neighbours, and his descendants recall that the Hack children loved to ride their horses on the beach and through the paddocks with their Aboriginal friends.[288]

The Ngarrindjeri tribes of the Lower Murray Lakes and the Coorong had once numbered about 3000 people,[289] but since the arrival of Europeans their population had been drastically reduced. They were destroyed by European diseases such as smallpox, influenza and syphilis and the introduction of alcohol. Barton told a parliamentary inquiry there were only about sixty to eighty individuals left near his station.

The Aborigines became valuable stockmen to South Australian settlers and guides to the explorers. An 1860 report by the Sub-Protector of Aborigines at Wellington, George Mason, noted, 'there are about 35 young men in constant employment as stockkeepers and general servants with the settlers, and they appear to give great satisfaction to their employers'.[290]

While the Hacks were on the Coorong, a mission station was established at Point McLeay on the shores of Lake Alexandrina, with an enlightened superintendant, George Taplin. This was an establishment for Aborigines who were willing to adopt a 'Christian' lifestyle, with a farm and ration depot. But when Taplin wanted a small site for his mission on the Narrung Peninsula, he ran into conflict with John Baker, who had a large estate there.[291]

Baker criticised the administration of the mission, which led to the first full-scale inquiry in 1860 into the Aboriginal people in South Australia, by a Select Committee of the Legislative

Council. Barton Hack was invited to give evidence, probably at the request of John Baker. Barton must have felt constrained in what he could say, given that Baker was one of the five members of the inquiry. The Hacks knew Baker well, and he employed Stephen and Bedford around this time.

Barton explained that he was in contact with the Aborigines Protection Society in London. He said nothing could be done to prevent the decrease in the Aboriginal population, and commented: 'I have never been able to suggest any feasible plan to ameliorate their condition ... nothing but a native missionary travelling with them would do them any good. No European could ever do them any material good'.

Barton was asked about the former school for native children in Adelaide, run by the Protector of Aborigines Matthew Moorhouse, which had closed in 1852. Barton said the children ran away from school at a certain age and forgot everything which had been taught them. He said several of Mr Moorhouse's scholars had lived with his family at Parnka, and they also had a half-caste boy living with them, who could read and write. Barton said he gave the boy's father flour and tobacco every month as an inducement to leave him there.

The report of the select committee was stark. It noted that the Aboriginal people were dispossessed of their land, and said 'all the evidence goes to prove that they have lost much, and gained little or nothing, by their contact with Europeans'. It recommended that a chief protector be appointed alongside sub-protectors to oversee the provision of food and clothing to those who were elderly, sick or infirm, and to dispense justice. The protector would be responsible for instilling morals and Christianity, and this would require removing the children from their parents into a special school, a policy similar to the later 'stolen generation'.

Barton queried the forcible separation of the children and said, 'how far it would be justifiable is another question'. He said the parents 'become exceedingly attached to their children, indeed they are just like white people in this respect'.

Barton's relationship with the local Aborigines is further revealed in the report by George Mason, the Sub-Protector of Aborigines at Wellington. Mason visited a native encampment with fifty-five adults and twelve children situated between Magrath Flat and Salt Wells. These people were there he said, for the sake of the fishing, and when they wanted drinking water they crossed the Coorong to Barton's wells. He added, 'the natives all speak in praise of Mr. Hack and his family for the kindness shown by them to the natives when in want'.

A new direction
After two years at Parnka, it was clear that the dairy farm was not making a profit. Barton continued for the time being to make cheeses, but decided a change in direction was necessary. Stephen had come south again, and they decided to take up some leases further inland, for grazing or land speculation.

Chapter 24

Coonalpyn

Barton and his family remained on the Coorong, but gave up the dairy. In 1860 Barton and Stephen began to take leases in the Ninety Mile Desert region. To finance this, each found a wealthy backer. Barton established a sheep station at Coonalpyn, with Stephen establishing one near Tintinara. Barton's sheep speculation failed and he returned to Adelaide in 1863. Stephen stayed on for a few more years, but his farming ventures were also unsuccessful.

Stephen comes south again

In March 1860 Stephen Hack once again returned to the south; Bedford Hack went north to work as superintendant of John Baker's station at Pernana. The following year Bedford went into partnership with Sir Thomas Elder and Henry Dean to run cattle at Lake Hope, staying north for several years.[292]

Barton and Stephen were attracted to the Ninety Mile Desert region, formerly called the Hundred Mile Scrub. It was the only land in the south-east that had not been taken up for pastoral runs, mainly because it was dry and marginal. In those days it was not cleared or fenced; it was just a vast emptiness with sandy soils and low vegetation. Today, with the introduction of fertilizers the land is much richer. This area had been opened up in the gold rush of 1852, when a track, roughly parallel to the present-day highway and railway from Victoria to South Australia, was etched across the desert to the diggings. Barton had travelled along it on his return from the goldfields.

Land speculation

There are no remaining family letters or diaries from this period, but some of what happened can be reconstructed from the business letters of 1861–1862 at the back of Barton's diary and from old government records of pastoral leases. Barton and Stephen's land claims at this stage were mainly for speculation purposes: they planned to take up runs, pay rent on them and sell them later at a profit. But if the land was not occupied it could be forfeited, so in some instances they lost it. Another problem was that boundaries often changed, because the region was not yet surveyed accurately.

During 1860 and 1861, the brothers applied for at least seventeen claims in the south-east, amounting to several hundred square miles[293] and stretching from Salt Creek on the Coorong to the 56-Mile Well on the inland track and across the Mallee country towards the Victorian border.

Claims cost money and Barton had very little, so once again he resorted to loans. It appears that his claims were financed initially by the stock and station agency Elder, Stirling & Co., known as Elders. Barton already had twenty square miles at Bonney's Camp, in 1860 taking out three claims for land near there. He sold the first two claims to the Cookes, which helped clear a debt of £300 Barton had with Elders.

The Cookes then purchased Barton's original lease at Bonney's Camp and this enabled Barton to pay off the £300 mortgage on Bonney's Camp which he had taken with the agent Bayne. But he was still short of cash and immediately borrowed £300 from Bayne by taking out a second mortgage on Parnka.

The third claim near Bonney's Camp was later referred to as 'Palcolatin'. It went to Stephen Hack and his new partner, the wealthy and influential businessman Robert Barr Smith (later the benefactor to Adelaide University), who was with the pastoral firm of Elders and was Thomas Elder's brother-in-law. Barr Smith put up the capital and this enabled Stephen to make several claims.

In July 1860 Stephen lodged a claim close to where the town of Tintinara now stands, later selling this to George Boothby, one of the sons of the Judge of the Supreme Court of South Australia.[294] Another claim, near the 56-Mile Well, was split into two leases, the first going to Stephen and Barr Smith, with the second sold to Thomas and James Boothby, George's brothers. The Boothbys later called this property Tintinara, after an Aboriginal employee named Tin Tin.[295]

By far the biggest claims Barton and Stephen made were to the north and south of Tintinara, Stephen taking a run of 171 square miles just south of Tintinara, with Barton taking the other two runs, one for 125 square miles and one for 104 square miles. These were not for speculation, but for their own use.

Sheep farming

At the beginning of 1861, Barton and Stephen decided to try their hands at sheep farming on their large inland runs, and again they gave them Aboriginal names. Barton called the smaller of his runs, Coonalpyn, a corruption of the Aboriginal word Kunayalpe.[296] His second run was located near Emu Springs. According to his son Wilton, Stephen had two blocks, next to the Boothbys' Tintinara property, called Karlgurra and Baroona.[297] Despite these new acquisitions, Barton and his family continued to live at Parnka. Stephen's family was in England and he lived on his head station at Karlgurra, which would have been similar to the head station Barton built at Coonalpyn, shown in a sketch by Charles Babbage in 1862.

The business letters show that when Barton decided to become a sheep farmer, he still had about 150 cows at Parnka and nearby. He gave up cheese-making, selling twelve of his largest cheese vats. He sold his cows to Thomas Matthews, a farmer on the Upper Sturt River.

Barton's land speculation was patently inadequate funding for a sheep station, which meant that a partner was urgently required to supply the capital. In June 1861 he wrote to Peter Prankerd, an Adelaide land agent, explaining that he wanted to buy two to three thousand sheep; he considered the most appropriate way would be to find a partner, for whom it would 'involve a very temporary advance of capital and would afford a good commission on the transaction'. Barton must have kept good contacts in Adelaide and still had powers of persuasion, because he found the partners by October. They were Henry Giles and James Smith, flour and grain merchants in West Terrace, Adelaide. Part of the deal was that Barton purchased most of his supplies from them.

Coonalpyn had to be made ready for the sheep and William Hack was put in charge as overseer. As there were no fences and feed was scarce, the sheep wandered over the scrub for miles and were difficult to round up. Shepherds were needed and huts had to be built for them and water found. Surface water was not permanent as far inland as this and deep wells had to be dug, which was costly.

In September, Stephen advertised in Adelaide for two well-sinkers. A well was dug on his run at a place called Hidden Island, followed by a well on Barton's run. Well-digging in the sandy soil was a difficult and dangerous task, as Stephen's son Wilton described later in his memoirs.[298] Not only was there the danger of the well collapsing on the men below, but harmful gas could be released lower down. At the end of 1861 Barton's first well was finished. Two further wells were dug, with a shepherd's hut and yards built at each well.

While the run was being prepared, Barton obtained finance from Giles and Smith and purchased about 3000 ewes from a Dr Browne in Mount Gambier, for £1500. The sheep were moved to the Cooke brothers' run at Maria Creek and left in charge of Theodore. Barton joined him and they had the sheep shorn there, producing over 2000 fleeces, weighing on average 3½ lbs. Later on Barton and his partners were paid about three shillings per fleece, so this first clip should have been worth £300. The wool was very fine but 'short staple', so Barton suggested some Merino rams to improve the fleece. The 3000 ewes were moved to Coonalpyn just before Christmas.

As the sheep were somewhat aged, Barton decided it would be best to select 2000 of the best ewes for breeding, sell the remaining 1000 and replace them with 2000 best quality ewe lambs. Giles and Smith however were less than enthusiastic with this suggestion. Barton split the 3000 sheep into two flocks. He took out the best for breeding and the rams were brought up from Parnka to service them, placing the cull (about 300) on Boothby's run at Tintinara, in the care of an Aboriginal boy.

Finances

Barton tried every conceivable way to earn income. In 1860 he planted wheat at Parnka, and early in 1861 it was harvested. By February 1862 the second harvest was underway and he had around forty bags ready for Captain Kruse to take to the Port Adelaide mill, but his annual income from this source was less than £100. He tried to sell his boat for £25 but failed.

Barton could draw on Giles and Smith for capital associated with sheep farming, but not for private purposes, which meant he was constantly in financial difficulties. He still had two mortgages on Parnka: £180 from Stephen and £300 from the agent Bayne. Barton suggested that Bayne provide him with a new combined mortgage of £500 so that he could pay off Stephen and make Bayne the first mortgagee, and Bayne agreed.[299]

Barton owed Elders £300 and hoped to pay this by selling some of his smaller runs. He was struggling to pay overdue interest on two mortgages on his house in Lefevre Terrace in North Adelaide, and he owed the Atlas Building Society about £230 for a loan he had taken out back in 1855.

So at the beginning of 1862, Barton had debts of at least £1658. He struggled to pay the interest and to meet the bills for day-to-day needs such as flour, tea, sugar, soap and footwear. He was constantly postponing payment and paying interest instead. His letters are peppered with phrases such as, 'I am indebted to you for your forbearance towards me'; 'I have been so long your debtor'; and 'I hope I shall not again try your patience so far'.

Decline and fall

Lambing began in mid-July 1862, but by the end of August about sixty per cent of the lambs had died and many of the aged ewes as well, although some of Barton's neighbours had suffered worse losses, including Stephen Hack, Morphett and Tolmer. The main cause was the winter weather and dingoes. Barton wrote to his partners that it was a bad season for aged ewes and that Tolmer and his sons 'have only 230 left out of 7000 and others have suffered in a similar way'. Tolmer decided to sell up, but Barton, as usual the optimist, purchased the remnants of Tolmer's flock with finance from Giles and Smith.

Barton now had to prepare for shearing, running the sheep and lambs on the large islands in the Coorong, where there was abundant grass. The sheep venture must have been a significant drain on Giles's and Smith's resources and they contemplated taking out a loan to help them through. Barton supported this move and said for security there was: '3 government claims of 104, 125 and 26 miles, 4 summer stations with deep wells, huts and yards, 4 winter ditto at native wells with huts, yards, 33 rams, 3000 sheep of which about 700–800 lambs'.

He explained that, if the property was sold, it would show a profit because of improvements such as the construction of wells and huts. As usual, he based his argument on the notional value of the investment, seemingly blind to the fact that the value of the land had dropped, given the woeful experience of all the pastoralists in the area.

Shearing began the first week of November, and bales were packed ready for forwarding. Barton's bales were shipped via Goolwa, while Stephen's were sent to Milang and then taken by dray to Adelaide. Barton must have had extraordinary powers of persuasion, because he then convinced Giles and Smith to buy more sheep, a purchase of a further 1000 ewes.

At this point the letter book ceases because Barton had run out of blank pages. We don't know exactly what happened next, except that by the end of the year Barton was planning to return to Adelaide. Presumably Giles and Smith decided to pull out of the venture. In winding up the business, the wool and the 3000 sheep could have been sold, but not the land. All the money and effort Barton had put into improving the land had been for nothing. When he returned to Adelaide, he would have carried with him significant debts.

Summing up his years in the south-east in his memoirs, Barton wrote:

> We took up scrub country about forty miles inward from the Coorong, and sank several wells, finding good water 60 to 100 feet deep. I purchased, in partnership with Mr G M [Messrs Giles and] Smith, 3,000 ewes at Mount Gambier from Dr. Brown[e]. These were aged and troubled with footrot, and did not turn out well ... The sheep speculation was discouraging and the dairy business altogether unsuccessful, so the end came; and at the close of 1862 we determined to return to Adelaide, which I reached with my family in July, 1863.

Karlgurra

Stephen Hack worked just as hard on his own sheep farm, and in January 1862 his son Wilton arrived in Adelaide on the *Claramount* from London. Wilton was eighteen, and after finishing school in England and Germany, had come to join his father. Stephen, now aged forty-seven, battled on a bit longer in the south-east after Barton and his family had returned to Adelaide, in November 1863 making four new claims totalling just over fifty square miles. However, he failed to sell them and a month later he travelled to the north again, near Lake Hope.[300]

By February 1864 Stephen may have been back in the south-east, because he made four new claims at Pine Hill near Bordertown, which he later sold. By the end of 1864 he was planning to 'sell the country'[301] and this may have been when he sold his runs (Baroona and Karlgurra) to the Boothbys.

Stephen finally gave up farming around 1865 and returned to England. Before doing so, he bought some land in the Mallee, near the Victorian border, which he called Pinnaroo. As Wilton wrote in his memoir, 'He went home to England to join my mother, leaving me Pinnaroo, the mob of horses and oddments'. Wilton stayed at Pinnaroo for about a year, and spent most of his time trying to find water and sink a well. He hired some men and took in two young relatives, William's son Barton John Hack, and Henry Watson's son George. A period of severe drought, it was around this time that George Goyder the Surveyor-General, drew the famous 'Goyder's line' across the north of the state to indicate the areas which were too dry for farming.

Wilton, like his father and uncle, was forced to give up in the south-east, and was back in Adelaide by February 1867. As he wrote in his memoir, 'I . . . came out of it rich in experience, but with empty pockets'.

Neighbours

The Hacks were not alone in their struggles in the south-east. The Dodd brothers, who grazed on the peninsula just north of Barton, also found it difficult, and by the 1860s they had turned to horse breeding.[302] The Boothby brothers at Tintinara also struggled. In a memoir published at the end of his life, James

Boothby wrote, 'One excuse for going into such poor grazing country was that it was all being taken up by richer, wiser men than ourselves, including the late R Barr Smith who thought there was money in it. I do not know one who made any out of it, but many that it ruined'.[303] Alexander Tolmer and his sons also failed in the south-east.

As for the Parnka lease, when Barton left in 1863 it was reissued at his request to the Hon. John Baker. When Baker died in 1872, it was sold to Robert Barr Smith for £3 an acre.[304] It was not until thirty years after the Hacks had left, that anyone tried living there again. In 1895 William Ashby purchased a lease at Parnka and had 200 dairy cattle. He lived in the ruins of Barton's house while he built his own.[305]

Nowadays there are only small traces left of Hacks' station on the Coorong. The large waterhole near the house, some foundation stones and a long concrete trough remain. Everything is grown over with native grass and bushes. Hack's Crossing is the site of the Coorong Wilderness Lodge, built by the South Australian Government and run by descendants of the original Ngarrindjeri. The Coorong is now a national park, well known to bird watchers and home to over 200 species of birds.[306]

Chapter 25

Final years

In 1863 Barton returned to Adelaide and worked as an accountant for several employers. In 1869 he joined the railways department and rose to become Comptroller of Railway Accounts, a position he held until his retirement in 1883. He died in 1884, aged seventy-nine, at his home in Semaphore. Barton's memoirs became a valuable record of the early days of the colony and established him as a significant pioneer. He is known as the founder of Echunga, and a commemorative ceremony was held there in 1984, one hundred years after his death. Stephen Hack farmed in the south-east until about 1865; then returned to England and remained there until his death in 1894 aged seventy-eight.

Barton returns to Adelaide

In July 1863 Barton returned to Adelaide from the Coorong, leaving behind his dreams of being a successful pastoralist. He was fifty-eight and was once again facing a desk job. Adelaide had grown and the population was now over 127,000.[307] Barton began work as an accountant with H. Hill & Co., railway contractors, and in 1867 with another contractor, John Rounsevell.

Barton rented a house at 120 Childers Street, North Adelaide and became active in the local Wesleyan chapel in Archer Street.[308] When Barton and Bbe left the Coorong, their children largely went their separate ways. William stayed on farming in the south-east, Edward was farming in Victoria at Yackandandah, and Bedford was in the far north, managing cattle at Lake Hope. Theodore, aged twenty-four, joined the Customs Department as a boarding officer at Semaphore, and later became the harbour master at Willunga, south of Adelaide. In November 1864 he married Elvira Ansell and set up house in Willunga.

Only a tiny number of letters remain from this later period.

One is a letter from Bbe written in December 1864 to 'Darling Tods' (Theodore) and Ellie (Elvira) just after their marriage.[309] It is full of domestic detail. Bbe was concerned that Ellie was unwell and was thinking of going to nurse her or send Emmie (Emily) instead. Alfred and Frank were at home, along with Bbe's youngest child Jessie, now sixteen, who was going to Willunga with some medicine for Ellie.

Bbe thanked Theo for sending 'a very nice lot of wine', which was probably for medicinal purposes, as the Wesleyans were not drinkers. Bbe's married daughter Emily had called in with a snook (a type of fish) and the cook had prepared it for dinner. The letter shows Bbe as loving and affectionate to her children, but with a firm hand. She asked Theo if he had written to Charlie and added, 'by the way I hear many complaints that Tods does not give answers asked him in letters – a bad plan that my boy, and one to be avoided in future'.

Bbe's married daughter Louisa was travelling through France, and in her letter to Theo Bbe wondered why she had not sent her usual monthly letter. Louisa's husband Patrick Tod had died in 1855 and she was now married to Hingston Lindon, a merchant in Plymouth, Louisa giving birth to a baby named Harold a year earlier.[310] In August 1865 Louisa died in London at the age of thirty-four, from tuberculosis. Her baby son Harold was only two. Little is known of her husband and child, except that the following year Hingston Lindon married again, in Lancashire. The tragedy of Louisa's death was followed two years later by the death of Barton and Bbe's daughter Jessie in Adelaide on 31 March 1867, when she was only eighteen. She also died from tuberculosis.

Bbe's oldest son William was still in the south and she was waiting to hear of his intentions, when Stephen 'sold the country'. This suggests William was working for Stephen, and Bbe was perhaps still looking after William's five young children. William's intentions were to marry again. On 5 May 1865, he married Emma Harding, at the Manse, Mosquito Plains, near Naracoorte. William was thirty-seven and Emma was the nineteen-year-old daughter of William Harding, who had pastoral leases near Stephen's and had just purchased Tintinara. William and Emma stayed on in the south-east, and three months after the wedding Emma gave birth to her first child, Charles Herbert, on 7 August 1865, at Kincraig, near Naracoorte.

Emma's descendants described her as a tiny woman with rosy cheeks. She may have been small, but she was strong in spirit. When she married William, his oldest child Mary Louisa was eleven, and the youngest Arthur William was only five. Emma became a devoted stepmother to these five children, going on to have eleven children of her own. It was not easy – one of her step-daughters, Annie, who was rather wild, would ride off and spend the day with the Aborigines on the Coorong.[311]

Stephen Hack's son Wilton wrote in his memoirs that around 1868 he went to live with Barton and Bbe in Childers Street. Wilton had left Pinnaroo and in 1867 got a job as an assistant bookkeeper to James Brown and lived with Brown's family. The following year Wilton became a drawing teacher at his old school, the Adelaide Educational Institute, being paid 19 shillings a week. According to Wilton's memoir:

> Uncle Barton ... said I ought not to be lodging with strangers ... and for me to go and live with him. I thanked him and thought him very kind. I was still only earning my 19 shillings per week. This went on for some months ... One day my Aunt [Bbe] presented me with a bill and I was charged I found a pound a week from the day I entered the house, even the holidays when I was away ... I remonstrated at this, and 10s per week for the holidays ... was knocked off ... Then I got the drawing mastership of Prince Alfred College and also Caterer's School Norwood [December 1868], until at length this hideous debt to my uncle was paid off.

It is interesting that Wilton claimed it was Bbe who asked for the rent. Barton must have made the offer out of kindness, but in 1868 he had a falling-out with John Rounsevell and left his employment. Barton then tried to work for himself as an accountant, opening an office in Gresham Chambers, but he was not successful and they were probably desperately short of money at this time.

In his memoir, Wilton wrote that around 1869 he joined the Baptist church and that the eighty-year-old George Fife Angas paid the Reverend George Stonehouse £100 a year for two years to train Wilton as a Baptist preacher. Wilton then left Barton's house and went to live with the Stonehouse family, on 10 May 1870 marrying Stonehouse's daughter, Anna Maria. When Wilton became a pastor of the Baptist church at Hilton, a suburb of Adelaide, the couple went to live there, after which they moved to Providence in the Barossa Ranges. Wilton said that it was around this time that he invited William Hack's son Barton John to live with him.

> I was to feed the boy and look after him, Uncle [Barton] was to clothe him and Theodore to pay his school fees ... I sent him to Fred Caterer's school in Glenelg ... at the end of twelve months I saw Uncle Barton and Theodore and they both repudiated and I had to face the music myself.

If Wilton's account is true, it is another example of Barton making a generous offer and then not being able to deliver, because of a shortage of money. However when Barton joined the railways, he found a job for his grandson Barton John, who then stayed in the railways for forty-nine years.[312] He became station master at Lucindale, and later was station master at Yarcowie, near Burra.

In Adelaide, Barton was active with the Wesleyans and supported their campaign against alcohol. In 1868 when the South Australian Total Abstinence League was established, he was elected chairman and his son Charles to the committee. [313]

By the 1860s Barton and Bbe had several grandchildren, and each year more of their children were marrying; over the following decade or so Charles, Bedford, George and Alfred married. In 1873 Frank married and was the last of Barton's children to do so.

Burnside

Barton's attempt to work for himself was not successful, and the following year he sought a job in the railways, in July 1869 at the age of sixty-four becoming an accountant in the goods department at £400 a year. He must have performed well because a year later he became Assistant Accountant in the Railway Department, and in February 1873, at the age of 67, he was appointed Comptroller of Railway Accounts, where he stayed until his retirement in 1883.[314]

During this time, Barton and Bbe left Childers Street and moved around, living in rented houses. By 1871 Barton could afford better accommodation, and they moved to Hazelwood Cottage in Burnside. This was a nine-room stone house on thirteen acres, leased from John Howard Clark, the editor of the *Register*. The house still stands at 34 Howard Terrace, facing Hazelwood Park. Barton also leased twenty-five acres on the same estate from George Chinner.[315] Charles Hack also moved to Burnside (probably living with Barton), and his next three children were born there. In 1874 he was listed as a 'collector' (collecting money due) for the *South Australian Advertiser*.[316]

Six of Barton's eight sons were now scattered, but Theodore and Charles stayed near their parents and helped them as they grew older. When Barton moved to Burnside, Theodore and Elvira moved closer, to a seven-roomed stone house on fifteen acres on the other side of Glynburn Road.

During this time Barton and Bbe had another blow when their daughter Emily died on 7 January 1873 at the age of thirty-six, from cirrhosis of the liver.[317] She was living at College Town with her husband Cornelius Mitchell, and they had no children. This must have been particularly hard for Bbe, who had now lost all her daughters – Annie, Gulielma, Lucy, Louisa, Emily and Jessie.

In 1874 Barton and Bbe moved again, to Rosebank, a ten-roomed stone house on seven acres in Burnside, next to the Magill estate, owned by the Penfold family who ran the Grange Vineyard Company. Once again it was a large house, probably shared with Charles and his family. The following year Barton added another twelve acres to the lease. Theodore also moved to the estate, to a seven-roomed stone house on Magill Road.

Semaphore

Theodore's sister-in-law Stella had married Theophilus Robin, who ran a large timber yard in Lipson Street, Port Adelaide. When Robin died unexpectedly in September 1874, Theodore resigned from the Railways Department and joined the business, running it in conjunction with Stella Robin.

In September 1876 Theodore purchased a house with Stella Robin at Lot 66 (now number 30) Coppin Street in Semaphore, a wooden house with eight rooms. Two months later, Theodore purchased a house roughly opposite at Lot 47 (now number 23) Coppin Street, for his own family.[318] Two years later Barton purchased 30 Coppin Street from Theodore and Stella, and he and Bbe (and presumably Charles and his family) then moved to Semaphore, where once again the three families lived near one another. In May 1880 Barton purchased the vacant property to the rear of 30 Coppin Street (now 29 South Terrace).

Why Semaphore? It was a remote place at the time, divided from Adelaide by the Port River, with very few people living there. The attraction may have been that the land was cheap and it was close to Theodore's timber business in Port Adelaide. Barton would have visited Semaphore when John Hart was the premier and lived there in his large house, Glanville Hall.

When Theodore purchased the second Coppin Street house, it was an old stone house nestled among the sand dunes. The house must have been abandoned because it was almost buried in sand. Someone (probably Theodore) removed the roof and built a twelve-room wooden house on top, at the level of Coppin Street. Today the wooden house has been restored and is partly covered in brick. Old wooden stairs at the back of the house show how it was connected to the stone house, which may have been used as a cellar. The house is an architectural curiosity, a relic of Semaphore's history.

Theodore needed a large house. When he purchased 23 Coppin Street he and Elvira had five children and went on to have more. In December 1880 Theodore and Stella Robin, as Barton had done, purchased the block behind his house in Semaphore Road (now 28 Blackler Street).

Theodore shared Barton's interest in public affairs and in 1876, when he moved to Semaphore, he was elected to the Port Adelaide Council, and was the mayor from 1878 to 1880 when the railway was extended to Semaphore, attracting holiday-makers. In 1880 Semaphore became a separate municipality, with Theodore as its first mayor from 1883 to 1884.

Barton moved to Semaphore when he was seventy-three and

Bbe a year younger. Wherever he lived, he remained involved with the Wesleyans, in Semaphore becoming one of the principal officers of the church. Some of his sons were also Methodists, and Edward and Theodore became local preachers.

In 1881 Barton was still working as the head of Railway Accounts when Bbe became ill. She died on 20 July at their house in Coppin Street, aged seventy-four, from Bright's disease of the kidneys. On the same day Charles's youngest son Mervyn Vincent died, aged three years, from diphtheria. Bbe and her grandson were buried side by side in Woodville Cemetery (now Cheltenham cemetery.) Theodore took out a ninety-nine year lease on the family grave in the Methodist section.[319]

Retirement and memoirs

After Bbe died, Barton continued to live in Semaphore, presumably with Charles and his family. Barton was feeling old, and decided to set down an account of his life. The first version was 'Recollections of a Pioneer' published in the *Methodist Journal* in three parts, in September 1877.[320] It was forty years since the founding of the colony, and there was a great deal of interest in the stories of the early settlers.

In June 1883 Barton retired from the railways with a payout of eight months' leave of absence. It was reported in the *Register* that he was presented with a framed portrait of those working under him and an address which showed the respect in which he was held by his staff. The Acting Comptroller, Mr Pickering, commented on Barton's 'equanimity' and Barton said this was because he acted on the principle, 'Be unto others the same as you would they should be unto you'.[321]

In September that year Barton purchased a property on The Parade, Semaphore (today 106 The Esplanade). It faced the sea and consisted of two allotments. Lot 28 was vacant but there was a ten-room stone house on Lot 27 and Barton moved in there, presumably still with Charles and Annie and their seven children.[322] Drawing on extracts from his diary of the early years, Barton began to write once again and in April 1884 a three-part account of his life appeared in the *Register* with the title, 'A chequered career, reminiscences of a pioneer'.[323] The *Register* said Barton was:

A colonist known and respected during almost the whole of the last half-century throughout South Australia ... Mr Hack has had many ups and downs. He has experienced vicissitudes which would have utterly subdued the spirit of many a less brave and determined man. But with him, buffeting seemed to give increased endurance; and he stands today, after nearly fifty years of very varied colonial life, a thoroughly hale, hearty and sturdy South Australian veteran, of whom we are all justly proud.

The articles were so popular that the *Register* asked him to write a fuller version. It appeared in five parts between July and August 1884, with the title, 'Early settlement in South Australia, experiences of a pioneer'.[324] The *Register* said it 'added considerably to the fund of information regarding the opening up of the colony' and that Barton was 'amongst the honoured band of pioneers'. The articles were reprinted in the weekly *Observer*.

After chronicling his life in the colony, Barton wrote: 'Being now 79 years old, I have only to wait for my final retirement from the scenes of a very chequered life, in which I trust I have made very few enemies and many friends'.

Barton's death

Not long after writing those words, Barton became ill with heart disease, and died on 4 October 1884, aged seventy-nine. He was buried on 6 October in the family grave at Woodville Cemetery. The *Register* reported that the procession included about thirty vehicles, and that Barton's sons and grandsons, some of the early colonists and fellow civil servants attended the graveside, with 'several Wesleyan ministers, the Congregational minister at the Port and a great many gentlemen from the city, the Port and the Semaphore' also in attendance'. The Reverend James Bickford conducted the burial and was 'much moved while reviving personal reminiscences'.[325]

A long obituary appeared in the *Register* on 6 October and also in the weekly *Observer*.[326] Until the last few months, the paper said, Barton had enjoyed fairly robust health, 'especially for one, who 48 years ago, left England to save his life'. The obituary summarised Barton's life, drawing on his memoirs, and said 'in his domestic and social relations John Barton Hack was a pattern to all'.

A funeral service was held at the Semaphore Wesleyan Church on the evening of 12 October with a sermon by the Reverend Bickford. An obituary by the Reverend H.H. Teague was read to the 'deeply-affected' congregation and published later in the *Methodist Journal*.[327] The Reverend Teague said 'during the 38 years of his connection with Methodism, Mr Hack filled nearly all the leading lay offices of our Church . . . every one of which he performed with fidelity and ability'. Speakers referred to Barton's work as co-treasurer of the Foreign Missionary Society and his kindness to many poor families at the Semaphore church as the almoner of the Church Poor Fund. Mr John Bray, another Methodist, perhaps carried away by the event, spoke of him as 'a perfect saint'.

Barton's will

Barton's will was written in March 1884, six months before he died. The estate was valued at under £1050 and he appointed Theodore and Charles as executors. He bequeathed a house and land on the Parade (106 The Esplanade) and a house and land at 30 Coppin Street, Semaphore, surprisingly to Charles's wife, Annie Hack, 'for her sole use and free from the debts, control and engagements of her present and any future husband'. The rest of Barton's estate went equally to his seven other sons, except that George's inheritance was to be held in trust by the executors.

Why did Barton leave his two houses to Annie? It may be because she had lived in his house for nearly twenty years and looked after him and Bbe. The South Australian *Married Women's Property Act 1883* had been passed the year before and for the first time married women could acquire property, rather than its becoming the property of their husband.[328]

But why leave it to Annie and not Charles? The reason may be explained by a family secret uncovered in our research. In 1880, the year before Bbe died, a baby named John Howard Millard Hack was born to Harriet Amelia Millard, who had been a pupil-teacher at a school on the Lefevre Peninsula, not far from

Semaphore. The father was a Charles Hack, and the baby died five months later at Clifton. It seems that Charles had fathered an illegitimate child, and this may explain Barton's choosing to favour Annie rather than Charles. Despite this, Annie and Charles continued to live in the house on the Esplanade, and rented out the house in Coppin Street.

Stephen Hack

On the other side of the world, Barton's brother Stephen was living in Gloucestershire. Stephen had left Pinnaroo and returned to England around 1865. There he rejoined his wife Bessie and daughter Julia, now a young married woman of twenty-three. The following year he and Bessie were living with her brother George Wilton at Walbrook House, Longhope, in Gloucestershire.[329] Little is known of Stephen's later years, except that he and Bessie stayed in Gloucester for the rest of their lives.

Two letters survive from Stephen and Bessie's later years, written by Bessie to her nephew Theodore Hack.[330] The first, dated 10 November 1879, was a reply to a letter from Theodore (who was now Mayor of Port Adelaide) with news and photographs of his family. Bessie wrote, 'Above all was I pleased with your own photo . . . notwithstanding the dignity of your magisterial robes it was the same old Tods looking at me with the very same eyes that twinkled always merrily in the old days that seem so far away now . . . How I should like to see you all! What changes since I left the Colony!'

Bessie wrote that she and Stephen led a very monotonous life, 'Sometimes we get a peep at our dear Julia, but her numerous family claim her home so much that we see such little of her, her health is very delicate'. Bessie said Wilton had been 'in very, very low waters, and in a most depressed condition of spirits . . . I do not think Wilton will ever do well or be anything but a poor man, he is a source of the greatest anxiety to us'. (Wilton was at the time trying to set up a utopian settlement in South Australia.)

The second letter was dated 4 December 1881.[331] Stephen was now sixty-five, and according to Bessie he was nearly blind and could not occupy himself in any way, so he 'sits and broods over old troubles and scenes long past'. Bessie expressed her 'very great grief' that Stephen had written a letter to Barton blaming him for past events.

We do not know how Barton reacted to this, but Bessie wrote, 'I knew nothing about it, I had hoped and believed that all chance of discord between the two brothers was past and gone'. She said the only excuse she could make was 'the exact and peculiar condition of his mind, which is undoubtedly weakened by his epileptic attacks and on some points, is morbid and diseased'. She added, 'Dear Tods, for the sake of the past when you all loved me, let this sad episode be forgotten and forgiven'. Bessie added 'give him [Barton] my fond love, he ever was, and is to me still, as a dear brother'.

In 1891 Stephen and Bessie were living at 48 Kingsholm Rd, St Catherine's, Gloucester, and a photo taken in front of the house, shows Stephen with a white beard and Bessie in a wheelchair. Stephen died there on 14 May 1894 aged seventy-eight. Wilton must have returned to England after his father's death, as he was in Gloucester in December that year, when he drew some sketches for his sister Julia.[332] Bessie lived until 1915 and died in Gloucester at the age of ninety-nine.

Thomas Sanden Hack

Barton's brother Tom remained an architect in Southampton after his mother died. He had some successes, but like Barton, he ran up debts and in 1850 was in the debtors' prison in Southwark. In 1853 he and Lydia were living in Bristol when Lydia died of tuberculosis, aged forty-four. Tom returned to his career as an architect and in 1860 married Mary Chamberlain. He died in Bristol aged fifty-three, of Bright's disease of the kidneys.[333]

Gates Darton

Gates and Margaret Darton had six children, although only four survived to adulthood. Gates gave up the ironmongery business and was back in London by 1855, where he became an accountant. In 1871 he returned to the book trade as a manufacturing bookbinder, employing 230 people. In 1881 they were living in Peckham. Margaret died there in 1886 and Gates in 1887.[334]

Their great-great grandson Lawrence Darton (1914–2008), a teacher and author, spent much of his life working on the Darton and Hack papers. He wrote a book on the family publishing companies called *The Dartons*,[335] and an unpublished manuscript based on the Hack family letters, which he called *A Letter from Adelaide*.

Henry Watson

Barton's brother-in-law Henry Watson remained a chemist in O'Connell Street, North Adelaide, for the rest of his working life.[336] He and Charlotte had eleven children, four of whom died in infancy. Charlotte died in 1892 aged eighty and Henry died in 1894 aged ninety-two.

After Henry's death, his son-in-law John Sanderson Lloyd presented Henry's diary of his voyage to Australia in 1838–1839 to the South Australian archives.[337] In an accompanying letter, Lloyd wrote about the financial crash of the early 1840s which caused Barton and Henry to become insolvent. He wrote:

> People have to a great extent forgotten the crash and general ruin occasioned in Col Gawler's time by the dishonour of his bills, but neither Mr Hack nor Mr Watson was able to recover afterwards from these troubles. They were not very successful in business although capable, respectable, industrious and religious, the one having associated himself with the Wesleyans, the other with the Church of England. They lived to be old men, Mr Hack to be 79, Mr Watson to be 92, but during their long lives they were always struggling men, with difficulty making ends meet and never in easy circumstances.

Some of Henry Watson's descendants were Quakers, including Henry's granddaughter Helen Robson, who married Fred Coleman, the son of Lucy May. Fred was a noted agriculturalist and according to his family, refused an OBE from the King saying that in the Quaker view all men were equal. Fred Coleman and his son Watson Coleman were both on the board of the Friends' School in Hobart.[338]

The centenary in 1984

One hundred years after the death of John Barton Hack, in October 1984, a celebration was held at Echunga to commemorate its founder. The event was organised by Jean Bates, president of the Echunga Memorial Institute. More than 250 people attended the centenary, including about seventy-five direct descendants from South Australia, Victoria and Western Australia. Amongst the descendants were several who carried the name of their ancestor – John Barton Hack of Melbourne, John Barton Hack of O'Sullivan Beach, and John Barton Wagener of Crafers.[339]

Wreaths were laid on the Hack family grave in the Cheltenham cemetery and a service was held in the Echunga Uniting Church. John Barton Hack of Melbourne gave an address about the life of his great-grandfather, and a portrait and plaque commemorating John Barton Hack were unveiled in the foyer of the Echunga Memorial Institute by the MP for Murray, David Wotton.

Summing up

At the centenary service John Barton Hack's great-grandson described the many ups and downs of his ancestor's 'chequered life' to his audience. In assessing John Barton Hack he said, 'my overwhelming impression is that he was an enterprising and hard-working optimist, and that when the fates moved against him as they often did, he did not give in, but fought to revive his fortunes in one capacity or another, as best he could. He was also a deeply religious man, and a generous one'.[340]

At the afternoon tea following the service, a descendant of Wilton Hack took me aside and questioned whether Barton Hack was indeed a fine and worthy man. She showed me a copy of Wilton's diary, and pointed out Wilton's account of Barton taking him in and Bbe asking for rent. I was shocked, and asked my father why he had 'cleaned up' his ancestor's story. My father looked surprised, but on a later occasion he wrote of his great-grandfather, 'my personal opinion is that he had poor judgement, was vain and rather sanctimonious, and created many problems for his family, not the least being the father of his poor wife's fifteen children'.[341]

How do we sum up anybody's life, including our own? When

Barton Hack wrote his memoirs he did not hide the truth of his ups and downs, but nor did he dwell on his failures. His brother-in-law Gates Darton, by keeping the ledgers and letters between the family in England and Australia, revealed a different story. Without that correspondence we would never have known the extent of Barton's imprudence in money matters and the hardship he caused Gates in England. As a strict Quaker, Gates believed in absolute integrity in business matters and was embarrassed by Barton's casual and sometimes negligent attitude. It is tempting to think that Gates kept all of this material and passed it down to his children, in the hope that one day someone would read it and understand what he went through.

Barton's sons inherited his casual attitude to financial matters, and most of them became insolvent at one time or another. In my own family I found there was a reaction to this. My grandfather Clement Hack, according to my father, 'believed in a strict code of ethics in both personal and business life, and was very critical of anyone who deviated from it'. My father also was scrupulously honest and conservative in financial matters. He frequently told us not to do business with friends or relatives, and quoted the line from Shakespeare, 'neither a borrower nor a lender be'.

J.B. Hack: remarkable Quaker pioneer

Barton took huge risks in business and often acted to serve his own interests without thinking of the consequences for other people. But it was precisely because he was optimistic and took risks that he achieved a great deal, especially in the six years between 1837 and 1842, when he was in his thirties.

He took a long voyage to a colony barely born, and he and his family contributed to its growth. When he arrived, he brought with him a bullock team and dray and performed a service that was extremely useful – not to mention essential – for the colonists. He imported much-needed goods and established the first dairy for fresh milk, butter and cheese. He undertook the first public works at the port and in Adelaide when no one else had the resources, and built the first bridge over the Torrens.

In those early years he promoted the pastoral, agricultural and horticultural development of the province by importing stock, seed and trees. He ensured the continuation of the whaling industry, which along with wool was the only real source of export income for the colony before the discovery of minerals.

Believing passionately in his new country, he assisted in the establishment of many of the colony's business and social institutions, including the Adelaide Botanic Garden, the Agricultural Society, the Literary and Scientific Association and Mechanics Institute (which later became the State Library and Museum), and the Chamber of Commerce.

He was the first person to establish an 'agribusiness' in South Australia, encompassing beef and dairy production, horse-breeding, crop-growing, market-gardening, and viticulture. His wine, made from grapes from vines imported by him, was the first made in the colony, wine now being a mainstay of the South Australian economy.

His enthusiastic assessment of the fledgling colony was used to promote emigration in England and he gave assistance and advice to a stream of immigrants, not only Quakers, on their arrival.

All this was achieved in a very short time. His downfall in 1843 was partly due to the economic crash of 1841–1842, but his own flaws played a part, in particular his reckless borrowing and over-reaching. After he lost everything he experienced a physical breakdown and was forced to start all over again, although he still persisted in his habit of borrowing money. It was not until he was sixty-four that he settled down to a job in the railways and gave up his business schemes. In joining the Methodists he found a new source of strength, and according to the eulogies at his funeral, he became a changed man, with a new thoughtfulness and gentleness, while retaining his essential sense of justice and kindness.

While Barton's achievements have been praised, the contribution of his wife has been overlooked. It is clear that a good deal of credit must go to Bbe for her pioneering spirit. Stephen understood this, and told his mother they could not have managed in the early days without Bbe's resilience. After their arrival she had to live in fairly rough conditions and endure almost-continual childbearing, while being responsible for their large family, although on occasions, when finances allowed it, she had some domestic help. She also took charge of the dairying part of the business.

After the crisis in 1843 Bbe had to manage with almost no money or domestic help, and in 1852 when Barton and his four oldest sons went to the goldfields, she managed on her own with the six younger children for nearly a year. In 1858, in her early fifties, she had to 'rough it' again for five years on the Coorong, an isolated and inhospitable place, and also care for the children of her son William, after the death of his wife.

Barton's children seem to have been loyal to him, which must say something about him as a father. When he went to the Coorong they rallied around to help him get established, and most of his sons worked for him at various times in the south-east. Later on when Barton and Bbe moved to Burnside and Semaphore, Theodore and Charles lived nearby and gave continual support to their parents.

Barton had plenty of energy and determination, and these kept him going when another man would have given up. He is remembered as the founder of Echunga, and his name lives on in Barton Terrace in North Adelaide, Hack Street and Barton Place in North Adelaide, Hack Range Road in Echunga and Hack Street in Mount Barker. Barton Hack achieved widespread recognition through the very readable memoirs he published towards the end of his life. In later years they were consulted by those who wanted to know more about the early days of the colony, and the memoirs were quoted by historians.

Had Barton had stayed in Chichester it would have been an entirely different story. Most importantly, he would probably have died of tuberculosis. Unhappy in the family currier business, he was overshadowed by his father and uncles, who were prominent in business and humanitarian causes. In South Australia he was able, with determination and immense hard work, to play a significant role and raise a large family. When he and Stephen arrived in the colony they had about £2000 between them. When the crash came their assets were worth about £30,000, a remarkable feat in five years – even if eventually it was all lost.

Particularly in their attitude to the Aborigines, Barton and Stephen were influenced by their Quaker background – in much the same way as their ancestors had championed the campaign against the slave trade. Being a Quaker did not harm their business dealings in South Australia, and in some ways it advantaged them, in that they were Dissenters, along with leading colonists like Robert Gouger, John Brown and Charles Mann.

Friendship was very important to Barton, evidenced by the words he wrote at the end of his life, 'I trust I have made very few enemies and many friends'. Despite Jacob Hagen and John Baker engineering his downfall, Barton remained on reasonably friendly terms with them. Ironically, Hagen and Hart raised the money for Barton to start a carrying business following his forced departure from Echunga, and Hagen and Baker were probably amongst those who gave Barton the mining job at Kapunda. Hagen left South Australia in 1854, but Barton remained in contact with Baker, who employed Bedford and Stephen Hack on his properties, and it was to Baker that Barton later sold his lease on the Coorong.

Barton would probably best like to be remembered in the words of George Morphett, who in 1940 was the President of the Pioneers Association of South Australia. In a pamphlet titled, *John Barton Hack, A Quaker Pioneer*, he summed up Barton:

> He was a man of excellent character, energetic and enterprising in this young community, but destined to be a victim of adverse circumstances. J.B. Hack was deeply interested in everything that made for the social, educational, and spiritual welfare of the community ... [He] deserves to be held in grateful remembrance by this State.

Stephen Hack: frontier man and explorer

Barton's brother Stephen Hack died a sad and disappointed man, but perhaps he was wrong to think he had failed. Stephen was aged a mere twenty-one when he arrived in South Australia. He had not settled to any occupation in England, and emigration allowed him to fulfil his dream of being a 'frontier' man, and in that respect he was very successful. On his arrival in South Australia he soon became an expert bushman and explorer, venturing into areas where no white man had been before. He befriended the Aborigines, learned the local language, and used native guides whenever he was exploring.

He was the first man to set out to overland cattle from New South Wales to South Australia – a journey which took him over largely unexplored land. He went on to manage the properties at Echunga and Yankalilla, supervising a large number of employees. After his insolvency he displayed his resourcefulness by turning his hand to whatever he could, driving a bullock dray and establishing a little farm on Echunga Creek.

We know little about Stephen's time in England or South Africa, but on his return to South Australia his pioneering spirit again came to the fore: he managed large stations in Victoria and outback South Australia and undertook explorations around the Gawler Ranges and Lake Gairdner. He also explored in the North Flinders ranges, where Mount Hack was named after him. His sheep farming with Barton in marginal land in the south-east may have failed, but the pioneer brothers played a crucial part in opening up that part of the province.

Stephen's life ended unhappily, but this was probably because he was old and unwell. He blamed Barton for their 'ruin' in 1843, and was rightly angry that he had spent time in jail and lost all his belongings But blaming Barton for their downfall was not entirely fair, since Stephen seemed not to take into account the economic crash that destroyed so many others at the time. Nor did he accept any responsibility for what happened. In his twenties Stephen enjoyed the life of a gentleman farmer, but showed an irresponsible disregard for how that life was supported, even running up substantial debts of his own in England.

We know almost nothing of Stephen's life after he returned to England for good, but it seems probable that he was supported by Bessie's family. Stephen may have become difficult in old age, but he was much admired by his son Wilton, who wrote on the back of his father's portrait 'a good man, a true friend and a general favourite.'

Stephen and Barton Hack led very chequered lives, but they made a significant contribution, in their different ways, to the founding of South Australia. They were true pioneers.

Appendix
Barton and Stephen's children

Barton's sons became farmers, businessmen and government employees. Some of them followed him into the Methodist church, and took an interest in community affairs. Two sons became involved in local government, one in state parliament and several became justices of the peace.

Barton's children and grandchildren.
The story of John Barton Hack would not be complete without a brief look at what happened to his children and some of their descendants. When Barton's sons were growing up, he made sure they had a classical education (Greek and Latin being the custom of the day), but said it would be of little use in the colony as they would end up being stockkeepers. And that is what several of them did, while the others mainly worked in government service or some form of business, like their father. Their success in commerce was little better than Barton's, and most of them became insolvent at some stage in their lives.

By 1873 Barton and Bbe had lost all their daughters. All of their eight sons married, and several of their grandchildren and great-grandchildren were named John Barton, after their pioneering ancestor.

William Hack
William, the eldest son, remained a farmer throughout his life. He had five children with his first wife Grace, and eleven with his second wife Emma. He and Emma stayed in the south-east after their marriage. They lived near Naracoorte on and off, and William worked on Emma's father's property Tintinara.[342] After William Harding died in 1874, William and Emma travelled to the Riverland in South Australia, where they moved from one

place to another. Children were born at Pooginook, Wigley's Flat and Cobdogla, all near the Murray.

A letter survives from Emma to her stepdaughter Annie in February 1876, when they were living near Wigley's Flat.[343] William was working on a station on the River Murray and they were living close to the river, having come up on a steamer from Adelaide. Emma said they bought all their things off the steamers, which had nice little shops. At this stage there were nine in the family, William, Emma, their five small children and two of William's older children, Barton John and Arthur William.

They were still on the Murray in 1884 when William was working as a wood merchant.[344] By 1887 William had a farm of 1200 acres at Stewart's Range, near Naracoorte, and in June Emma's eleventh child was born, whom they named Harry. Harry's descendants say that around 1889 William and Emma's son Wilfred (known as Freddie) died when he was dragged by a horse some paddocks away from home. He was about seven years old, and when Emma found him she carried him home in her arms.[345]

William became insolvent in 1891, but did not lose the farm, remaining there until his death on 2 April 1900 at the age of 71. Emma remained on the farm until she died in 1928 aged 83. Her obituary in the *Border Watch* said she was 'widely esteemed for her kindly and generous disposition and for her good works'.[346] William and Emma's son Harry Hack took over the farm and it is still in the family; today it is 2000 acres and run by Harry's grandson Brenton Hack (known as Ben). Hack's lagoon, a nature reserve south of Naracoorte, is named after Harry Hack.

One of William's granddaughters, Irene Ethel Hack, married Frank Godolphin Bonython, son of Sir John Langdon Bonython, the wealthy philanthropist and proprietor of the *Advertiser*.

Edward Hack

Edward had four children, three with his first wife Elizabeth and one with his second wife Sarah. His first child, Annie Mary, was born while he was at the goldfields in 1852, and on his return he established a home in Beulah Road, Norwood, while he and Bedford worked for Stephen Hack on the Murray during

1853–1854. Edward then returned to Victoria with his wife and child. They had two more children, Charles Edward and Louisa Bridget, and by 1857 were living in Yackandandah in the northeast of Victoria. In 1861 Edward's step-daughter Emma Hackett (Elizabeth's daughter) married John Bennett, a watchmaker, when she was 15 and he was 28. In 1870 Edward and his family were living at Chiltern in central Victoria, where he worked as a water carrier.[347]

In January 1874 Elizabeth died at Beechworth, aged 49. Edward returned to Adelaide and joined the government service.[348] On 31 August 1875, he married Sarah Ann Dall and the following year their son Robert Dall Hack was born in Norwood. In 1884 Edward was described as a porter and in 1885 he was foreman for the railways survey department, living at Rose Street, Prospect. From 1896 on, after being retrenched from government service, he had a draper's shop (Edward Hack & Son) in Pulsford Road at the north corner of Prospect Road. Edward died at his home in Prospect on 25 September 1904 aged 75. For 26 years he was a Methodist local preacher.[349]

One of Edward's great-granddaughters, Betty Hack, married an Aboriginal man, Malcolm Clothier, from the Wirangu people on the west coast of South Australia. Their grandson, Ben McKeown, is an artist who draws on his Aboriginal and European heritage.[350]

Alfred Hack

Alfred left his name in the south-east at 'Alf's Flat' near the Coorong. He married Susan Pengilly and was engaged in auctioneering and farming in the district of Aldinga,[351] probably because Susan's father had a farm there. Alfred and Susan had four children, born between 1871 and 1877 at Aldinga or nearby Port Willunga. Alfred became chairman of the Aldinga Council and a Justice of the Peace, but in 1883 during the recession he became insolvent and had to resign from the council and as a JP.[352]

In 1884 the family moved to Mill Street, Goodwood, where Alfred was still an auctioneer and agent, and from 1887 onwards he was a sanitary inspector for the Adelaide Council, living first in Mann Terrace, North Adelaide, then Finniss Street, North Adelaide, and finally at 54 Miller Street, North Unley, the same street as his brother Theodore. Susan died there in 1906, aged about 57, and Alfred died there on 7 June 1908, aged 74.

Alfred and Susan's two surviving children were John Barton Hack and Frederick Theodore Hack. Fred became a state and international cricketer. In 1905 he married a cousin, Rosa Pengilly, and went into business with another cousin, Fred Pengilly, building horse-drawn coaches. In 1907 Fred Hack became a pioneer in the new motor car industry, building individual cars and fire trucks. After selling the business to Holdens in 1917, Fred is rumoured to have taken off with the maid from the family's Glenelg home, leaving Rosa to raise their four children.[353] He ended up in Queensland, changed his name, and died in 1939, leaving nothing to Rosa and the children. His son Alfred Hack became a state and international cricketer, playing with Bradman.

Bedford Hack

In 1869, the year that he was 'droughted out' in the far north, Bedford married Frances Bishop and rented a property near Milang and grew wheat, but it was ruined by rust. In 1871 he joined the civil service and went to the Northern Territory to finish the overland telegraph line, returning at the end of 1872. He then joined the survey department and served as crown lands ranger and later as a warden of goldfields. In 1882 he made an inspection of the Echunga goldfields, and later became government arbitrator of the 1888 leases.[354] From 1887 he was a JP. In 1889 he was appointed manager of the Adelaide Sewage Farm at Islington, holding that position for 19 years and retiring in 1908 at the age of 73. At his retirement he was congratulated for making it profitable and enlarging the area by 160 acres.[355]

Bedford and Frances had five children, born between 1870 and 1878, at Milang, College Town, Melrose and Fullarton. From 1886 to 1889 the family lived at Woodville. Bedford died on 26 April 1912 at the age of 76. Three of his sons (Percy, Guy and Ralph) moved to Western Australia.

Charles Hack

Charles and his wife Annie had eleven children, born between 1867 and 1889. In 1884 when Barton died, he left Annie his two houses in Semaphore, and they remained in the house on The Esplanade. From 1882 to 1887 Charles was described as a broker, and in 1892 he was listed as a timber broker at 147 North Terrace East, Adelaide. From 1894 to 1895 he was at the Royal Exchange, King William Street, and from 1896 at 2 Palm Place, Hackney. Two of his daughters were married from this address in 1902 and 1910.

Charles died on 22 April 1915 at the age of 72, described as a 'collector' living at Edwin Terrace, Gilberton. His obituary said he was best known through his musical talent, and was a life member of the Orpheus Society. He was a member of the Anglican Cathedral Choir for twenty-two years and figured in nearly every oratorio given in Adelaide.

Annie died in October 1929 at Gilberton, aged 85. In her obituary she was described as an interesting personality who read extensively, took a deep interest in current events and politics and loved her garden.[356] Charles left no will and nor did Annie, but in 1956 their estate was granted to their daughter Winifred Bbe Skottowe, of Edwin Terrace, Gilberton.[357]

Charles's love of music was passed on to his eldest daughter Gulielma, who became a well-known singer. In 1887 she won the Elder scholarship which took her to the Royal College of Music, London.[358] In 1910 at the age of 43 she married William Ashley Magarey, lawyer and sportsman, the donor of South Australia's most prestigious football award. Guli became the Conservatorium's first female teacher of singing and her memory is perpetuated in the Guli Magarey Scholarship for a female singer at the Elder Conservatorium, University of Adelaide.

Charles had four sons who lived to adulthood: Gerald was the manager of the Guardian Insurance Co. in Adelaide, Leonard was a manager with Elder, Smith & Co. and a prominent state tennis player,[359] Noel worked for James Bell & Co. and Lionel was with the Eastern Extension Company.

Francis Hack

Francis (Frank) married Maria Boland in February 1873 and became an overseer at Mount Templeton. A son, Theodore Barton, was born there in November the same year. A second son, Thomas Philip, was born in August 1875. The following year, in September 1876 Maria died, aged only 26.

Two years later, on 13 February 1879, Frank married his second wife, Mary Anne Pedler. He worked as an agent in Adelaide and became insolvent on 3 August 1882. In 1884 he became manager of the Goodwood tramway until 1888, when he was listed as a sharebroker living at Gilberton. From 1896 he lived at Clifton Parade, Goodwood Park and died there on 17 August 1903 aged 59. At the time his wife was living at the Union Hotel, Waymouth Street. Francis won several literary competitions and was on the committee of the Unley Institute and Library.[360] His son Theodore Barton moved to Western Australia.

George Hack

Barton's youngest son George did not fare as well as his brothers. He married Elizabeth Ann Johns in 1869 and they had nine children, born between 1871 and 1885, when the family were living at various times in Kent Town, North Adelaide, Hackney, Norwood and Kensington. In 1884 George was described in Barton's will as a labourer, and his inheritance was controlled by his brothers Theodore and Charles.

Between 1887 and 1890 George twice became insolvent, and must have been separated from his wife, because she took him to court repeatedly for failure to pay maintenance of 15 shillings a week. In February 1891 the court was told that Mrs Hack had 'her lord and master' in jail for over two-and-a-half years out of the past three.[361] Elizabeth died in 1907 aged 58.

George's son Barton William Henry Hack had similar misfortunes. He married Helen (Nellie) Sayer in 1900 and had three children, but in 1910 Nellie issued a public notice saying that if he did not contact her within three months, she intended to marry again.[362] In 1914 she married Henry Thomas Watkins, by whom she already had two children. There is no record of the death of George or of his son Barton William Henry.

George's descendants fared better. A great-great-grandson Lindsay Richards is Professor of Dentistry at the University of Adelaide and another great-grandson Don Hack works for Resthaven retirement homes in Adelaide.

Theodore Hack

I have left to the last, Barton's fifth son, Theodore, my great-grandfather. It was to Theodore that Barton entrusted his diary, and Theodore passed it on to his son Clement, who placed it in the South Australian archives. Theodore was the son most like Barton in his business activities and civic-mindedness. He was the Mayor of Port Adelaide from 1878 to 1880 and the first Mayor of Semaphore from 1883 1884. As a local businessman and councillor, he had a street named after him in Port Adelaide (next to the Portland canal).[363]

Theodore became a member of the Legislative Assembly (MP for Gumeracha 1890–1893) and was a Justice of the Peace. He was a member of the Central Road Board and the Fire Brigades Board, chairman of the committee of the Prisoners Aid Society, and on the governing board of Prince Alfred College. Like Barton before him, he was on the committee of the Chamber of Manufactures. He supported the federation of the colonies and in 1891 was a delegate to an interstate conference to discuss one aspect of federation. He was active in the Methodist Church as a local preacher and in the Australasian General Methodist conference.[364]

Theodore inherited Barton's interest in business, but also his habit of over-reaching, and was three times declared insolvent. In 1884 Theodore was a timber merchant with timber yards at Port Adelaide, North Terrace and Port Augusta. In August 1884 the Port Adelaide yard failed and the creditors allowed him to buy out his sister-in-law Stella Robin and run the Port Adelaide yard in his own name.[365] In September the Port Augusta timber yard became insolvent. Then in November that year there was a massive fire at the Port Adelaide yard, which destroyed most of it.[366] Theodore struggled on for two years, but conditions in the colony were not good, and in October 1886 he became insolvent again. This time he lost the business, which was purchased by two employees, Theophilus Walter and Charles Morris.

In 1881 Theodore paid off his house at 23 Coppin Street, but immediately took out a new mortgage on it and the block behind. These mortgages were discharged in 1887, but as he was insolvent at the time, he lost both properties. In 1889 he moved to Konkalara, a ten-roomed stone house at 41 Miller Street, North Unley, first renting, and then in 1890 purchasing the property. His brother Alfred lived across the road at number 54.

After losing the timber yard, Theodore commenced business in Adelaide as a valuator and commission agent and later as an architect, with an office in King William Street. From 1891 to 1895 his business address was Marlborough Chambers in Waymouth Street, and from 1896 to 1902, the Royal Exchange, King William Street.

Theodore and Elvira had nine children and they also raised a granddaughter of William Hack, who was orphaned as a baby. This was Elsie Earl, whom Theodore and Elvira brought up as one of their own. But on 7 October 1890, Elvira died aged 49, from ascites (fluid in the abdomen, from liver disease or cancer). She left eight children as well as Elsie. Her oldest child Ernest Barton Hack, 23, was married and the youngest was eight-year-old Roy Darton Hack.

Theodore was 49 and hired a housekeeper, Elizabeth Jane Almer, a 32-year-old widow with one son. Theodore's children took a dislike to both of them and left home as soon as they could.[367] Despite this, Theodore married Elizabeth in October 1898 when he was 57 and Elizabeth was 40.

Theodore died at the age of 62, on 27 December 1902, after suffering for a long time from Bright's disease of the kidneys, like his mother. Theodore's will, made out while he was sick, left everything to Elizabeth. She stayed on in the family home until 1905 and died in Wayville in 1914.

Theodore's third son, Clement Alfred Hack (my grandfather, known as Clem) studied at the South Australian School of Mines and became a patent attorney. In 1904 at the age of 27 he moved to Melbourne and set up the firm of Clement Hack & Co., working for many of Australia's leading mining companies. He became president of the Institute of Patent Attorneys of Australia. Like his father, he took a keen interest in public affairs and was President of the Australian Natives Association, a founder of the Australian Industries Protection League, and member of several Victorian Government committees. He died young, at the age of 53, from Bright's disease, like his father.

His eldest son John Barton Hack (1911–1996, my father) became a partner in Clement Hack & Co. and was later President of the Institute of Patent Attorneys of Australia, Founder and President of the Australian Group of the International Association for the Protection of Industrial Property, represented Australia at several international conferences on patents and trademarks, and wrote a history of the patent profession in colonial Australia. He was also involved in community service throughout his life.

The firm of Clement Hack & Co. is now called Griffith Hack (Patents, Trade Marks and Intellectual Property Law) with offices in Melbourne, Sydney, Perth and Brisbane.

Another of Theodore's grandsons, Colin Ballantyne (1908–1988) was a well-known theatre director in Adelaide. He was chairman of the Board of the SA Theatre Company, co-founder of the Arts Council of SA and a prime force behind the Adelaide Festival. He was a president of the Arts Council of Australia and was awarded the CMG in 1971.[368] His daughter Elspeth Ballantyne is a well-known actress; her sister Jane Ballantyne is a film producer and their brother, Guy Ballantyne, is a former ABC television producer.

It is also worth mentioning what happened to Stephen Hack's children, Julia and Wilton.

Julia Hack

Stephen and Bessie's daughter Julia was married to the Reverend Charles Cutler, the vicar of Hathersage, on the Yorkshire moors. She had married in 1862, at the age of 20. The vicarage was famous for the fact that Charlotte Bronte stayed there in 1845 while writing Jane Eyre.[369] Julia may have found inspiration in that because she also became a writer. Under the name Julia Hack she produced numerous 'charming domestic stories', mainly for children. Like her grandmother Maria Hack, Julia's books had a strong moral theme. Julia was an invalid for much of her life, but despite this had ten children.[370]

Wilton Hack

Wilton Hack had an extremely colourful life, which he recounted in his memoir in 1907.[371] Like his father he was a restless soul, frequently leaving his wife and children for long periods. He tried numerous ventures, most of which failed, and was often supported financially by Stephen and Bessie.

Wilton Hack and his wife Anna Maria (Annie) had five children, one of whom died in infancy. Wilton's descendants report that he also had an illegitimate son. His granddaughter Helen Hack said the child was born to a servant girl while Wilton was in England at school, still in his teens. At the time his mother was keeping house for her brother-in-law in Derbyshire and perhaps the servant girl was there when Wilton visited on school holidays. Helen said the child was a Billy Ethridge or Etheridge; that Wilton acknowledged him, and Billy was later with Wilton and his family on the goldfields. According to Helen, Billy turned out to be 'a poor affair', fond of the drink and visiting brothels.[372]

After marrying and becoming a Baptist minister, in 1873 Wilton went to Japan as a missionary and later as a teacher of English. In 1876 he returned to Adelaide and negotiated with the South Australian Government for the admission of a few hundred Japanese families into the Northern Territory, but the project was later rejected by the Japanese Government.[373] He then floated some gold mines in New South Wales, and in 1870 returned to South Australia and attempted to establish a cooperative settlement for the unemployed at Mount Remarkable in the Flinders Ranges. The scheme collapsed and he had a breakdown.

Wilton was attracted to theosophy and visited India and Ceylon several times, studying Eastern religions, on which he wrote and lectured. In 1890 he went to England to promote gold mines in Western Australia, but had to borrow from his father for his return fare to Adelaide. In the 1890s he and Annie settled in Parkin Terrace, Glenelg, where he worked as a bookbinder and devoted himself to painting. When Anna Maria died in 1916, Wilton moved to Western Australia to stay with his son Will. The same year Wilton had a serious accident and was nursed by Minnie Alice Wierk, whom he married. He died at Beverley, Western Australia, in 1923.[374]

APPENDIX: BARTON AND STEPHEN'S CHILDREN

This appendix has only mentioned a small number of the many descendants of Barton and Stephen Hack. There are others scattered all over Australia, in cities and on farms. We are proud to be descended from these hard-working pioneers, and deeply grateful that the diaries, letters and memoirs of this extended family were preserved for so long, so that we can know more about their lives.

Notes

Introduction
1. John Barton Hack, 'Diary of J.B. Hack, with letters', manuscript and typewritten transcript of diary in State Library of South Australia, PRG 456/6.
2. Bbe was pronounced Beeby; Mrs Aileen Treloar, a descendant of John Barton Hack, pers. comm., 20 January 2011. This pronunciation was also the view of Lawrence Darton, a descendant of Gates Darton.
3. John Barton Hack & Bridget Hack, 'Letters to and from members of the Hack family 1837–1844', manuscripts and typewritten transcripts in State Library of South Australia, PRG 456/1.
4. Conservation Team, State Library of Victoria, pers. comm., 10 July 2010.
5. J. Gilchrist, 'Hack, John Barton (1805–1884)', *Australian Dictionary of Biography*, National Centre of Biography, Australian National University, http://adb.anu.edu.au.

Chapter 1
6. *Age*, 1 February 2007, obituary, Nick Vine Hall, genealogist, author, broadcaster.
7. See www.ancestry.com; www.houseofnames.com.
8. John Highfield, librarian, Liverpool Quakers, pers. comm., 7 September 2010. Chris Durrant has found some errors in transcriptions of Quaker records and has corrected them by checking images of original certificates. He also found that some of the dates attributed to documents before 1753 were wrong because the Quaker calendar changed in that year, from March being the 'first' month to January being the 'first' month. For an accurate family tree see his website www.durrant.id.au.
9. James Walvin, *The Quakers: Money and Morals*, John Murray, London, 1997, p. 11.
10. Walvin, p. 16.
11. Walvin, p. 210.
12. See www.quakers.org.au.
13. 'A history of the Chichester Bank (taken over by Barclays in 1900)', typescript in West Sussex Record Office, MP 714.
14. Chichester Tourist Information Centre, see www.chichester.gov.uk.
15. Bernard Price, *Chichester: The historic city and countryside*, Pitkin Pictorials, London, 1975.

16 The museum in Little London closed in 2011 when it moved to larger premises in Tower Street, Chichester.
17 Thomas Clarkson, *The History of the Rise, Progress, and Accomplishment of the Abolition of the African Slave-Trade by the British Parliament*, Longman, Hurst, Read & Orme, Paternoster-row, London, 1808.
18 Gordon Goodwin, 'Hack, Maria (1777–1844)', *Oxford Dictionary of National Biography*, Oxford University Press, 2004.
19 Ann Stillwell Griffiths, 'John Barton of Chichester, Stoughton and East Leigh 1789–1852', *Chichester History: The Journal of the Chichester Local History Society*, no. 17, 2000, p. 12, and no. 18, 2001, p. 16. Also accessible on the website of Dr David B.H. Barton, a descendant of John Barton, bartonhistory.wikispaces.com.
20 Edward FitzGerald, 'Memoir of Bernard Barton', in *Memoir, Letters, and Poems of Bernard Barton*, ed. Lucy Barton, Lindsay and Blakiston, Philadelphia, 1850.
21 Gordon Goodwin, 'Hack, Maria (1777–1844)', *Oxford Dictionary of National Biography*, Oxford University Press, 2004.
22 All but the first title by Maria Hack are available in Google books.
23 Jack Zipes (ed.), *Oxford Encyclopedia of Children's Literature*, Oxford University Press, 2006.
24 Griffiths, www.bartonhistory.wikispaces.com.
25 *Friends' Intelligencer*, Society of Friends, Philadelphia, vol. 51, 1894, p. 258.
26 John Marsh, 'Diaries 1752–1828', manuscript in Huntingdon Library, California, microfilm copies in West Sussex Record Office, MF 1170.
27 Karl Marx, *Capital. Vol 4: Theories of Surplus Value*, ch. 18, 1863, www.marxists.org/archive/marx/works/1863/theories-surplus-value. Marx wrote: 'Indisputably, Barton has very great merit'.

Chapter 2

28 John Highfield, librarian, Liverpool Quakers, pers. comm., 7 September 2010.
29 John Sanderson Lloyd, letter of 1911 attached to the diary of his father-in-law, Henry Watson, in State Library of South Australia, PRG 456/13.
30 C. Clement, 'Quaker Education and Schooling 1775–1840. Part IV: Richard Weston's school 1820–29', *The Clock Tower*, no. 22, 2011, p. 37.
31 See Chichester District Council; www.graylingwellchichester.com.
32 Honoria Williams, *Syllabic Spelling or a Summary Method of Teaching Children to Read*, 4th edn, Whittaker, Treacher & Arnot, Ave-Maria-Lane, London, 1829.
33 Lawrence Darton, 'A letter from Adelaide, an account of early settlement in South Australia from the journals and letters of John Barton Hack, Stephen Hack and Henry Watson, 1836–1844', typescript dated 1947 in West Sussex Record Office, MP 1372, and revised introduction, MP 1377. A revision dated 1980 is in the possession of Iola Matthews.

Chapter 3

34 Ann Stillwell Griffiths, 'John Barton of Chichester, Stoughton and East Leigh 1789–1852', *Chichester History: The Journal of the Chichester Local History Society*, no. 17, 2000, p. 12, and no. 18, 2001, p. 16. Also accessible on the website of Dr David B.H. Barton, a descendant of John Barton, bartonhistory.wikispaces.com.

35 Miles Fairburn, 'Wakefield, Edward Gibbon (1796–1862)', in *Dictionary of New Zealand Biography, Te Ara–the Encyclopedia of New Zealand*, www.teara.govt.nz/en/biographies/1w4/wakefield-edward-gibbon.

36 Douglas Pike, *Paradise of Dissent: South Australia 1829–1857*, 2nd edn, Melbourne University Press, Melbourne, 1967, p 3.

37 'Hindmarsh, Sir John (1785–1860)', *Australian Dictionary of Biography*, National Centre of Biography, Australian National University, http://adb.anu.edu.au.

38 Elizabeth Kwan, *Living in South Australia: A Social History*, vol.1, South Australian Government Printer, Netley, 1987, p. 166.

39 Lawrence Darton, 'A letter from Adelaide, an account of early settlement in South Australia from the journals and letters of John Barton Hack, Stephen Hack and Henry Watson, 1836–1844', typescript dated 1947 in West Sussex Record Office, MP 1372, and revised introduction, MP 1377. A revision dated 1980 is in the possession of Iola Matthews.

40 Fairburn, www.teara.govt.nz/en/biographies/1w4/wakefield-edward-gibbon.

Chapter 4

41 It was 72°F in London; National Meteorological Archive, UK, pers. comm., 25 May 2010.

42 The crib belongs to Mrs Aileen Treloar, a descendant of John Barton Hack's son William.

43 *Launceston Advertiser*, 12 January 1837.

44 Douglas Pike, *Paradise of Dissent: South Australia 1829–1857*, 2nd edn, Melbourne University Press, Melbourne, 1967, p. 112.

45 Don Charlwood, *The Long Farewell*, Allen Lane, Ringwood, Victoria, 1981, ch. 2.

46 Charlwood, pp. 134–5.

47 Charlwood, ch. 10.

48 Henry Watson, *A lecture on South Australia; including letters from J. B. Hack, Esq. and other emigrants*, 2nd edn, J. Gliddon, London, 1838.

49 John Stephens, *The Land of Promise*, Smith, Elder & Co., London, 1839.

Chapter 5

50 The cost of living in Australia changed roughly as follows: £1 in 1850 was equivalent to $110 in 2003 (calculation by Chris Durrant).

51 These ledgers were passed down to Lawrence Darton, great-grandson of Gates Darton, who passed them on to John Barton Hack, great-grandson

of John Barton Hack, who placed them in the State Library of South Australia (PRG 456/16).

Chapter 6

52 Tracey Lock-Weir, *Visions of Adelaide*, Art Gallery of South Australia, Adelaide, 2005, p. 3.
53 The population of South Australia at the end of 1836 was 546 according to Wray Vamplew et al., *South Australian Historical Statistics*, Historical statistics monograph no. 3, Australia 1788–1988: A bicentennial history, Kensington, NSW, 1984. But a tally of the passengers on the various ships that arrived would make it more like 700.
54 John Barton Hack, 'Chequered Career: Recollections of a Pioneer', *Methodist Journal*, 7 September, 21 September, 28 September 1877. He later elaborated on these memoirs in three parts in the *South Australian Register*, 22 April, 23 April, 28 April 1884, and in five parts in the *South Australian Register*, 3 July, 12 July, 19 July, 29 July, 9 August 1884.
55 Skipper painted this on 14 March 1837, Lock-Weir, p. 20. Although more bullocks had arrived earlier, nobody else had a cart or dray at this time.
56 Letter from Bridget Hack to Henry Watson, 26 March 1837, quoted in Gates Darton to Maria Hack, 11 September 1837, typewritten transcript in State Library of South Australia, PRG 456/3/65.
57 James Chittleborough, 'Recollections of the early days', *Advertiser*, 29 November 1912.
58 *South Australian Yearbook*, Commonwealth Bureau of Census and Statistics, South Australian Office, Adelaide, 1986, p. 6.
59 See reference to this in chapter 23, The Coorong.

Chapter 7

60 A lighthouse was erected later on Port Nelson and a plaque about the wreck of the *Isabella* is located next to the lighthouse. The cafe in the lighthouse is called the *Isabella*. In 1998 divers found some remains of the wreck, including the anchor. It is the oldest shipwreck on the Victorian coast. Heritage Victoria and History House, Portland, person. comm., 15 November 2011.
61 *A Pioneer History of South Australia*, Pioneers Association of South Australia, Adelaide, 2001, p. 25.
62 Letter from William Suter to his family, 24 May 1837, in Henry Capper, *South Australia*, 3rd edn, London, 1839; *South Australian Record*, 27 November 1837.
63 *South Australian Gazette & Colonial Register*, 29 July 1837.
64 *South Australian Register*, 9 December 1843. See this reference also for John Barton Hack growing grapes and making wine at Echunga. In 1836, before the proclamation of the colony, a few vine cuttings were brought from England to Kangaroo Island by the South Australia Company. Hack's

vines in North Adelaide in 1837 were the first on the mainland and the first private vineyard in the colony.
65 Letters to the Colonial Secretary in London, State Records of South Australia, GRG 24/1/1837 and 24/1/1838.
66 *South Australian Register*, 16 February 1892, William Wren Ellis.
67 Letter from Harriet Staker to her mother, 18 February 1838, *South Australian Record*, 14 November 1838.

Chapter 8
68 *South Australian Gazette & Colonial Register*, 10 March 1838.
69 James Backhouse, *A Narrative of a Visit to the Australian Colonies*, Hamilton, Adams & Co., Paternoster Row, London, 1843.
70 Wray Vamplew et al., *South Australian Historical Statistics*, Historical statistics monograph no. 3, Australia 1788–1988: A Bicentennial History, Kensington, NSW, 1984.

Chapter 9
71 Letter from John Barton Hack to Gates Darton, 31 August 1844.
72 James Monckton Darlot, 'Reminiscences', *Victorian Historical Magazine*, no. 71, 1940.
73 'Journal of Mr Darlot's route to Portland Bay, with five hundred and sixty five head of cattle, the property of Messrs W. and F. Dutton', *Supplement to The Australian*, 26 June 1838, and reproduced in the *South Australian Record*, 14 November 1838.
74 Joseph Hawdon, *The Journal of a Journey from NSW to Adelaide*, Georgian House, Melbourne, 1952.
75 Marnie Bassett, *The Hentys*, 2nd edn, Melbourne University Press, Melbourne, 1955, p. 426.

Chapter 10
76 *A Pioneer History of South Australia*, Pioneers Association of South Australia, Adelaide, 2001, p. 115.
77 Letter from Harriet Staker to her mother, 18 February 1838, *South Australian Record*, 14 November 1838.
78 Display in the Migration Museum, Adelaide.
79 John Brown, 'Letters relating to the foundation of the colony', manuscript in State Library of NSW, A271, copies in State Library of South Australia, PRG 1002/1.
80 *Portonian*, vol. 29, no. 3, September 2001.
81 *South Australian Gazette & Colonial Record*, 31 August 1839.
82 G.C. Morphett, 'John Banks Shepherdson, Pioneer Schoolmaster and Stipendiary Magistrate', Pioneers Association of South Australia, Booklet no. 43, Pioneers Association of South Australia, Adelaide, 1947.
83 *Southern Australian*, 2, 16 June 1838.

84 E. Kwan, *Living in South Australia: A Social History*, South Australian Government Printer, Netley, 1987, p. 23.
85 J.W. Bull, *Early Experiences of Colonial Life in South Australia*, Adelaide, 1877.
86 *South Australian Gazette & Colonial Register*, 4 August, 11 August 1838.
87 John Barton Hack, 'A Chequered Career: Reminiscences of a Pioneer', *South Australian Register*, 22 April, 23 April, 28 April 1884. Hand-corrected cuttings are pasted in the journal, State Library of South Australia, PRG 456/6.
88 John W. Bull, *Early Experiences of Life in South Australia and an Extended Colonial History*, 2nd edn, E.S. Wigg & Son, Adelaide, 1884.
89 Wray Vamplew et al., *South Australian Historical Statistics*, Historical statistics monograph no. 3, Australia 1788–1988: A bicentennial history, Kensington, NSW, 1984.
90 *Southern Australian*, 1 December 1838.

Chapter 11

91 Douglas Pike, *Paradise of Dissent: South Australia 1829–1857*, 2nd edn, Melbourne University Press, Melbourne, 1967, p 104.
92 Report of Governor John Hindmarsh to Lord Glenelg, 21 June 1838, State Records of South Australia, GRG2/69.
93 Letter of Governor John Hindmarsh to Admiral Sir Pulteney Malcolm, 22 June 1838, typescript in State Library of South Australia, PRG 456/39.
94 *Australian*, 2 October 1838.
95 Papers relating to the dispute, Supreme Court of South Australia, GRG 36/56 (accession 995).

Chapter 12

96 J.L. Ewens, 'The little ships of the pioneer years', Pioneers Association of South Australia, Booklet no. 77, Pioneers Association of South Australia, Adelaide, 1952. A copy of the Certificate of Registration of the *Hero* is in the State Records of South Australia, GRG 4/1/45.
97 For a full description of Barton's involvement in the whaling industry see the report by Captain Hart, *Southern Australian*, 4 January 1842; J.S. Cumpston, *Kangaroo Island 1800–1836*, Roebuck Society, Canberra 1970; K.T. Borrow, 'Whaling at Encounter Bay', Pioneers Association of South Australia, Booklet no. 53, Pioneers Association of South Australia, Adelaide, undated.
98 Charles W. Stuart, 'Diaries, 1833–1843', manuscript in State Library of South Australia, D 6872 (L).
99 R. Hetherington, 'George Gawler (1797–1869)', *Australian Dictionary of Biography*, National Centre of Biography, Australian National University, http://adb.anu.edu.au.
100 No relation to John Finnis, who spelled his name with one 's'.

101 John Barton Hack, 'A Chequered Career: Recollections of a Pioneer, Part II', *Methodist Journal*, 21 September 1877.
102 G.C. Morphett, 'Early Mount Barker', Pioneers Association of South Australia, Booklet no. 33, Pioneers Association of South Australia, Adelaide, undated.
103 *South Australian Gazette & Colonial Record*, 26 January 1839.
104 Henry Watson wrote on 4 April 1839 that the Three Brothers were the 'hills from which the farm takes its name'.
105 'Papers Relative to the affairs of South Australia: Statement of the extent and cultivation of land, water supply, remarks on crops and buildings, and the population of the province: compiled from official returns for 1840', Her Majesty's Stationery Office, London, 1843. Reprinted as 'Official Returns of the Country Sections Cultivated', *South Australian Register*, 12, June, 19 June; 3 July, 10 July, 24 July, 31 July; 7 August 1841.
106 R.F. Williams, *To Find the Way: Yankalilla and District 1836–1986*, Yankalilla and District Historical Society, Yankalilla, 1985.

Chapter 13
107 Letter from Henry Watson to Gates Darton, 12 March 1846.
108 See www.australiancemeteries.com/sa/adelaide/quakermeetinghouse.htm.
109 Henry Watson, 'Diary, 1838–1839', manuscript and typewritten transcript in State Library of South Australia, PRG 456/13.
110 *Southern Australian*, 11 August 1838.
111 Stephen Hack, 'Notebook', manuscript in State Library of South Australia, PRG 456/11.
112 Lucie Barritt, *The Barritt Family Genealogy and Biographies 1600–1986*, Bonnells Bay, NSW, 1988.
113 May family papers, State Library of South Australia, PRG 131.
114 Letter from Lucy Coleman (née May) to Lewis May, 8 June 1921, manuscript in State Archives of Tasmania, microfilm in State Library of South Australia, PRG 131/4.
115 Letter from Henry Watson to Gates Darton, 20 February 1841.

Chapter 14
116 R. Hetherington, 'George Gawler (1797–1869)', *Australian Dictionary of Biography*, National Centre of Biography, Australian National University, http://adb.anu.edu.au.
117 Wray Vamplew et al., *South Australian Historical Statistics*, Historical statistics monograph no. 3, Australia 1788–1988: A bicentennial history, Kensington, NSW, 1984.
118 *South Australian Register*, 31 August 1839.
119 John Barton Hack, 'Chequered Career: Recollections of a Pioneer, Part III', *Methodist Journal*, 28 September 1877.

NOTES

120 M. Colwell & A. Naylor, *Adelaide, an illustrated history*, Lansdowne Press, Melbourne, 1974.
121 Today it is known as 'Business SA' and has an office in Unley. A photo of John Barton Hack hangs in the foyer and there is an internal meeting room named 'The Hack Room' with his photo and some background information on him.
122 *South Australian Register*, 22 June 1839.
123 *Southern Australian*, 30 October, 1839.
124 *South Australian Gazette & Colonial Register*, 21 December 1839.
125 *South Australian Gazette & Colonial Register*, 11 May 1839.
126 *South Australian Register*, 9 October 1839.
127 Elizabeth Kwan, *Living in South Australia: A Social History*, South Australian Government Printer, Netley, 1987, p. 33.
128 Henry Owen Philcox was baptised at Burwash, Sussex, on 8 December 1824.
129 John Barton Hack, 'Early Settlement in South Australia: Experiences of a Pioneer. Part IV', *South Australian Register*, 29 July 1884.

Chapter 15
130 John Barton Hack, 'Early Settlement in South Australia: Experiences of a Pioneer. Part IV', *South Australian Register*, 29 July 1884.
131 'Papers Relative to the affairs of South Australia: Statement of the extent and cultivation of land, water supply, remarks on crops and buildings, and the population of the province: compiled from official returns for 1840', Her Majesty's Stationery Office, London, 1843. Reprinted as 'Official Returns of the Country Sections Cultivated', *South Australian Register*, 12 June, 19 June; 3 July, 10 July, 24 July, 31 July; 7 August 1841.
132 John Barton Hack, 'Early Settlement in South Australia: Experiences of a Pioneer. Part V', *South Australian Register*, 9 August 1884.
133 Land grants, State Records of South Australia, GRG 35/217.
134 The original watercolour sketch by Governor George Gawler is held in the State Library of South Australia, PRG 50/34/2. Two lithographs of this sketch exist; one is from a drawing by George French Angas, in the National Library of Australia, and the other by J. Hitchen, in the Art Gallery of South Australia.
135 Mainly from a close reading of the letters of George Sanders to Jacob Hagen in 'Outgoing letterbooks of George Sanders, 1855–1864', manuscript in State Library of South Australia, PRG 1392/1. See also reference to wine cellar in chapter 22.
136 The 2006 census said population 846.
137 *Southern Australian*, 16 October 1840.
138 C.S. Sanders, 'The Settlement of George Sanders and his Family at Echunga Creek, 1839–40, from the journal of Jane Sanders', *Pioneers Association of South Australia Booklet*, no. 86, Pioneers Association of South Australia, Adelaide, undated.

139 The Quaker birth records show Hagen was born on 19 January 1809.
140 Jack Whimpress, *Echunga 1839–1939*, Adelaide, 1975, p. 18.
141 Documents in General Registry Office, Old System Title Section, Netley, OS 9559.
142 Letter from Samuel Darton to John Barton Hack, 16 October 1839, State Library of South Australia, SRG 103/23/1.
143 C. Stevenson, *The Millionth Snowflake, the History of Quakers in South Australia*, Religious Society of Friends, Adelaide, 1987.
144 W.N. Oates, *A Question of Survival, Quakers in Australia in the Nineteenth Century*, University of Queensland Press, St Lucia, 1985.
145 Display inside St Peter's Cathedral.
146 William May, *Australian Friend*, December, 1891.
147 Gavin Walkley, *St. Mark's College, the Buildings and Grounds*, Lutheran Publishing House, Adelaide, 1985, p. 21.
148 Walkley, p. 28. Mr Walkley, an architect and benefactor to St Mark's College, worked on the restoration of the cottage and it was named after him.

Chapter 16

149 Wray Vamplew, et al., *South Australian Historical Statistics*, Historical Statistics Monograph no. 3, Australia 1788–1988: A bicentennial history, Kensington, NSW, 1984.
150 R. Hetherington, 'George Gawler (1797–1869)', *Australian Dictionary of Biography*, National Centre of Biography, Australian National University, http://adb.anu.edu.au.
151 Land title in General Registry Office, Old System Title Section, Netley, OS 9559.
152 John Hart, Jacob Hagen & John Baker, 'Report on whaling', *Southern Australian*, 4 January, 7 January 1842.
153 E.A.D. Opie, *South Australian Records prior to 1841*, Hussey & Gillingham, Adelaide, 1917, p. 95.
154 J.B. Hack, 'A Chequered Career: Reminiscences of a Pioneer. Part II', *South Australian Register*, 23 April 1884.
155 R. Cockburn, *Pastoral Pioneers of South Australia*, Lynton Publications, Blackwood, 1925, p. 123.
156 Max Slee, *Inman, First Commander of the South Australian Police*, Seaview Press, West Lakes, 2010, p. 200.
157 Opie, p. 108.

Chapter 17

158 *South Australian Register*, 1 May 1841.
159 R. Hetherington, 'George Gawler (1797–1869)', *Australian Dictionary of Biography*, National Centre of Biography, Australian National University, http://adb.anu.edu.au.

160 *South Australian Register*, 15 May 1841.
161 Hetherington, http://adb.anu.edu.au/biography/gawler-george-2085.
162 Douglas Pike, *Paradise of Dissent: South Australia 1829–1857*, 2nd edn, Melbourne University Press, Melbourne, 1967, p. 192.
163 H.J. Finniss, 'The Great Eastern Road', Pioneers Association of South Australia, Booklet no. 103, Pioneers Association of South Australia, Adelaide, 1968.
164 Letter of John Barton Hack to Gates Darton, 30 April 1842.
165 Documents in the Old System Title Section, General Registry Office, Adelaide.
166 Documents in the Old System Title Section, General Registry Office, Adelaide. Manuscript copies are in Hagen papers, Bodleian library, Oxford, MS Eng. Misc. c285-6.
167 Lawrence Darton, 'A letter from Adelaide, an account of early settlement in South Australia from the journals and letters of John Barton Hack, Stephen Hack and Henry Watson, 1836–1844', footnote to letter from John Barton Hack to Jacob Hagen Senior, 10 May 1841, typescript dated 1947 in West Sussex Record Office, MP 1372, and revised introduction, MP 1377. A version with revised introduction (1980) is in the possession of Iola Matthews.
168 They were in Gloucester in the June 1841 census.
169 Quaker birth, death and marriage records for England are held at the London Family History Centre, National Archives, Kew.
170 Darton, footnote to letter from Henry Watson to Gates Darton, 17 December 1841.

Chapter 18

171 Douglas J. Whalen, 'Torrens, Sir Robert Richard (1814–1884)', *Australian Dictionary of Biography*, National Centre of Biography, Australian National University, http://adb.anu.edu.au.
172 Mortgage, 2 March 1842, Old System Title Section, General Registry Office, Adelaide.
173 Mortgage, 2 March 1842.
174 R. Preston, 'Thomas Sandon Hack: Architect of Southampton, 1841–49', Southampton Occasional Papers, Local History Forum, Southampton, no. 3, March 2011.
175 Jacob Hagen, 'Copies of deeds, etc.', manuscript in Bodleian Library, Oxford, MS Eng. Misc. c285-6.
176 Jacob Hagen, 'Copies of deeds, etc.'.
177 Bartley v. Hagen, *Southern Australian*, 31 October 1843.
178 John Barton Hack, 'Early Settlement in South Australia: Experiences of a Pioneer, Part V', *South Australian Register*, 9 August 1884.
179 Douglas Pike, *Paradise of Dissent. South Australia 1828–1857*, 2nd edn, Melbourne University Press, Melbourne, 1967, p. 190.

Chapter 19

180 John Barton Hack, 'A Chequered Career: Recollections of a Pioneer, Part III', *Methodist Journal*, 28 September 1877.
181 Elizabeth Kwan, author of *Living in South Australia: A Social History*, pers. comm., 10 December 2009.
182 John Barton Hack, 'Chequered Career: Recollections of a Pioneer, Part III', *Methodist Journal*, 28 September.
183 Bartley v. Hagen, *South Australian Register*, 2 September 1843.
184 Insolvency documents relating to John Barton Hack, State Records of South Australia, GRG 66/5/74.
185 Bartley v. Hagen, *Southern Australian*, 3 November 1843.
186 *Southern Australian*, 17 February 1843.
187 Bartley v. Hagen, *Southern Australian*, 1 September 1843.
188 Jacob Hagen, 'Copies of deeds, etc.', manuscript in Bodleian Library, Oxford, MS Eng. Misc. c285-6.
189 Documents in the Old System Title Section, General Registry Office, Adelaide.
190 John Barton Hack, 'A Chequered Career: Recollections of a Pioneer, Part III', *Methodist Journal*, 28 September 1877.
191 Letter from Samuel Davenport to Miss Maria Davenport, 9 March 1843, State Library of South Australia, PRG 40/18/2.
192 *Southern Australian*, 21 March 1843.
193 Insolvency documents relating to John Barton Hack, State Records of South Australia, GRG 66/5/74.
194 Insolvency documents relating to Stephen Hack, State Records of South Australia, 66/5/83.
195 *Southern Australian*, 31 March 1843.
196 *Register*, 11 February 1905.
197 Margaret May, 'Journal with copies of letters, 1843–45', typewritten transcription in State Library of South Australia, PRG 131/2.
198 James Allen, *The South Australian Almanack and General Directory for 1844*, James Allen, Adelaide, p. 233.
199 Wilton Hack, 'Sketch of My Life', 1907, photocopy of manuscript in State Library of South Australia, PRG 456/35.
200 Allen, p. 233.
201 There are two almanacs from 1844 (using data from 1843): Thomas Young Cotter, *The South Australian Almanack and Adelaide and Colonial Directory for 1844*, Archibald MacDougall, Adelaide; James Allen, *South Australian Almanack and General Directory for 1844*, James Allen, 1844.
202 Emily Phillips, introduction to 'Journal with copies of letters, 1843–45', 1906, typescript in State Library of South Australia, PRG 131/2. Emily was a daughter of Margaret May.
203 *South Australian Register*, 22 November 1843.
204 *South Australian Register*, 22 November 1843.

Chapter 20

205 *South Australian Register*, 17 May 1843.
206 *Southern Australian*, 3 November 1843.
207 *South Australian Register*, 9 December 1843.
208 George Sanders to Jacob Hagen in 'Outgoing letterbooks of George Sanders, 1855–1864', manuscript in State Library of South Australia, PRG 1392/1.
209 *South Australian Register*, 27 January 1844.
210 *South Australian Register*, 18 December 1844.
211 *South Australian*, 4 March 1845.
212 *South Australian Register*, 10 October 1840.
213 *South Australian*, 21 November 1845.
214 Jack Whimpress, *Echunga 1839–1939*, Adelaide, 1975, p. 91.
215 *Advertiser*, 30 December 1927, letter from W.J. Purvis.
216 Pat Kavanagh, oral history recorded 5 April 1975, State Library of South Australia, OH354.
217 The average temperature in winter in the hills is 5°C at night, www.bom.gov.au.

Chapter 21

218 Douglas Pike, *Paradise of Dissent: South Australia 1829–1857*, 2nd edn, Melbourne University Press, Melbourne, 1967, p. 300.
219 Pike, pp. 300–2.
220 Pike, Appendix A.
221 George Henry Wilton, death certificate.
222 J. Gilchrist, 'Hagen, Jacob (1805–1870)', *Australian Dictionary of Biography*, National Centre of Biography, Australian National University, http://adb.anu.edu.au.
223 J. Gilchrist, http://adb.anu.edu.au/biography/hagen-jacob-2141.
224 George Sanders, 'Outgoing letterbooks of George Sanders, 1855–1864', manuscript in State Library of South Australia, PRG 1392/1.
225 See www.burrahistory.info/BurraMining.
226 Uniting Church History Centre, pers. comm., July 2012.
227 'The Late Mr J.B. Hack', *Christian Weekly and Methodist Journal*, 17 October, 1884.
228 *Christian Weekly and Methodist Journal*, 17 October, 1884.
229 Society of Friends, 'Papers relating to changes of membership, 1836–1924', State Library of South Australia, SRG 103/5/4; 'Burial notes, 1843–1946', State Library of South Australia, SRG 103/6/2.
230 Now All Saints Uniting Church, on the corner of Marion Road and Mooringe Avenue, Plympton.
231 Christ Church, North Adelaide, www.ccna.asn.au.
232 *South Australian Register*, 31 December 1857.
233 'Mr Bedford Hack's career, on his retirement', *Advertiser*, 25 June 1908.

234 There is no record of this marriage in South Australia or Victoria. The date September 1851 (in a family history) is probably calculated by nine months back from the birth of their daughter Annie Mary.
235 Robert Stein, 'Torrens, his Chief Clerk of Customs, and the Press', *South Australiana*, vol. 21, no. 1, March 1982.
236 Pike, p. 448.
237 John Barton Hack, 'A Chequered Career. Reminiscences of a Pioneer. Part III', *South Australian Register*, 28 April 1884.
238 Graeme Butler & Associates, *Eaglehawk and Bendigo Heritage Study*, vol. 2, 1993, www.bendigo.vic.gov.au.
239 Pike, p. 447.
240 *Advertiser*, 25 June 1908.
241 Tod's house Spring Grove at Fourth Creek was on the market in February 1853.
242 John Barton Hack, 'A Chequered Career: Reminiscences of a Pioneer, Part III', *South Australian Register*, 28 April 1884.
243 *South Australian Register*, 19 December 1857.

Chapter 22
244 Alice Owen Hack, death certificate.
245 See www.sahistory.org.za.
246 'Mr Bedford Hack's career, on his retirement', *Advertiser*, 25 June 1908.
247 *Advertiser*, 25 June 1908, retirement, Bedford Hack.
248 Report by G.W. Goyder, *South Australian Register*, 10 July 1857.
249 Report by A.H. Freeling, *South Australian Register*, 26 September, 1857.
250 *Parliamentary Papers, South Australia, 1857–58*, no. 156, Government Printer, Adelaide.
251 Wilton's memoir confuses this with the *Fortune*.
252 Norman A. Richardson, *Pioneers of the North-West of South Australia*, W.K. Thomas & Co., Adelaide, 1925, p. 10–11.
253 Bessie Threadgill, *South Australian Land Exploration, 1856 to 1880*, The Hassell Press, Adelaide, 1922, p. 34. Her book covers a full report of Hack's exploration and maps.
254 Geoffrey H. Manning, 'A Compendium of the Place Names of South Australia', www.slsa.sa.gov.au/digitalpubs/placenamesofsouthaustralia.
255 *Parliamentary Papers, South Australia, 1857–58*, no. 156.
256 Threadgill, p. 34.
257 *South Australian Register*, 3 February 1858.
258 *Advertiser*, 25 June 1908, retirement, Bedford Hack.
259 *South Australian Register*, 1 March 1859.
260 *South Australian Register*, 2, 7 March 1860.
261 *South Australian Register*, 2 March 1860.
262 Richardson, p. 27.
263 *Advertiser*, 25 June 1908, retirement, Bedford Hack.

Chapter 23

264 John Barton Hack, 'A Chequered Career: Reminiscences of a Pioneer, Part III', *South Australian Register*, 28 April 1884.
265 *The Tattler*, National Parks and Wildlife, Department for Environment and Heritage, South Australia, edn 12, August 2006, www.parks.sa.gov.au.
266 Noted in letter from Barton Hack, 24 March 1862.
267 John Barton Hack, 'Diary of J.B. Hack, with letters', manuscript in State Library of South Australia, PRG 456/6. The letters cover the time on the Coorong, 1861–1862.
268 R. Baker, M. Baker & W. Reschke, *Coorong Pilot*, Fullers Services, Adelaide, 1977, p. 44.
269 R. Luebbers, 'The Archaeology of Chinamens Wells and Hacks Station, the Coorong, South Australia', unpublished report for Department of Environment and Planning, South Australia, 1996, p. 76.
270 Letter from Stephen Hack at the Coorong, 27 January 1858, *Register*, 3 February 1858.
271 'Returns of pastoral leases, 1851 to 1864', *Parliamentary Papers, South Australia, 1865–66*, no. 39, Government Printer, Adelaide; 'Pastoral claims between Coorong and east boundary of the Province', *Parliamentary Papers, South Australia, 1868–69*, no. 155, Government Printer, Adelaide.
272 Letter from Emily Hack to Minnie, 1858, manuscript and typewritten transcript in State Library of South Australia, PRG 456/18.
273 Luebbers, p. 20.
274 Land tax evaluations by G.W. Goyder, 1864, summarised in Luebbers.
275 Luebbers, pp. 81ff, 87.
276 Elizabeth Nicholls, *Shut Six Gates: A History of Tintinara, Culburra and District*, Tintinara Historical Society, Tintinara, 2006, p. 19.
277 H.H. Teague, 'Obituary at funeral of J. B. Hack', *Christian Weekly and Methodist Journal*, 17 Oct 1884.
278 Luebbers, p. 76.
279 *Advertiser*, 31 August 1858.
280 Letter from Corporal A. Burt, *Advertiser*, 19 March 1859.
281 'Pastoral lease maps of south-eastern region 1876–1913', State Records of South Australia, GRS 6910/328.
282 Captain Kruse said the run belonged to Archibald Cooke and Alfred was the overseer, *Advertiser*, 20 May 1908.
283 Old System Title Section, General Registry Office, Adelaide, Memorial 211, book 161.
284 This mortgage was payable on 1 January 1863, with interest of 10 per cent per annum, Old System Title Section, General Registry Office, Adelaide.
285 *Register*, 14 March 1862.
286 Lucy Treloar, a descendant of Annie Wagener, William and Grace's daughter, pers. comm., 20 January 2011.

287 'Report of the Select Committee of the Legislative Council upon the Aborigines', *Parliamentary Papers, South Australia, 1860*, no. 165, Government Printer, Adelaide. Barton gave evidence on 9 Oct 1860.
288 Luebbers, p. 22; descendants of William Hack, pers. comm., 20 January 2011.
289 Graham Jenkin, *Conquest of the Ngarrindjeri*, Rigby, Adelaide, 1979.
290 *South Australian Register*, 26 November 1860.
291 Jenkin, p. 83.

Chapter 24
292 *Advertiser*, 27 April 1912, obituary, Bedford Hack.
293 'Returns of pastoral leases, 1851 to 1864', *Parliamentary Papers, South Australia, 1865-66*, no. 39, Government Printer, Adelaide; 'Pastoral claims between Coorong and east boundary of the Province', *Parliamentary Papers, South Australia, 1868-69*, no. 155, Government Printer, Adelaide; 'Registers of Pastoral Leases First Series', Book 1, State Records of South Australia, GRS/3519.
294 1851 UK Census; www.tintinara.com/tourism.
295 J.H. Boothby, '"Dead Yesterday": Reminiscences of an Old Colonist', *Register*, 22 April 1919.
296 Elizabeth Nicholls, *Shut Six Gates: A History of Tintinara, Culburra and District*, Tintinara Historical Society, Tintinara, 2006, p. 6.
297 Wilton Hack, 'Sketch of My Life', 1907, photocopy of manuscript in State Library of South Australia, PRG 456/35.
298 Wilton Hack, p. 27.
299 Old System Title Section, General Registry Office, Adelaide, Memorial 223, book 165.
300 *South Australian Register*, 10 December 1863.
301 Letter from Bridget Hack to her children, 13 December 1864, manuscript and typewritten transcript in State Library of South Australia, PRG 456/9.
302 R. Baker, M. Baker & W. Reschke, *Coorong Pilot*, Fullers Services, Adelaide, 1977, p. 40.
303 Nicholls, p. 27; Boothby, *Register*, 22 April 1919.
304 R. Luebbers, 'The Archaeology of Chinamans Wells and Hacks Station, the Coorong, South Australia', unpublished report for Department of Environment and Planning, South Australia, 1996, p. 22.
305 Luebbers, p. 23.
306 *The Tattler*, National Parks and Wildlife, Department for Environment and Heritage, South Australia, edn. 12, August 2006, www.parks.sa.gov.au.

Chapter 25
307 Wray Vamplew, et al., *South Australian Historical Statistics*, Historical statistics monograph no. 3, Australia 1788-1988: A bicentennial history, Kensington, NSW, 1984.

NOTES

308 *Christian Weekly and Methodist Journal*, 17 October 1884, funeral sermon and obituary, John Barton Hack.
309 Letter from Bridget Hack to her children, 13 December 1864, manuscript and typewritten transcript in State Library of South Australia, PRG 456/9.
310 Harold Lindon was born in the September quarter of 1863, www.freebmd.org.uk.
311 Aileen Kelly, great-granddaughter of Annie Hack, pers. comm., 20 January 2011. The event may have been when they lived at Kingston and Annie was about fourteen.
312 Grace Kingsborough, 'Biographical notes on John Barton Hack and family', 1934, State Library of South Australia, PRG 456/32. Grace was a great-great granddaughter of John Barton Hack.
313 *South Australian Register*, 15 January 1868.
314 *South Australian Register*, 22 April 1884, obituary, John Barton Hack.
315 Burnside rate books, held at Burnside Library, City of Burnside; Josiah Boothby, *The Adelaide Almanac and Directory for South Australia, Adelaide*, J. Williams, Adelaide.
316 Boothby.
317 Cirrhosis cited on death certificate.
318 Port Adelaide rate books, Port Adelaide Library, City of Port Adelaide Enfield; Old System Title Section, General Registry Office, Adelaide.
319 *South Australian Register*, 21 July 1881.
320 John Barton Hack, 'Chequered Career: Recollections of a Pioneer', *Methodist Journal*, 7, 21, 28 September, 1877.
321 'Retirement of Mr J.B. Hack', *South Australian Register*, 18 July 1883.
322 There is no record of where Charles Hack lived in 1883, but we can assume it was with Barton, who was a widower and needed assistance, and because he left the house to Charles's wife Annie in his will and they lived there after Barton's death.
323 John Barton Hack, 'A Chequered Career: Reminiscences of a Pioneer', *South Australian Register*, 22 April, 23 April, 28 April 1884.
324 John Barton Hack, 'Early Settlement in South Australia: Experiences of a Pioneer', *South Australian Register*, 3 July, 12 July, 19 July, 29 July, 9 August, 1884.
325 'Funeral of the Late Mr J.B. Hack', *South Australian Register*, 7 October 1884.
326 *South Australian Register*, 6 October, 1884, obituary, John Barton Hack.
327 'The Late Mr J.B. Hack', *Christian Weekly and Methodist Journal*, 17 October 1884.
328 *Married Women's Property Act 1883*, www.samemory.sa.gov.au.
329 UK census, 1871.
330 Letters of Elizabeth Hack to Theodore Hack, 1879 and 1881, manuscript and typewritten transcript in State Library of South Australia, PRG 456/12.
331 Letters of Elizabeth Hack to Theodore Hack, 1879 and 1881.

332 Wilton Hack, 'Album of sketches and verses', 1894, manuscript and photocopy in State Library of South Australia, SLSA PRG 456/20.
333 UK census; R. Preston, 'Thomas Sanden Hack, Architect of Southampton 1841–9', *Southampton Occasional Papers*, no 3, March 2011.
334 UK census.
335 Lawrence Darton, *The Dartons, An Annotated Check-list of Children's Books, Issued by Two Publishing Houses, 1787–1876*, Oak Knoll Press, New Castle, Delaware, 2004.
336 *Observer*, 21 July 1894, obituary, Henry Watson.
337 John Sanderson Lloyd, letter of 1911 attached to the diary of his father-in-law, Henry Watson, in State Library of South Australia, PRG 456/13.
338 Jennie Coleman, Watson Coleman's daughter-in-law, pers. comm., 20 February 2013.
339 *Courier* (Mt Barker, South Australia), October 1984; *Southern Argus*, October 1984.
340 *Echunga Community Times*, October 1984.
341 Actually fourteen children. He thought Jessie had a twin who died at birth, but there is no record of such a birth or death.

Appendix

342 William and Emma's son Theodore Hack was born in Dec 1873 at Tintinara; *South Australian Register*, 12 January 1874, mentions William Hack of Tintinara.
343 Letter from Emma Hack to her stepdaughter Annie Wagener, 23 February 1876, manuscript in State Library of South Australia, PRG 456/27.
344 In Barton Hack's will William was described as a wood merchant on the River Murray.
345 Meredith Boddington, Harry's granddaughter, pers. comm., 2011.
346 *Border Watch*, 13 August 1929.
347 A.G. Bannister, *Her Pioneers: Hack, Winchester, Carvosso, Püschner*, Walkerville, 2001.
348 *Adelaide Observer*, 1 October 1904, obituary, Edward Hack.
349 *South Australian Register*, 27 September 1904, obituary, Edward Hack.
350 See www.benmckeown.net.
351 *Advertiser*, 8 June 1908, obituary, Alfred Hack.
352 Christopher Hack of Little River, Victoria, Alfred's great-grandson, pers. comm., 11 June 2012.
353 Christopher Hack, Fred's grandson, pers. comm., 11 June 2012.
354 Jack Whimpress, *Echunga 1839–1939*, Adelaide, 1975, p. 56.
355 *Advertiser*, 25 June 1908; *Advertiser*, 27 April 1912; *Public Service Review*, June 1908.
356 *Advertiser*, 28 October 1929, obituary, Annie Brooks Hack.
357 Testamentary Causes Jurisdiction, November 1956, Supreme Court of South Australia, A30558.

358 *Advertiser*, 10 August 1951, obituary, Mrs Guli Magarey.
359 *Advertiser*, 10 July 1912, obituary, Leonard Hack.
360 *South Australian Register*, 18 August 1903, obituary, Francis Hack.
361 *South Australian Register, Advertiser*, 1887–1891, numerous references, George Hack.
362 *Advertiser*, 13 June 1910.
363 Port Adelaide-Enfield library, pers. comm., 2009.
364 *South Australian Register*, 29 December 1902; *Observer*, 3 January 1903, obituaries, Theodore Hack.
365 *South Australian Register*, 18 October 1884.
366 *South Australian Register*, 11 November 1884.
367 Bobbie Coyne, daughter of Roy Darton Hack, pers. comm., 2008.
368 Peter Ward, 'Ballantyne, Colin Sandergrove (1908–1988)', *Australian Dictionary of Biography*, National Centre of Biography, Australian National University, http://adb.anu.edu.au.
369 www.derbyshireuk.net/hathersage.
370 Julia Hedley, great-granddaughter of Wilton Hack, pers. comm., 2009; N. Roden, 'The death of Mrs Cutler, a talented Derbyshire authoress', *High Peak News*, 4 October 1913.
371 Wilton Hack, 'Sketch of My Life', 1907, photocopy of manuscript in State Library of South Australia, PRG 456/35.
372 Julia Hedley, Wilton's great granddaughter, pers. comm., 22 September 2012. We have not been able to find a birth record for a Billy Ethridge or Etheridge in Derbyshire when Wilton was at school.
373 Wilton Hack, 'Correspondence 1876–1877', typescript in State Library of South Australia, PRG 456/19; J. Cross, 'Wilton Hack and Japanese Immigration into North Australia', *Proceedings of the Royal Geographical Society of Australasia: South Australia Branch*, vol. 61, 1959–1960.
374 'Hack, Wilton (1843–1923)', *Australian Dictionary of Biography*, National Centre of Biography, Australian National University, http://adb.anu.edu.au; Julia Hedley, pers. comm., 2 April 2009.

Index

A

Aboriginal people
  South Australia and 35; new Adelaide settlers and 67–8; Hack family and 74, 87, 216, 218, 252–3, 254; disputes with colonists 102–3, 139–40; Coorong farm and 223–4, 226–8
Aborigines Protection Society 67, 227
Adelaide 3, 5, 33, 35, 54, 61, 71, 72, 85, 89, 90, 93, 96, 97, 104, 105, 106, 109, 117, 118, 121, 122, 124, 125, 129, 142, 144, 165, 179, 194, 198, 201, 212, 213, 214, 217, 220, 223, 224, 225, 227, 231, 234, 240, 242, 250, 256, 259, 262, 264
  naming of 60; first Barton Hack trip to 63–7; town lots allocation 64, 85–6; Aboriginal people and 67–8; business expansion 69–81; Light's layout 71; first schools 102; emigration crisis 136; lack of sewage 143; debt crisis and 161; barter system 1842 175; Barton Hack return to 1863 237–41
Adelaide 111, 114, 135, 136, 141
Adelaide Auction Company 157, 176, 181, 183, 190
Adelaide Chamber of Commerce 134, 138, 156, 161, 252
Adelaide Hills 5, 6, 202
Adelaide Railway Station 63
Adelaide Survey Association 123
Agricultural and Horticultural Society 138, 185, 195, 251
Albury 92, 211, 214
Aldinga 104, 257
Alf's Flat 225, 257
Allen's Creek 207, 208
Angas, George Fife 31, 32, 239–40
  South Australian land sales and 33–4
Angepena 214
Ann 84, 91
anti-slavery movement 14, 17, 20
Archer Street 209, 237
Association for the Introduction of Vines 195
Association for the Prosecution of Felons 157
Atkinson, Alfred 211
Atlas Building Society 233
Augustus 204, 211

B

Babbage, Benjamin Herschel 214, 217
Babbage, Charles 223, 231
Backhouse, James 86–7
Baker, John 157, 176, 177, 180, 181, 190, 198, 206, 207, 214, 218, 221, 224, 226, 227, 229, 236, 253
Balhannah 117, 118, 121
Ballantyne, Colin 263
Ballantyne (née Earl), Elsie Miriam 262
Ballantyne, Elspeth 263
Ballantyne, Guy 263
Ballantyne, Jane 263
Bank of Australasia 55, 120, 122, 190
Bank of South Australia 91, 101, 105, 120, 175, 176
Barker, Alfred 129, 147
Baroona 231, 235
Barritt, Joseph 129–30, 148, 150, 179, 180
Barritt (née Harrison), Mary Ann 150, 170, 180
Barr Smith, Robert 230, 236
Bartley, William 181–2
  Hack family and 175–6; Bartley v. Hagen case 191
Barton (née Woodrouffe Smith), Anne 19–20
Barton, Bernard 13, 14, 15, 16, 17, 23, 25
Barton, Elizabeth 13, 18
Barton(née Horne), Elizabeth 14
Barton (née Rickman), Fanny 23
Barton, John (1754–1789) 13–14
Barton, John (1789–1852) 15, 18, 19–20, 38, 39, 21, 23, 29, 31, 37, 72, 126, 133, 154, 196, 197, 205, 213
Barton, Lucy 17
Barton (née Done), Mary (Maria) 60
Barton family, origins 8
Barton Terrace 72, 252
Bates, Jean 249
Bayne, David 225, 230, 235
Beaconite controversy 86, 131
Bedford's Well 225
Bickford, Reverend James 244, 245
Birkbeck College 20
Blanchewater 214, 218
Blenkinsop, Captain John William Dundas 73, 89, 99
Bliss (née Hack), Elizabeth Barton 12, 15, 18, 19, 22, 23, 24, 197, 199, 203, 213

284

INDEX

Bliss, Reverend George 19, 22, 203, 141
Bonney, Charles 90, 93–4, 97
Bonney's Camp 220, 224–5, 230
Bonython, Sir John Langdon 256
Bonython (née Hack), Irene Ethel 256
Boothby, George 230
Boothby, James 230, 231, 232, 235–6
Boothby, Thomas 230, 231
Botanical Gardens 138, 157
Breeze, Robert 208–9, 211
Brocklesbury 214
Brown, John 35, 89, 101, 140, 162, 169, 183, 190, 207,253
Browne, Drs William James and John Harris (brothers) 232, 234
Buffalo 35, 36, 54, 58,65, 72, 77
Burnside 241, 252
Burra 5, 202, 240
Burwash Farm 146, 176

C

canal construction 76, 78, 101, 110
Capetown 43, 168, 174, 214
Carter, Caroline; *see* Woodforde, Caroline
Chamberlain, Mary 247
Chichester 4, 8, 9, 12, 15, 18, 19, 20, 21, 22, 23, 24, 26, 27, 36, 37, 38, 40, 48, 52, 55, 62, 77, 88, 100, 106, 118, 120, 129, 133, 252
Chichester Gardens 77–8, 100, 144, 190, 193
Chichester Savings Bank 11, 19
Childers Street 237
Chittleborough, James 62–3
Christ Church 209
Clothier (née Hack), Betty 257
Clothier, Malcolm 257
Coleman, Frederick (Fred) 248
Coleman (née May), Lucy 131, 248
Coleman, Watson 248
Cooke, James and Archibald 225, 230, 232
Coonalpyn 231–2
Cooper, Judge Charles 184, 189, 191
Cooper's Creek 218
Coorong 5, 212, 230, 233, 234, 237, 239, 252, 253, 257
    Barton Hack at 219–28
Coppin Street 242, 245, 246, 262
Corder, Thomas 200, 204
Coromandel 58
Cotter, Dr Thomas Young 66, 75
Crafers 118, 142, 143, 249
Curraghmore estate 55
Customs Office 115, 169, 205, 209, 237
Cutler, Reverend Charles 263
Cutler (née Hack), Julia Africaine 168, 174, 175, 176, 186, 213, 214. 215, 247, 247
    short biography 263

D

Darlot, James Monckton 92–3, 94, 96
Darton, Edward Hack 82
Darton, Edward Lawrence (Lawrence) 2, 3, 13, 22, 24, 248
Darton, Emily Jane 82
Darton (née Hack), Margaret Emily 47, 50, 82, 100, 162, 163, 197, 203, 213
    marries Gates Darton 26–7; death of 247
Darton, Margaret Elizabeth 163
Darton, Samuel 25, 111, 148–9
Darton, Thomas Gates (Gates) vii, 25, 36, 37–8, 39, 40, 46, 47, 50, 56, 61, 64, 65, 70–1, 85, 91, 104, 123, 124, 135, 147, 148, 149, 152, 155–6, 160, 162, 163, 165–6, 167, 169, 170, 171, 174, 176, 189, 192, 199, 200–1, 202–3, 205, 206, 207, 213, 250
    marries Margaret Hack 25, 26–7; South Australian land sales and 33–4; financial disputes with Hack family 51–4, 55, 111–15, 125, 140–2, 153, 157–8, 195–7; letters from 82–5; last years 247
Darton, publishers with Harvey 15, 16, 111, 163
Davis, Tom 56, 74, 80, 103, 105
Dean, Henry 229
Deane, Ellen 188, 197, 198
Deane, George 107, 151, 181, 183, 184, 197–8
Deane (née Greenwood), Rachel 107, 151, 188
Devlin, Captain Arthur 90–1, 96, 99, 100, 110, 111, 115, 116, 132, 135, 136, 138, 155
Dixon, Esther 41, 46–7, 55
Dixon, James 41, 55
Dodd, Thomas and James 235
Draper, Reverend Daniel James 208
Duffield, Walter 148, 185
Duffield, William 194–5, 204
Dutton, Francis 217
Dutton, Frederick Hansborough 91, 92, 217
Dutton, John 137
Dutton, William Hampden 91, 120–1, 122, 217

E

Earl (née Hack), Mary Louisa 223, 239
Echunga 130, 142, 147, 153, 161, 168, 179, 184, 204, 205, 206, 253, 254, 258
    departure from 201; Barton Hack centenary 249; Barton Hack and 252
Echunga Creek 143, 183, 184, 254
Echunga Dairy and Old Dairy Farm 186, 188, 199, 203
Echunga Gardens 146, 183
Echunga Springs 5, 146, 156, 159–60, 165, 166, 188, 190, 192, 206–7
    move to 143–51; description 1842 173–4; mortgage 162, 169–70, 176; sole business of Hacks 171–4; Stephen Hack and family and 175, 183, 184; foreclosure 180; sale of 181–3; Hagen and 185, 186, 193–4; first wine from 193–5
Elder, Sir Thomas 229
Elder, Smith & Co 230, 233, 259
Emu Springs 231
Encounter Bay 5, 31, 73, 80, 88, 96, 99, 103, 104, 105, 115, 137, 155, 164
Esplanade, The (Semaphore) 243, 246, 259
Ethridge, Billy 264
Eyre, John 215

F

Field, Captain William George 129, 147
financial crisis, South Australia 155–6, 159–67
Finniss, Boyle Travers 119
Finnis, Captain John 118, 119, 120
Finniss Flats (Ashbourne) 209, 211, 223
Fisher, James Hurtle 35, 66, 73, 76, 85, 89, 100, 102, 109, 110, 157, 162, 169, 182, 183, 190, 191
Fisher, James and Charles Brown 78, 90
FitzGerald, Edward 15
Flinders Ranges 264
Foley, Jack 105–6, 154
Forster, Josiah 17, 148, 149
Fourth Creek 117, 118, 119
Fox, George 9, 10
Freeling, Captain Arthur Henry 214–15
Friends Burial Ground 124, 150
Froyle 9
Fry, Elizabeth 30, 149
Funtington 19, 24

G

Gawler, Governor Colonel George 111, 120, 121, 122, 145, 146, 161, 164, 248
  appointment of 109; visit to Mount Barker 119; public works and 134–5; early years as Governor 137–8; recall of 159–60
Gawler Ranges 215, 216, 217, 254
Gem 78, 84, 91
Giles, Henry 231, 232, 233, 234
Gilles, Lewis William 54, 56, 207
Gilles, Osmond 54, 77, 101, 120–1, 122, 138, 207
Gleeson's Hill 142
Glenelg 54, 58, 59–63, 65, 69, 72, 75, 240, 264
Glen Osmond 161, 202
Gloucester 2, 4, 27, 36, 50, 99, 163, 213, 247
Glynburn Road 241
goldfields, Victorian 209, 210–11
Goodwood (Mount Barker) 118–19, 121, 122
Goolwa 220, 224, 234
Goshawk 115, 125, 140
Gouge, Robert 30, 31, 32, 33, 60, 66, 71, 76–7, 78, 89, 101, 110, 137, 253
Goyder, George 223, 235
Grand Jury, first 70
Granite Island 137
Grant, Billy 215, 216
Graylingwell House 26–8, 36, 39, 40, 128
Great Eastern Road (toll) 161
Grey, Governor George 167, 206
  arrival of 159–60; South Australian debt crisis and 161–2; Watson and 169; Hack brothers and 172;
Griffith Hack 6, 263
Griffiths, John 58
Gurney, Samuel 149, 150

H

Hack, Alfred 27, 173, 177, 201, 203, 211, 221, 225, 238, 240, 258, 262
  short biography 257–8
Hack, Alice Owen 213
Hack (née Stonehouse), Anna Maria 240, 264
Hack (née Meyrick), Annie Brooks 239, 243, 245, 246, 259
Hack, Annie 26, 124, 126, 241
Hack, Annie Catherine; *see* Wagener, Annie Catherine
Hack, Annie Mary 211, 256
Hack, Arthur William 225, 239, 256
Hack, Barton John 223, 235, 240, 256
Hack, Barton William Henry 260
Hack, Betty; *see* Clothier, Betty
Hack (née Watson), Bridget (Bbe) 5, 17, 26, 27, 34, 36, 37, 39, 65, 79, 86, 99–100, 124, 125, 127, 130, 131, 142, 151, 162, 163, 166, 168, 172, 177, 186, 188–9, 192, 197, 203, 205, 210, 245, 249, 255
  voyage to Australia 2, 3; marriage to Barton Hack 22–3; voyage to Van Diemen's Land 40–50, 54; Holdfast Bay settlement 62–3; new Adelaide home 66–7, 69–81; birth of Emily 75; activities 1838 98–9; birth of Gulielma 107; move to Echunga 143–51; birth of Theodore 147; Watsons and 153; resilience 173; poverty and 198, 200, 201; move to North Adelaide 207; last child 209; grandmother for the first time 211; Coorong and 220, 221–2; Wesleyan Methodism and 224; care of William's children 226; return to Adelaide 1863 237–8; move to Semaphore 242–3; death of 243; life's achievement 251–2
Hack, Bedford 34, 46, 67, 100, 173, 177, 201, 203, 209, 211, 214–15, 218, 221, 225, 227, 229, 237, 240, 253, 256
  short biography 258
Hack, Brenton (Ben) 256
Hack (née Wilton), Elizabeth Marsh (Bessie) 168, 172–3, 174, 175, 176–7, 182, 184, 186–8, 203, 246–7, 254, 264
  marries Stephen Hack 163; poverty and 198–9; voyage to England 204; to South Africa 213, 214; return to South Australia 1854 214; return to England 1857 215
Hack, Charles 173, 189, 211, 214, 222, 238, 240, 241, 242, 243, 245–6, 252, 260
  short biography 259
Hack, Charles Edward 257
Hack, Charles Herbert 239
Hack, Charlotte Helen (Helen) 264
Hack, Clement Alfred 250, 261, 262–3
Hack, Don 261
Hack, Edward 26, 98, 102, 124, 173, 177, 198, 201, 204, 205, 209, 211, 214, 237, 243
  short biography 256–7
Hack, Edward Janson 13, 19, 21

INDEX

Hack (née Johns), Elizabeth Ann 260
Hack, Elizabeth Barton; *see* Bliss, Elizabeth Barton
Hack (née Hackett), Elizabeth 209, 211, 256
Hack (née Almer), Elizabeth Jane 262
Hack, Ellen; *see* Knott, Ellen
Hack (née Ansell), Elvira Louisa (Ellie) 237, 238, 241, 242, 262
Hack, Emily Margaret; *see* Mitchell, Emily Margaret
Hack (née Harding), Emma 238–9, 255, 256
Hack, Ernest Barton 262
Hack (née Bishop), Frances Harriet 258
Hack, Francis (Frank) 192, 211, 238, 240
  short biography 260
Hack, Frederick Theodore 258
Hack, George Bliss 205, 240, 245
  short biography 260–1
Hack, Gerald 259
Hack (née Stanlake), Grace 223, 225, 255
Hack, Gulielma (1802–29) 12, 23
Hack, Gulielma (1867–1951); *see* Magarey, Gulielma
Hack, Gulielma Mary 107, 124, 126–7, 241
Hack, Guy 258
Hack, Harry 256
Hack (née Sayer), Helen (Nellie) 260
Hack, Irene Ethel; *see* Bonython, Irene Ethel
Hack, James 9, 11, 15, 18, 22, 23
Hack, Jessie Maria 209, 226, 238, 241
Hack, John Barton (Barton) (1805–84) 12, 13, 14, 15, 18, 24, 26–7, 29, 31, 208
  diary and letters of 1–3; early years 4; arrival and first settlement in South Australia 3–4, 58–9; Quakers and 11, 148–51; schooldays 17; tuberculosis and 21, 26–7; marriage to Bridget (Bbe) Watson 22–8; partnership with Smith 22; journal 1836 36; voyage preparations 37–9; voyage to Van Diemen's Land 40–50, 51–7; bullock carrying businesses 61, 72–5, 115, 199–200, 202–3, 205–6; first Adelaide trip 63–7; first land purchases 64–5; family move to Adelaide 65–6; Aboriginal people and 67–8, 139–40; business dealings 69–81, 87; early Adelaide disputes 76–7; Hack's bridge construction 78–9; disputes with Gates Darton 82–5, 111–15, 195–7; Hindley Street venture 1838 98–100; debts and 155–6; early Adelaide disputes 77; Mount Barker and 80–1, 117–23; financial crises 84, 185–6, 232–5, 248; Stephen Hack and 95–6, 175, 203, 204, 214, 247, 258; Adelaide organisations and 100–2; arrival of relatives 1838 107–8; recall of Governor Hindmarsh and 109–10; Governor George Gawler and 109, 159–60; merchant business 110–11, 135–6, 152–4; Little Para River survey and 121–2; Mount Barker and 127–33; Adelaide politics and 137–8; move to Echunga 143–51; public life and 156–7; Governor Grey and 161–2; family matters 162–3, 164, 173; end of Hack, Watson & Co 165–7; South Australian financial crisis and 169–78; insolvency 179–92; Echunga Springs 188, 197–201; poverty and 192; wine making 193–5; inheritance 205; Kapunda manager 207; Wesleyan Methodism and 207–8; timber business 208–9; Bendigo goldfields and 210–11; accountancy 1852–7 211–12; return to South Australia 1853–7 214–15; Coorong and 218, 219–28; building of Parnka 222–4; land claims 1861–62 229–31; sheep farming 1861 231–2, 233–4; return to accountancy 1863 237–41; joins Railways Department 240–1; move to Semaphore 242–3; retirement and reminiscences 243–4; death of 244–5; will 245–6; centenary of death 249; summary of life and character 249–53; descendants 255–65
Hack, John Barton (Barton) (1911–96) 2, 4–6, 8, 249, 258
  short biography 263
Hack, John Barton (Barton) (b. 1943) 249
Hack, Julia Africaine; *see* Cutler, Julia Africaine
Hack, Julia Emily 223
Hack, Leonard 259
Hack, Lionel 259
Hack, Louisa; *see* Tod, Louisa
Hack, Louisa Bridget 256
Hack, Lucy Barton 127, 142, 143
Hack (née Bigg), Lydia 36, 99, 125, 163, 172
Hack (née Boland), Maria 260
Hack (née Barton), Mary (Maria) 2, 6–7, 11, 13, 14, 13, 18, 24, 25, 27, 30, 34, 36, 38, 39, 50, 51, 52, 53, 75, 84–5, 86, 94–5, 100, 103, 116, 132, 140, 159–60, 163, 172, 173–4, 177, 181, 205, 263
  children's educational publications and 15–17; widowhood 18–19, 20, 23–4; Gates Darton and 82; leaves Quakers 86; financial affairs and 111–12; death of 196–7
Hack (née Pedler), Mary Anne 260
Hack, Mary Louisa; *see* Earl, Mary Louisa
Hack, Mervyn Vincent 243
Hack (née Wierk), Minnie Alice 264
Hack, Noel 259
Hack, Percy 258
Hack, Priscilla; *see* Philcox, Priscilla
Hack, Ralph 258
Hack, Robert Dall 257
Hack, Roy Darton 262
Hack (née Dall), Sarah Ann 256, 257
Hack, Stephen (1775–1823) 11–13, 16, 18–19
Hack, Stephen (1816–94) 3, 4, 5, 8, 9, 14, 15, 18, 22, 24–6, 114, 138, 176–7, 189, 191, 212, 227, 233, 251, 252, 253, 256
  Quakers and 11, 149; South Australian land sales and 33–4; voyage from England

36, 37, 38, 39; Tasmania and 40–50, 51, 53–4; arrival in South Australia 59, 61; Glenelg settlement 65; Aboriginal people and 67–8; business dealings 69–81, 84, 87–9; bullock driving 72–5; inheritance and 56, 82–5, 116, 196, 197, 205; overland Sydney expedition 89, 90–7; partnership 1838 99; explorations 6, 103–6, 215–17, 218; reading choices 104; move to Hindley Street 106–7; South Australian Bush Club and 107–8; merchant business 1838 110–11; dispute with Darton 112; Mount Barker squatting enterprise 117–23, 127–33; Three Brothers Farm and 122–3, 130–2; division of family business and 132–3; letters to Britain 141; move to Echunga 143–51; debts and 153; voyage to England 1840 154; Echunga Springs and 162, 170–1; marriage to Bessie and visit to England 163–4; end of Hack, Watson & Co 165–7; visit to Capetown 168; return to South Australia 172–3, 174–5; insolvency 179–92; bark trade and 197–8; poverty and 198–9, 200; carrying business 200; voyage to England 1844 203–4; dairying at Brocklesbury 211; Cape of Good Hope 213–14; Coorong farm and 219–20, 222; dissolution of partnership with Barton Hack 224, 225; land claims 1861–62 229–31; sheep farming 1861–2 231–2, 233–4, 235; return to England 1865 235; last years and death 246–7; career tribute 253–4; children of 263–5

Hack (née Pengilly), Susan 257

Hack, Theodore 98, 100, 147, 163, 173, 211, 214, 221, 232, 237, 238, 240, 241–2, 243, 245, 246–7, 252, 258, 260
  short biography 261–3

Hack, Theodore Barton 260

Hack, Thomas Philip 260

Hack, Thomas Sanden (Tom) 13, 22, 24, 27, 36, 48, 56, 84, 104, 116, 125, 154, 163, 172, 197, 213
  last years 247

Hack, William (1759–1826) 11, 18, 21

Hack, William (1828–1902) 23, 26, 79, 98, 102, 173, 177, 198, 200, 201, 203, 204, 205, 209, 211, 222, 223, 225–6, 237, 238–9, 252, 262
  Coonalpyn and 231–2; short biography 255–6

Hack, Wilton 186–7, 213–14, 215, 231, 232, 235, 239–40, 249, 254
  short biography 264

Hack, family origins 8–9

Hack's Crossing 78–9, 145, 220, 222, 236

Hack's Lagoon 256

Hack Range Road 252

Hack, Watson and Co. 132, 134–42, 163, 186
  collapse of 165–7, 177, 205

Hagen, Jacob 148, 150, 152, 155, 165, 175, 176, 177, 179, 189, 192, 193–4, 195, 197, 198, 201, 206, 207, 253
  Hack property foreclosure 169–70, 180–1, 182, 183–6; at Echunga Springs and 188; Bartley v. Hagen case 190–1

Hagen (née Baker), Mary 180, 198

Hagen Arms Hotel 206

Hahndorf 121, 128, 129, 161

Hall, Lieutenant George 119, 121

Harcourt, Reverend John 208

Harding, William 238, 255

Hart, Captain John 38, 41, 42, 44, 45, 46, 49, 54, 57, 58, 59, 62, 69–70, 71, 83, 85, 91, 95, 96, 97, 99, 106, 110, 111, 114, 115, 116, 123, 132, 133, 137, 138, 139, 154, 155, 156, 165, 166, 170, 177, 203, 204, 207, 242
  rise to premiership 211–12

Harvey, Robert 52, 53, 83, 157

Hawdon, Joseph 90, 93–4, 97, 118

Henty family 55, 78, 94–5, 99

Hero 115, 155

H. Hill & Co 237

Hill, Bella 56, 62, 80

Hill, Joseph 56, 63

Hind Cove 73, 99, 137

Hindley Street 5, 85, 122, 146, 152, 154, 156, 186, 210

Hindley Street residence 98–100, 106–7, 127, 130, 132, 133, 142, 143, 162

Hindmarsh, Governor John 33, 35, 36, 54, 58, 60, 64, 66–7, 71, 76–7, 78, 88–9, 102
  recall of 109–10

Hodding, Fred 147

Holdfast Bay 54, 58–60, 63

Hope 91, 95, 96, 110, 115

Howard, Reverend Charles Beaumont 65, 66

Howard Terrace 241

I

Inman, Henry 105, 119, 139

insolvency cases 179–92, 185–6, 189–91

Isabella 3, 38, 51, 52, 53, 54, 63, 85, 135
  voyage to South Australia on 40–50; Launceston–South Australia voyage 56–7; arrival at South Australia 58, 59; offloading from 60–1; return trip to Launceston 62; loss of 69, 71, 114

J

Jacob Hagen & Son 136, 164, 165

Janson, Halsey 18, 20, 23, 52, 140, 154, 197

J.B. and S. Hack and Co. 132, 186

Jeffcott, Judge John William 42, 56, 66, 70, 89, 99

Jickling, Henry 66, 79

Joint Stock Cattle Company 117–18, 120, 121, 122–3, 129, 147, 157

Jones, Henry 41, 56, 59, 62, 70, 72, 83, 85, 111, 114, 135

INDEX

K
Kangaroo Island 54, 57, 58, 139
Kapunda 202, 207, 253
Karlgurra 231, 235
Katherine Stewart Forbes 132, 137, 141, 154
Kaurna nation 67
Kavanagh, Edward 199
Kavanagh, Pat 199
Kekwick, Daniel 147, 151
Kingston, George Strickland 35, 119
King William Street 71, 98, 150, 210, 211, 262
Knott, Charlotte 204
Knott (née Hack), Ellen 13, 22, 23, 24, 26, 27, 107, 141, 145–6, 162, 163, 172, 197, 204–5
Knott, George Gawler 162
Knott, Dr John 26, 27, 107, 108, 138, 141, 146, 172, 204–5

L
Lady Fitzherbert 168
Lady Wellington 91, 96, 110, 111
Lake Alexandrina 80, 81, 160, 219, 221, 226
Lake Gairdner 216, 217, 254
Lake Hope 218, 229, 237
Lake Torrens 214, 215, 217
Launceston 2, 41, 43, 48, 49, 51–7, 62, 69, 71, 77, 83, 84, 85, 94, 135, 196
Lefevre Terrace 209, 211–12, 233
Legislative Council 206, 212
Light, Colonel William 54, 60, 63, 70, 73, 76, 77, 88, 89, 101, 106, 110, 119, 137
  Adelaide survey and 35
Lindon, Hingston 238
Lines, Oscar John 129, 130
Literary and Scientific Association and Mechanics Institute 6, 102, 138, 157, 195, 251
Little London (Chichester) 12, 18, 24, 53, 85
Little Para estate 121–2, 123, 129, 142, 148, 150, 152, 153, 154, 185
Liverpool 2, 17, 22, 23, 27, 36
Lloyd (née Watson), Charlotte Emily (Apetty, Minnie) 88, 127, 146, 221
Lloyd, John Sanderson 221, 248
London 11, 13, 14, 27, 110, 121, 169, 183, 215, 247
Luebbers, Roger 223

M
Macdougall, Alexander 135–6
McEwin, George 194
McFarlane, Duncan 120
Macgowan, James 163, 172
McKeown, Ben 257
McLaren, David 99, 121, 138, 139, 140, 155
Magarey (née Hack), Gulielma 259
Magarey, William Ashley 259
Magarey (Gulielma) Scholarship 259
Magill Road 241
Magrath Flat 219, 220, 222, 223, 224, 228

Mann, Charles 71, 89, 191, 253
Manning cottages 58, 61, 63–4, 65, 106, 107, 127, 148, 151
Marx, Karl 20
Mason, George 226, 227–8
Mason, Samuel 91, 129, 144, 190
May, Frederick (Fred) 130
May, Hannah 130-1, 147, 185
May, Henry 130
May, Joseph 130, 147, 185, 192, 205–6
May, Lucy; *see* Coleman, Lucy
May, Margaret; see Phillips, Margaret
May, Maria; see Phillips, Maria
May, William 130
May family 151, 163, 179, 200, 206
Meadows Survey 181
Melbourne Street 77, 209
Milang 223, 234, 258
Millard, Harriet Amelia 245
Milnes family 214, 215
Mitchell, Cornelius Butler 225, 241
Mitchell (née Hack), Emily Margaret 75, 79, 127, 173, 225, 238
  Coorong and 220–2; death of 241
Mitchell, Major Thomas 92, 225
Morphett, George 253
Morphett, John 34, 59, 60, 63, 64, 71, 73, 76, 77, 80, 85, 101, 110, 136, 139, 140, 155, 157, 162, 169, 183, 190, 233
Morphettville 59
Mount Barker 97, 103, 106, 116, 122, 147, 160, 161, 176, 179, 194, 200, 201, 221, 252
  expedition to 80–1; squatting enterprise 117–23; Hack brothers and Henry Watson at 127–33; outlay on 142; Philcoxes at 146; Quaker presence 151
Mount Flint 218
Mount Hack 214, 215, 218, 254
Mount Lofty range 31, 79, 80, 81, 117, 127, 143
Mount Remarkable 216, 264
Mount Terrible 104
Mullengandra 91, 92, 93, 94, 96
Murray River 31, 73, 80, 88–9, 91, 93, 96, 97, 118, 129, 160, 210, 211, 214, 219, 220, 221, 256

N
Naracoorte 238, 239, 255, 256
Neales, Bentham 181–2
Newland, Richard Francis 120, 175, 176, 180, 190
New South Wales 31, 90, 92, 93, 103, 118, 133, 203, 215, 217, 254, 264
New Zealand 136, 169, 206
Ngarrindjeri people 226, 236
Ninety Mile Desert 210, 229
Nixon, Frederick 106
North Adelaide 5, 71, 72, 77, 78, 100, 148, 207, 208, 209, 219, 221, 233, 237, 248, 252, 258, 260
Northern Territory 217, 258

North Flinders Ranges 214, 218, 221, 254
North Kapunda 207, 209
North Terrace 3-4, 63, 64, 71, 75, 79, 98, 102, 103, 105, 107, 162, 211, 259, 261

O

Onkaparinga River 74, 104, 117, 118, 121, 142, 145
Opie, Edward Andrew 79
overland expedition 1837 90-7

P

Parade, The (Semaphore) 243, 245
Parnka 219-20, 222-8, 230, 231, 232, 233, 236
Pengilly, Fred and Rose 258
Pennington Terrace 6, 64, 75, 78, 80, 107, 119, 124, 126, 127, 132, 146, 149, 150, 153, 209
Peramangk people 147
Pernana 214, 229
Pfender family 40, 54, 56
Philcox, Anna Priscilla 146, 169, 176
Philcox, Edward O. 107, 108, 129, 141, 145-6, 157, 162, 163, 166, 167, 169, 176, 204, 213, 214
Philcox, James 169, 176
Philcox, Margaret Esther 162, 169
Philcox (née Hack), Priscilla 13, 22, 23, 24, 27, 108, 141, 145-6, 157, 162-3, 172
Phillips (née May), Maria 131, 185, 188, 206
Phillips, George 162, 179, 186, 206
Phillips, Henry Weston 150, 162, 179, 180, 185, 186, 206
Phillips (née May), Margaret 131, 185-6, 187, 189, 197-8, 200, 201, 203-4, 205, 206
Pike, Douglas 32, 176
Pinnaroo 235, 239, 246
Pioneers Association of South Australia 253
Port Adelaide 5, 31, 199, 212, 233, 241, 242, 246, 261
Port Augusta 215, 261
Portland Bay 55, 69, 78, 90, 92, 93, 94-6, 97, 99, 106, 117, 123
Port Lincoln 60, 215
Port Mills 212
Port Phillip 55, 93, 111
Port River 54, 58-9, 72, 75-6, 101, 242
Port Vincent 123
Port Willunga 257
Protector of Aborigines 87, 102, 140, 227
Pullen, William John Samuel 97

Q

Quakers (Society of Friends) 3, 5-6, 8-11, 12, 13, 17, 18, 19, 21, 22, 27, 39, 67, 71, 72, 84, 138, 139, 147, 148, 169, 174, 185, 198, 200, 206
Aboriginal people and 252-3; Barton family and 22-3, 40-1; burial practices 124; Echunga 179-80; Gates Darton and 250; Hack brothers and 24-5, 86-7, 208, 251; education and 15, 16; Maria Hack and 86; Meeting House 148-51, 168; Mount Barker area 129, 130, 131; slave trade and 13-14; South Australia and 32-3, 189; Wakefield and 30; Watsons and 248

R

Rapid 35, 58, 103, 129, 137, 155
Rapid Bay 58, 77, 104
Richards, Lindsay 261
Richardson, John 122, 154
Robe, Governor Frederick Holt 206
Robin (née Ansell), Stella Ann 241-2, 261
Robin, Theophilus 241
Robson, Helen 248
Rosetta Cove 73, 115, 137
Rothe family 147, 206, 207
Rounsevell, John 237, 239
Rundle Street 70, 123, 135, 225
Russell, John 123

S

Salt Creek 223, 224, 230
Sanders family 147-8, 179, 200, 206
Schah 53, 69, 70, 72
Select Committee inquiry into the Aboriginal People 1860 226-7
Semaphore 237, 243, 244, 245, 246, 252, 259, 261
Hack family move to 1878 242-3
Shepherdson, John Banks 102, 117, 147
Siren 78, 85
Skey, Russell 182, 183-4, 186, 199, 200, 204
Skipper, John Michael 59, 61
Skottowe (née Hack), Winifred Bbe 259
Sleaford Bay 115, 164
Smith, James 231, 232, 233, 234
Smith, Nathan 52-3
Smith, Thomas 4, 21-2, 36, 39, 52, 83
South Africa 193, 195, 254
South Australia 6, 7, 14, 20, 23, 25, 28, 49, 54, 55, 56, 93, 177, 215, 217, 229, 244, 255, 257, 264
creation of 12, 30-1, 32; land sale conditions 33-4; voyage preparations for 37-9; arrival in 58-68; initial optimism 1837 88-9; population increase 107; public works 134; financial crisis 5, 155-6, 159-67, 168-78; gold rushes and 210; debt to J.B. Hack 250-1; Stephen Hack and 253-4
South Australian Bush Club 107-8
South Australian Commissioners 32, 33-4, 38, 76, 77, 88, 102, 109, 135, 160, 169
land fund bankruptcy 159
South Australian Company 34, 60, 63, 65, 71, 73, 80, 90, 96, 99, 101, 115, 121, 123, 136, 137, 138, 155, 156
South Australian School Society 102, 117, 138
South Australian Total Abstinence League 240
special survey system 119-21, 135
Staker family 79-80, 99

INDEX

Stephen, George Milner 110, 138, 139
Stephens, Edward 64, 101, 105, 120, 156, 162, 207
Stephens, Samuel 34, 63, 73, 80
Stevenson, George 33, 64, 76, 78, 101, 194, 210
Stewart's Range 256
Stonehouse, Reverend George 240
Stow, Reverend Thomas Quinton 98, 102
Strangways, Giles 118
Strangways, Thomas Bewes 71, 77, 118
Strangways Valley 122, 130
Strathalbyn 211, 221
Streaky Bay 215, 216
Stuart, Charles William 65, 79, 80, 103, 108, 118, 119
Sturt, Captain Charles Napier 31, 80, 118
Suter, Emma 62, 80
Suter, William 62, 72, 144

T

Taplin, George 226
Three Brothers Estate 122–3, 127–9, 130, 154, 188
   move to 144–5; Stephen Hack and 153; partition 183
Tintinara 230, 231, 232, 235, 238, 255
Tod (née Hack), Louisa 26, 127, 172, 173, 188, 189, 198, 201, 203, 205, 210, 211
   marries Patrick Tod 209; marries Hingston Lindon 238; death 238
Tod, Patrick James 209, 211, 238
Tolmer, Alexander 210, 233, 236
Torrens, Colonel Robert 32, 169
Torrens, Robert Richard 169, 209–10
Torrens River 54, 60, 63, 64, 71, 72, 78–9
   town acres, Hacks and 113–14

U

Upper Sturt River 59, 73, 231

V

Van Diemen's Land 31, 38, 40–50, 160
Victoria 155, 210, 229, 230, 254, 256
vineyards and winemaking 5, 78, 144–6, 173, 177, 184–5, 193–5, 238, 251

W

Wagener (née Hack), Annie Catherine 223, 239, 256
Wagener, John Barton 249
Wakefield, Edward Gibbon 12, 20, 30–2, 38, 149
Wakefield, Priscilla 11–12, 30
Walker, George Washington 86–7
Walkley Cottage 151
Warburton, Major Peter Egerton 216, 217
Watergate 184

Watson, Charlotte Emily (Apetty, Minnie) Minnie; see Lloyd, Charlotte Emily
Watson (née Float), Charlotte 27, 88, 108, 125, 126, 127, 137–8, 143, 146, 153, 162, 166–7, 168, 205, 207
   reconciliation with Hacks 199; death of 248
Watson, Eliza Maria 205
Watson, Fanny Rogers 127, 143, 146, 153
Watson, George 235
Watson, Henry 17, 23, 39, 40, 49, 65, 66, 69, 72, 74, 77, 84, 85, 88, 108, 112, 124–5, 126–8, 130, 132, 133, 135, 136, 139, 141–2, 143–4, 145, 146, 151, 152, 153–4, 155–6, 157, 158, 160, 162, 166–7, 176, 189, 195, 200, 203, 205, 207, 221
   marries Charlotte Float 27; Hack debts and 52; end of Hack, Watson & Co 165–6; Customs job 169; reconciliation with Hacks 199; Watson v. Torrens 209–10; death of 248
Watson, Henry Edward 168
Watson, Louisa, death of 126
Watson, Martha 23, 27, 125, 127
Watson, William 22, 23, 27, 40, 125, 127, 163
Watson, William Woodman 162
Watson family 174, 179, 184
Wellington 210, 211, 220, 221, 226, 227
Wesleyan Methodists 5, 86, 237, 238, 244, 248
   Hacks and 207–8, 224, 240, 251, 257, 261; Semaphore 243
Western Australia 55, 159, 215, 264
Western Creek 183, 185
Western Flat 129, 151
West Terrace Cemetery 124, 150
whaling 99, 115–16, 137, 164–5, 171, 190
   difficulties 1840 154–5; withdrawal from 166, 177–8
Willunga 237, 238
Wilton, George Henry 175, 187, 198, 204, 246, 247
Wilton, John Pleydell 163, 175
Wilton, William Wilton Meora Stephen (Will) 264
Wirangu people 257
Woodforde (née Carter), Caroline 41, 54–5, 56, 62, 63, 65, 66, 75, 85, 99, 103, 127
Woodforde, Dr John 103, 127, 192, 201
Woods, Julia 37, 75, 95, 128, 131
   death of 83
Woodville Cemetery (Cheltenham Cemetery) 243, 244
Wright, Captain William 104
Wyatt, Dr William 87, 102, 103

Y

Yankalilla 104, 113, 119, 123, 143, 145, 176, 254
Young, John Lorenzo 211, 214

Wakefield Press is an independent publishing and
distribution company based in Adelaide, South Australia.
We love good stories and publish beautiful books.
To see our full range of books, please visit our website at
www.wakefieldpress.com.au
where all titles are available for purchase.

Find us!

Twitter: www.twitter.com/wakefieldpress
Facebook: www.facebook.com/wakefield.press
Instagram: instagram.com/wakefieldpress